# RELIGION IN THE MODERN WORLD

# RELIGION IN THE MODERN WORLD

## From Cathedrals to Cults

**Steve Bruce**

Oxford   New York

OXFORD UNIVERSITY PRESS

1996

Oxford University Press, Walton Street, Oxford OX2 6DP

Oxford New York
Athens Auckland Bangkok Bombay
Calcutta Cape Town Dar es Salaam Delhi
Florence Hong Kong Istanbul Karachi
Kuala Lumpur Madras Madrid Melbourne
Mexico City Nairobi Paris Singapore
Taipei Tokyo Toronto
and associated companies in
Berlin Ibadan

Oxford is a trade mark of Oxford University Press

Published in the United States
by Oxford University Press Inc., New York

British Library Cataloguing in Publication Data
Data available

Library of Congress Cataloging in Publication Data
Data available
ISBN 0–19–878152–0
ISBN 0–19–878151–2 (pbk.)

10  9  8  7  6  5  4  3  2  1

Typeset by Hope Services (Abingdon) Ltd.
Printed in Great Britain
on acid-free paper by
Biddles Ltd.,
Guildford & King's Lynn

# Preface

By tradition the preface of a serious book is the place where the author relaxes, drops his careful and measured prose, and reveals a little of himself. In order to honour a man who meant a great deal to me, I intend to take full advantage of that tradition.

One of the great insights, if not innovations, of sociology is the simple point that knowledge is not neutral. How we see the world is in good part a product of our experiences, and many of those are common to our culture and society and to the various smaller social groups in which we were raised and in which we live. All knowledge is partial and socially constructed. Try as we might, we can never completely rid ourselves of those values and beliefs into which we were socialized. Various sociological currents of a Marxist hue try to solve the problem of the relativity of all knowledge by claiming that there is an objective course to human history and that, by aligning ourselves with the 'right' social group, which is the working class—or more exactly what the Marxist intellectuals think the working class ought to be—one can achieve the correct vantage-point. By being on the side of history we can move from peddling ideology to discerning truth. There is a less popular but very similar position taken by Christian sociologists. For them the salvation from relativism is salvation in the traditional Christian sense. Get right with God and we no longer see through a glass darkly.

I had the good fortune to be taught sociology by someone who was committed to the pursuit of disinterested scholarship. Roy Wallis was a good enough sociologist to know that we are all products of our worlds and that our biographies cannot fail to affect how we see the world around us, but he was also a good enough philosopher to appreciate that there is a difference between saying that we are products of our past and saying that all our intellectual endeavours can be no more than a representation of our class interests. His response to the relativism problem was that which, until the excesses of the late 1960s, was the orthodoxy in social science. You work hard to leave aside your prejudices and preferences, do your best to clarify arguments, collect evidence as honestly as you can, present your work to your colleagues, and engage in debate over the findings, guided always by the best available evidence.

It is in this spirit that I have approached the subject of religion in the modern world. But my debt to Roy Wallis goes deeper than this. Our primary research was always separate; he was interested in new religious movements and I studied mainstream Christianity, but we brought our diverse materials to bear on common interests and authored a number of joint essays on theoretical issues. In the years from 1974 to 1990 I learnt so much from Roy Wallis that now I often cannot separate his ideas from mine. Worse, because we used identical word processors, I have pages of text which could be his words, mine, or a draft of a joint paper. Had he not died in 1990, this book would have been jointly authored. As it is, Chapter 7 is heavily dependent on his writings and almost everything else is an elaboration, revision, or extension of something we talked or wrote about together.

Neither of us was religious; our interest in religion was entirely professional. I cannot believe in life after death, but I have a large photograph of Roy over my desk and at times while writing this book I have found myself cheered by imagining his acerbic response to something I have just typed. As I correct each dreadful prose mistake, I remember that the first comment he ever wrote on a draft of mine was 'Is English your first language?' Had he been around to co-author, what follows would have been far far better. I only hope that those colleagues who know his work do not feel that I have let him down and that those readers who come new to the sociology of religion will sufficiently enjoy the book to accept my estimation of Roy Wallis and read his works.

# Acknowledgements

One way or another a large number of people and organizations played a significant part in the production of this volume and I would like to acknowledgement my debts by briefly mentioning them. Tim Barton of Oxford University Press has been a constant source of encouragement and the comments of the Press's anonymous referees greatly improved the final version, as did the painstaking copy-editing of Hilary Walford.

Over the years I have been the fortunate recipient of a number of small grants from the Nuffield Foundation, the British Academy, and the Economic and Social Research Council, and the work assisted by that funding has contributed to the argument of this volume. Most recently a grant from the Nuffield Foundation allowed me to employ Dr Sandra McIsaac to analyse the data from the 1991 British Social Attitudes Survey and I am extremely grateful to it and to her. Social and Community Planning Research and the Economic and Social Research Council's Data Archive at the University of Essex kindly supplied the original data, and the staff of the University of Aberdeen's Computing Centre assisted us with the practicalities of data transfer.

Dr Paul Heelas of the Department of Religious Studies, University of Lancaster, kindly commented on the material in Chapters 7 and 8, and many long conversations with him have much improved my thinking about new religious movements and the New Age.

# Contents

# 1

# INTRODUCTION

......................................................................................................................................

THIS book is an attempt to describe and explain what has happened to religion in the Western world since 1517. Such a task requires severe selection. As the great polymath Ernest Gellner says of his larger task of describing and explaining the structure of human history, 'reality is so rich and diverse that no unselective description could even be begun, let alone completed. Instead one chooses the crucial and elementary factors operative in human history, selected to the best of one's judgement, and then works out their joint implications'.[1] Fortunately, I have not had to begin from scratch. The central ideas that inform my argument are well known and many have been well established in social science since the 1950s. The originality of the work lies in the organization of those ideas and their extension to deal with recent phenomena. In a nutshell, I will argue that the basic elements of what we conveniently refer to as 'modernization' fundamentally altered the place and nature of religious beliefs, practices, and organizations so as to reduce their relevance to the lives of nation-states, social groups, and individuals, in roughly that order. A simple outline of those changes can be given by explaining why the book is subtitled 'From Cathedral to Cults'.

It was the job of the staff of the great Christian cathedrals of the Middle Ages to worship and glorify God by daily performing a set rota of services which themselves rotated through a fixed calendar during the year. At the English Reformation Archbishop Cranmer reduced the number of daily services to two: Matins and Evensong. Both 'offices', as they were called, were built around the same pattern of psalms and readings from the Old Testament and from the New Testament, separated by ancient songs (or canticles) drawn from scripture or from the history of the early Christian Church. From our vantage-point, the expected relationship between this sphere of activity and the lives of ordinary people is an interesting one. An explanatory card now given to visitors to Lincoln Cathedral contains the following paragraph on 'Sharing in the Service': 'When the choir is present, the traditional ideal of cathedral worship is that it makes as near perfect and therefore professional a musical offering to God as possible. We therefore ask the congregation to be together with the choir in their thoughts and prayers, but to remain silent.' Visitors are encouraged to join in the hymns (a modern innovation), but the request for silence inadvertently reminds us of the nature of formal religion in pre-Reformation Europe. A small number of highly trained officials, acting on behalf of the state and the people, glorified God. They did so with a liturgy and with music that was far too complex for the active participation of lay people. Religion was done, not in the local language, but in Latin, which united religious professionals across Christendom but separated them from the laity. Even in parish churches the service was conducted in Latin, spoken by a 'priest whose knowledge of the language may have been only slightly greater than that of the congregation'.[2] There were no hymns and only sometimes a sermon. Until the late fourteenth century, later in many places, there were no seats in the part of the church used by the audience; they either stood or knelt in an unheated building.

Ordinary people were expected to behave morally, to attend church on the great feast days, and to finance the professionals who did the serious religious work on behalf of the community and the nation. The Christian Church most closely touched lives through its administration of rituals which sanctified such crucial transitions in the lives of the community and its members as birth, marriage, and death; through the social standing of its clergy in their communities; and through the magic which it did not encourage but which it happily condoned. Saints and their associated shrines were held to offer powerful remedies for this or that ailment. St Wilgerfort could help wives be rid of their husbands. Other saints could protect men and cattle and visit plague on their enemies. Pregnant women could use holy relics to reduce the pains of labour.[3] Holy water, sprinkled on houses, fields, and livestock, protected or improved them. As Thomas explains, throughout the Middle Ages the attitude of church leaders to the credulities of their simpler followers was ambivalent: 'They disliked them as gross and superstitious but they had no wish to discourage attitudes which might foster popular devotion.'[4]

People also drew on the Christian sacraments to bless the common rites of passage. Babies were baptized and children were confirmed. A month after giving birth, women were welcomed back into the community and restored to their normal social roles by being 'churched', a service that combined thanksgiving with an element of ritual purification.[5] Couples were married in church, and, of course, death was surrounded by religious rituals.

It is a simplification, of course, but what one sees in pre-Reformation religious life is a sophisticated complex organization of formal religion laid over a mass of popular superstition, with the two worlds bridged by the complete and uncritical acceptance of a few simple Christian beliefs. It was universally held that God would judge us and banish us to heaven or to hell as appropriate and that the Church held the key. Only the prayers of the Church, the mediation of the saints, and the re-enactment in the Mass of the sacrifice of Jesus on the Cross would ensure the kingdom of heaven. Ordinary people used the magic of the Church to live their ordinary lives and supported the professionals who performed 'high' religion and acquired religious merit on behalf of the whole community.

The Reformation marked a break both with that division of labour and with the hierarchically structured feudal world which allowed it to make sense. The legacy of the religious innovations of Luther, Calvin, and the other reformers strengthened and hastened a variety of social changes which we can understand under the general heading of *individualism* and which we can see in changes to styles of worship and religious music. Local languages replaced Latin. Hymns sung to simple folk melodies that even the tone deaf could essay augmented the elaborate arrangements of the cathedral choir. Power shifted from religious professionals to the laity. A personal emotional response to the figure of Jesus and his sacrifice replaced the correct professional performance of the ritual of the Mass as the major expression of religion. Believing the right things came to be more important than making the right ritual actions, and, whereas right ritual could be delegated to others, right belief could not.

There was not an immediate increase of popular interest in Christianity. In some areas the Reformers' attacks on such superstitions as the devotions to saints led initially to a decline in popular engagement with religion, but, especially with the spread of literacy and the preaching endeavours of various competing sectarians, popular religion began to displace popular magic.

As we shall see, this change had a paradoxical effect. The need for ordinary people to take responsibility for their own salvation produced an increase in popular religious knowledge and involvement. For many people in the parts of Europe most affected by the Reformation, a rather shallow and conformist adherence to the single Church and a widespread but diffuse supernaturalism were replaced by enthusiastic commitment to one of a range of competing sects. Yet this flowering spread the seeds of its own decline. The fragmentation of the religious culture was, in time, to see the widespread, taken-for-granted, and unexamined Christianity of the pre-Reformation period replaced by an equally widespread, taken-for-granted, and unexamined indifference to religion.

Someone predisposed to see the social world and human nature as fundamentally unchanging might argue that our present lack of interest and attention to matters religious is merely a return to what characterized the pre-Reformation period: a lack of personal involvement in formal religion. This would be a mistake. Even those pre-Reformation Europeans who troubled the inside of a church only on 'high days and holy days' lived in a world whose rhythms and seasons were blessed by the Church, knew that the Church controlled entry to heaven, and had frequent recourse to the magic of the saints (and to older and darker arts). The common people of our day care nothing for blasphemy, allow most of their rites of passage to go unsanctified, and in so far as a small number of them resort to magic (the subject of Chapter 8), those practices take them further away from, not nearer to, the formal religion of the churches.

As Chapter 4 will argue, if the *church* was the dominant form of religion in the pre-Reformation world, the *sect* its embodiment in the early modern period, and the *denomination* its classic form in the twentieth century, the emblem of religion for the twenty-first century is the *cult*. The decline in the main traditions has allowed a flowering of new religions and 'New Age' innovations. Some (such as white witchcraft) are intended as re-creations of pre-Christian religion; others are imports from the East. Yet others are psychotherapies elevated from the mundane worlds of medicine and psychology by the adoption of quasi-supernatural claims and practices. What is obvious is that, for all that the exoticism of the New Age catches our eye, the direct social impact of these cultic practices is slight. The small numbers of people who get involved do so in a highly selective and picky way. Like the sovereign consumers they believe themselves to be in other spheres of their lives, they feel able to decide what works for them and how involved they will become. This is not the religion of necessity, of doing God's will because to do anything else is to court damnation. This is what US-government forms quaintly call 'the religion of your preference', and it is relativistic. There is no longer any idea that there is one truth, one correct body of knowledge. Instead there is individual preference. If it works for you, then it is true. In the New Age, everyone does what is right in his or her own eyes. Or, to turn it on its head, whatever anyone does is right. For reasons I will explore, New Age religion has little of the profound social impact of such previous religious innovations as the Quaker movement or Methodism.

At its simplest then, one theme of this book is individualism and the changes in what is implied by that notion. The individualism of the Reformation was the assertion of individual responsibility to do the will of God through learning and living the one true faith. That there could not be consensus about just what was God's will caused a shift, so that, by the second half of the nineteenth century, individualism meant the right to do what we wanted provided it did not harm others. For three centuries, competing convictions really competed; differences of opinion about God's will had to be argued because there was only one God. I am suggesting that the late modern period (by which I mean post-1945) has seen a further fundamental shift. Many people have resolved the competition of convictions by changing the rules of the game. Individualism has encroached on the definition of reality, what philosophers call 'epistemology'. We claim not only the right to do what is right in our own eyes but to assert that the world is as we variously see it. Religious evolution has moved through three phases: from the substantial one God, through an era of argument and competing Gods, to an immaterial and diffuse one God, a cosmic consciousness which can be claimed as the underlying 'reality' beneath whatever deviant and divergent visions one may have.

This is a skeletal account of my main direction. However, it should be obvious that 'religion' and 'modernization' are not simple unitary notions, that few societies have identical histories, and hence that any simple model of religious evolution will have almost as many exceptions as it has fitting cases. Even within the small and relatively homogenous British Isles, there is still civil conflict between peoples who define themselves in large part by their competing religions, as well as examples of ethnic and regional minorities holding their religions as communal rather than individual matters. Hence periodically there will be excursions from the main route of our journey to consider in what social circumstances religion retains its older forms or gains new roles. None the less, to recognize that the journey of religious change in the West has been a halting one, with periodic crossroads where a different direction could have been taken, is not to abandon the search for a unifying explanation. It is also worth adding, for those who know the contemporary sociology of religion literature, that this book is a robust defence of that body of ideas commonly designated the 'secularization thesis'. It is perhaps inevitable that each generation of scholars is tempted to advertise its work by revising previous orthodoxies. In the natural sciences such revisions are often driven by the need to reconcile prevailing ideas with new evidence. Sadly, in the social sciences revisionism seems more often to be driven by changes in intellectual fashion. Though the critics of secularization sometimes improve our understanding, much of the recent debate has been debased by the construction and demolition of straw men. One of the aims of this book is to clarify the arguments of such scholars as Weber, Durkheim, Parsons, Berger, Wilson, and Martin so that we can build on what is of enduring value in their work and not become trapped in a cycle of fashion-led revisions to revisionism.

As a final act of introduction, I want to clarify what is meant here by 'religion'. Social scientists have two very different ways of defining religion. Functional definitions identify religion in terms of what it does: for example, providing solutions to 'ultimate problems', or answering fundamental questions of the human condition. Substantive definitions identify religion in terms of what it is: for example, beliefs and actions which assume the existence of supernatural beings or powers.[6]

Both kinds of definition pose problems. Functional definitions may count as religious things which do not on the face of it look terribly religious and which their adherents regard as secular: for example, secular therapies or socio-political ideologies. Further, functional definitions have been difficult to use consistently. What is an 'ultimate' problem and ultimate in whose mind are questions that are not easily resolved. In practice, proponents of such an approach often fall back on an examination of beliefs and institutions which are religious in the more obvious substantive sense. Further, to define religion in terms of social or psychological functions is to beg what is often the most interesting question: just what functions does this or that religion perform in this or that setting. Moreover, given that human beings will always have questions which remain unanswered or problems which continue to raise issues of humanity's existential condition, functional definitions rather prejudge one of the questions most often asked about religion: is it possible for a society to operate without a religion?

Finally, while there are good reasons for wanting to explore the similarities between religions and other beliefs, and between institutions that perform similar functions, calling them all religions gains us very little except some arguable theoretical baggage and a loss of analytical clarity. One of my main interests is the exploration of the uses to which religion is put. Far from making the study of the 'functions' of religion easier, functional definitions of the phenomenon make it impossible by tautologically mixing into the designation of religion precisely those features of it which we want to establish empirically.

There are also difficulties with substantive definitions. They may be closer to the understanding of the average Westerner, but when we seek to unpack the notion of 'superhuman' or 'supernatural', we find difficulties with some non-Western or traditional cultures. Where people daily commune with the spirits of their ancestors or take steps to avoid ubiquitous witchcraft, it may not be easy to discriminate the natural from the supernatural in the minds of those concerned.

However, a definition that fits with broad contemporary common-sense reflection on the matter is usually not a very bad place to start. Moreover, the utility of a definition must in the end depend upon the success of the explanations in which it is employed. That is, the purpose of a definition is to bring together analytically similar phenomena, aspects of which we believe we can explain in the same terms. I define religion substantively because this allows me to formulate a number of theories which I believe have considerable explanatory scope. Religion, then, consists of beliefs, actions, and institutions which assume the existence of supernatural entities with powers of action, or impersonal powers or processes possessed of moral purpose. Such a formulation seems to encompass what ordinary people mean when they talk of religion.

## Notes

1. Ernest Gellner, *Plough, Sword and Book: The Structure of Human History* (London: Paladin, 1991), 13.
2. J. H. Bettey, *Church and Community: The Parish Church in English Life* (Bradford-on-Avon: Moonraker Press, 1979), 21.
3. Keith Thomas, *Religion and the Decline of Magic* (Harmondsworth, Middx.: Penguin, 1973), 29.
4. Ibid. 56.
5. David Cressy, 'Purification, Thanksgiving and the Churching of Women in Post-Reformation England', *Past and Present*, 141 (Nov. 1993), 106–46.
6. Peter L. Berger, 'Substantive Definitions of Religion', *Journal for the Scientific Study of Religion*, 13 (1974), 125–33. See also his *The Social Reality of Religion* (London: Faber & Faber, 1969), app. 1, 'Sociological Definitions of Religion'.

# 2

---

# THE FOUNDATIONS OF
# MODERNITY

......................................................................................................

Wars and football matches begin and end. Major social movements and cultural revolutions take their time to shuffle on
and off the stage, so that any division of history into named periods
involves a degree of artificiality. However, we have to start somewhere and any discussion that involves the notion of 'modernization' may as convincingly start with the Reformation as anywhere
else. That upheaval in the religious and political life of Europe can
be conventionally dated as starting on the last day of October 1517,
when Martin Luther nailed his list of complaints about the state of
the Church to the door of the cathedral in Wittenberg.[1]

In this chapter I want to explain briefly the origins of modern
rationality, the rise of individualism, the foundations of modern science, and the collapse of a unitary Christendom, all of which are
related in diverse ways to the Reformation.

Peter Berger has plausibly argued that the origins of the rationality of the West can be traced to the religious culture of ancient
Israel.[2] The religion of the Old Testament differed from that of surrounding cultures in a number of important respects. The religions
of Egypt and Mesopotamia were profoundly *cosmological*. The
human world was embedded in a cosmic order which embraced the
entire universe, without any sharp distinction between the human
and the non-human, the empirical and the supra-empirical. Such
continuity between people and the Gods was sharply broken by the
religion of the Jews. 'The Old Testament', Berger says, 'posits a God
who stands *outside* the cosmos, which is his creation but which he
confronts and does not permeate.'[3] The God of Ancient Israel was a
radically transcendent God. He was the only God who made radical

ethical demands upon his followers, and he was so distanced from them as to be beyond magical manipulation. We could learn his laws and obey them but we could not bribe, cajole, or trick him into doing our will. There was a gulf between humankind and God, with a thoroughly demythologized universe between.

As we see in the myths of ancient Rome and Greece, a horde of gods or spirits, often behaving in an arbitrary fashion and operating at cross purposes, makes the relationship of supernatural to natural worlds unpredictable. First Judaism and then Christianity were rationalizing forces. By having only one God (that is, being mono-theistic), they simplified the supernatural and allowed the worship of God to become systematized. Pleasing God became less a matter of trying to anticipate the whims of an erratic force and more a matter of correct ethical behaviour. Judaism was also a rationalizing force, in that, by elevating God, it removed him from the world. He created it and he would end it, but between start and finish the world could be seen as having its own structure and logic, an order that, because it existed independently of God, could be examined independently of God. This conception of God and the universe was carried over into Christianity.

As the Christian Church evolved, the cosmos was remytholo-gized in important ways. Angels and saints as semi-divine beings began to people the universe. Mary was elevated as a mediator and co-redeemer with Jesus. The belief that God could be manipulated through ritual, confession, and penance undermined the tendency to regulate behaviour with a standardized and rational ethical code.[4] No matter how awful one's life, redemption could be bought by funding the Church. However, as we shall see, this trend was reversed as the Protestant Reformation demythologized the world, eliminated the ritual and sacramental manipulation of God, and restored the process of ethical rationalization.

The German sociologist Max Weber devoted much of his schol-arly life to exploring the rationality of the West. In addition to the general cultural background of the above observations, he addressed in very specific terms the rationalizing effects of the Reformation and it is with his work that we will start.

## Weber's Problem: The Origins of Capitalism

The point of Weber's famous essay *The Protestant Ethic and the Spirit of Capitalism* is readily grasped if we are clear what it was that Weber thought needed to be explained about the West.[5] Many scholars (Adam Smith, for example, in his *Wealth of Nations*) assume that capitalism was a natural evolution from previous economic systems. Improved technology, knowledge, and the division of labour increased productivity, which in turn produced a change first in economic attitudes and later in economic structures. Although Marx expected the stages of change to be marked by increasing conflict between competing social classes and by periodic violent upheavals, he also saw the rise of capitalism as natural, as inevitable, as part of the onward march of history to its destiny in Communism. Weber readily conceded that the West had a number of peculiar advantages. It possessed an equitable climate which limited the impact of natural disasters and fluctuations in the weather. It possessed a geographical terrain which permitted relatively easy transport by land and sea. It had natural resources in abundance but not in such great abundance that people were discouraged from continuous labour. However, Weber believed that there were features of capitalism in its modern Western form that were so markedly different from what had gone before that they needed to be explained by finding the source of the new attitudes and patterns of behaviour.

To put his problem bluntly, whatever happened to that cluster of characteristics he calls 'economic traditionalism': sloth, recklessness, and habit? Pre-capitalist people were lazy; they were reckless in their attitude to the accumulation of wealth; and their working practices were heavily determined by tradition. The ancients did not like work; the Greeks despised it. It was done out of necessity. Slaves worked because they were slaves and poor Greeks worked because they did not have slaves.

As the great American anthropologist Marshall Sahlins has demonstrated, in most primitive and only slowly changing societies, people had fairly well-fixed notions of what they could expect by way of a standard of living.[6] If a hunter expected to catch one pig a week and caught it on the first day, he would probably stop hunting. One good reason for this is that there is limited value in a surplus. If it cannot be stored and there is little or nothing to exchange it for, then there is no point in acquiring and hoarding beyond immediate needs. But in addition to the practical problems, there is also a matter of attitude: many pre-industrial people seem to have lacked our interest in continuously increasing productivity. Once they had achieved what they expected out of life, their customary return, they stopped work. The early industrialists were thwarted when they tried to increase the productivity of their workers by paying them at a higher rate. The higher pay rate meant that they reached their customary standard of living earlier in the week and so stopped work earlier. Their income remained what it had been before and they had more non-work time.

The expectation of the 'traditional' rate of return was often accompanied by traditional notions of how to get it. Working methods were often hallowed by custom. The pig-hunter hunted a certain way because that is how pigs were always hunted. The custom might be given a religious gloss by being incorporated in a myth. Pigs were hunted this way because that is how the Gods told us to hunt. What is apparently missing from many simple economies is any concern with experiment and innovation. In part this is itself a result of a low level of productivity. One needs a surplus to consider ploughing some back into improvements. But it is again also a matter of attitude.

Now for recklessness. Even those who pursued wealth (and were successful) did so in a way which is foreign to modern capitalism. The early merchants were gamblers; Shakespeare's *Merchant of Venice* revolves around a good example. People put all their money into a ship and a cargo, sent it off, and hoped that it would return with goods which could be sold for a huge profit. Either the ship came in or it didn't! English privateers made fortunes for themselves and their sponsors through raids on enemy ships. Spanish and Portuguese conquistadors rampaged through South America amassing enormous riches in the form of booty. Conquerors of many kinds plundered wealth after military conquest. Such forms of booty capitalism had been a historical commonplace. So too had been the practice of grinding the poor through arbitrary taxation, or simply robbing weak or defenceless groups (such as Jews).

Weber was struck by the major differences to work and to wealth accumulation of pre-industrial and industrial societies. The former were bound by custom, tradition, a reluctance to work, and a fatalistic or opportunistic attitude to getting rich. In contrast, the early capitalists worked hard, reinvested their profits, abandoned customary practices and innovated, and subjected their business and manufacturing practices to detailed and systematic scrutiny. They measured the effectiveness of their procedures and, when they found something they could improve, they improved it. Instead of gambling their fortunes on merchant adventures or foreign wars, they devoted themselves to the painstaking and unglamorous business of making a decent profit; not a huge profit, just a decent profit. They governed their lives with an attention to discipline, to avoiding the dangers of sloth, intemperance, and over-indulgence of the senses, and they tried very hard to impose such disciplines upon their employees.

It is important to recognize the focus of Weber's argument. He was not suggesting that there was anything new in acquisitiveness as such; what was novel was the form into which it was channelled. What were the origins of the distinctly rational attitude to work and gain that Weber believed characterized modern capitalism? He found a clue in the distribution of capitalist development. Industrial capitalism took off, not in Italy, Spain, and Portugal, but in parts of Germany and Holland, England and colonial America—those places where the Reformation (and especially the Calvinist part of the Reformation) had had its greatest impact. Hence Weber suggests that there is some causal connection between what he calls 'the Protestant ethic' and what he calls 'the spirit of capitalism'.

It is worth pausing here to make a point about the logic of Weber's thesis, a logic which appears frequently in sociology and which is central to the argument of this book. Weber claims to identify causal connections that operate at the level of *unintended consequences*. He is not suggesting that such great Reformation leaders as Luther and Calvin told people to go out and make money. What he is suggesting is that the accidental and unforeseen combination of various Reformation ideas inadvertently and ironically produced a new attitude to work and industry, and I will now describe the key ideas.

## Vocation

The first and most important innovation of the Reformation was the rejection of the institution of religious professionals. Most societies have a religious division of labour. The majority of the population go about their business and leave religion to a small handful of professionals and virtuosi, who placate the Gods either on behalf of the whole society or on behalf of those who pay them. In many Buddhist countries, only a fraction of the population follow the highest calling and become monks. The religious activity of the rest of the population is largely confined to behaving decently, performing a few simple and undemanding rituals, and providing food for the monks.[7] The monks earn religious merit and pass it on to the common people. In some cultures people practise a division of labour within their own lives, becoming monks for a time either in early adulthood or once they have retired from conventional business and raised their families. But for most, religion is done by proxy. Though church leaders may have wished otherwise, much of pre-Reformation Christianity had a similar division of labour. The monks and the secular clergy did religion and piety and the lay people supported the clergy.

Too enthusiastic a religion destroys societies. A popular and enduring religion has to strike a balance between the demands that it makes on the people and their ability to sustain their families and do their jobs. The Protestant Reformers objected to the religious division of labour of the Church in medieval Europe because it placed too little premium on personal piety. Martin Luther insisted that every man be his own monk. We all have a constant obligation to live moral and religious lives. We cannot rely on others to do it for us. In particular, he argued against the idea that religious merit could be transferred from one person to another. The fact that your brother was a monk would not make any difference to your position. Paying others to say Masses for your soul would not ensure it was sent heavenwards.

The result was a new stress on the need for all people to behave in a consistently moral and religious manner. The potential conflict between widespread religious enthusiasm and the social and economic needs of the society was resolved by redefining virtuosi religious behaviour. Mundane roles and occupations were now promoted as expressions of piety, as being pleasing to God, provided that they were performed diligently and honestly. The stonemason who felt a religious vocation no longer left his hammer and chisel for the monastery or the priesthood. He remained a mason and cut stone to the glory of God.

The new understanding of vocation was neatly expressed by the English Puritan divine Matthew Perkins when he defined a 'calling' as 'a certain kind of life imposed on man by God for the common good':

> Whatsoever is not done within the compass of calling is not faith . . . [and] every man must do the duties of his calling with diligence. [There are] two damnable sins that are contrary to this diligence. The first is idleness, whereby the duties of our callings and the occasions of glorifying God are neglected or omitted. The second is slothfulness, whereby they are performed slackly or carelessly.

Of course not all mundane activity could be a calling. Perkins excludes making one's living:

> by usury, by carding and dicing, by maintaining houses of gaming, by plays and suchlike . . . [and] by making foreign and fond fashions of attire, which serve for no use but to be displayed; flags and banners either of folly, or pride, or wantonness . . . such miserable courses of living are contrary to the will of God.[8]

## Consistency

The second vital change in the Reformation was the abandonment of rituals of periodic purification and the insistence on a regular religious and ethical life. Before the Reformation, Christianity, in common with most major religions, operated a quite human system which accepted that people would fall short of the ideal and gave them various ritual tasks to perform which would restore them to pristine purity. The moral and religious life was cyclical. Despite their best efforts (or without any), people behaved badly. When the guilt got too much, they confessed their sins and were offered some religious exercise to perform which would restore the balance. Or, and this is what the Reformers found especially objectionable, sinners paid some religious people to perform such exercises. In certain times and places, the practice was thoroughly institutionalized, with the sale of 'indulgences' for a fixed and well-known tariff providing a major source of income for the Church.

For the Protestant Reformers, this religious 'crop rotation' made a mockery of morality by allowing the sinful to evade the consequences of their sins. So out went prayers and Masses for the dead. Out went penance and, for most Protestants, out went confession.[9] In came the idea that life was a ledger with a plus and a minus column and a running score at the bottom of the page. And there was no longer any magical device to alter the balance of good and bad. Each individual had to take a passionate interest in assessing his or her conduct. Many of the English Puritans kept detailed diaries in which they daily recorded evidences of their spiritual state.

This view of life as linear and irreversible had two important consequences. First, it made the Puritans anxious not to sin because there was no way of earning forgiveness. Here work was useful, because someone who was legitimately busy was less likely to fall prey to the sins of the flesh. Rather unfairly, because Puritans were not all killjoys, it was this aspect of Puritan teaching which made the name of the movement a synonym for regarding all pleasure as sinful. Secondly, and perhaps more interestingly, it changed the way that people viewed the course of their lives and the passage of time. The previous cyclical view of time had fitted well with an agrarian way of life in which seasons followed seasons; replacing it with a resolutely linear one provided a template which encouraged people to see all spheres of life in terms of progress and movements towards a goal.

## Predestinarianism

The Genevan Reformer, John Calvin, added a further element to this socio-psychological mix with his notion of 'predestination'. He arrived at his conclusion from his reading of the Scriptures, but I will argue the point on logic. Let us invent a God. What sort of characteristics ought a God to have? First, he should be all powerful; nothing else will do. If God really is all powerful, he must be free from all influences. That is, he must be beyond manipulation. He is thus not liable to be impressed by anything we do, especially as, since Adam disobeyed God and was expelled from the Garden of Eden, we have been mired in sin. So no amount of candle burning or rosary-saying is going to cause God to change his mind about us. A petty Baron or Lord might be impressed by such flattery; a just God is not going to be so moved.

Secondly, God must be all-knowing. If he knows everything, he knows the future as well as the past. Clearly not everyone is going to be saved. If there is a hell, it must have some occupants. The Reformers were not universalists; they believed that only some people would be saved and others would be damned. Furthermore, given the massive evidence of sin in the world, they not unnaturally concluded that the number of people who would be saved must be pretty small. But if God knows the future, he must know who among us is going to be saved.

Together these two principles lead us to the idea of predestination. Calvinists believed that, even before our birth, God knew which of us were destined for salvation and which of us were destined for hell. Nothing we could do during our lifetimes could change our fate. Christ had not died to redeem all of us; he had died as a sacrifice only for the elect. This is the part that seems most strange and cruel to our modern minds. Those who were not part of the elect could perform what good works they liked. Indeed, they had to perform good works; that was a duty that God placed on all his creatures. The unelect could even believe themselves to have had a conversion experience or, in modern parlance, to be 'born again', but they were still destined to hell.

Though logical, their predestinarianism put the Calvinist Puritans in an uncomfortable position. Some were saved and others were not. They wanted to know which side they were on. They knew that there was nothing they could do to change God's mind, but they wanted to know their position. They would have liked to believe that they were part of the saved, but they needed a sign. And they found it in the fact of material success. They reasoned that, just as a poisoned tree will not bear good fruit, so God would not allow sinners to prosper. Thus, if they worked diligently in their calling, avoided the temptations of the flesh, invested their money, and prospered, then surely they could take that prosperity as a sign from God that they were, after all, part of the elect. The Puritans were clear that works could not earn salvation—that was a free gift from God—but they could be a signal.

To summarize, Weber argues that the unintended consequence of certain Reformation ideas—the ending of the religious division of labour that allowed lay people to leave religion to professionals, the stress on consistency, and the salvation anxiety that resulted from a belief in predestination—created what he calls 'this-worldly asceticism': 'asceticism' because the Godly people avoided sin and the rich living that tempted them to sin and 'this-worldly' because the religious person no longer retreated from the world to the monastery but behaved righteously in the material world.

That this asceticism was not just a negative sanction but was also turned into a positive encouragement to a certain way of life can be seen in the Puritan notion of stewardship. Christ offers the parable of the master and the stewards. Before going off on a long journey, the master calls each of three stewards. To the most able, he left five *talents*; to the next three; and to the least able, he left one *talent*. The first traded with his five and made five more and the second also doubled his capital. But the third servant buried his one *talent*. On his return the master praised the first servant: 'Well done, good and faithful servant; thou hast been faithful over a few things, I will make thee ruler over many things.'[10] He was similarly pleased with the second, but he was vicious in his criticism of the servant who had been so afraid of incurring his master's wrath by losing his money that he had hidden it and returned it without any profit. In one conventional interpretation of this story, we all have an obliga-tion to make use of such talents (in the modern sense) as we have been given, for our own good and for the good of our fellows. But the Puritan divine Richard Baxter took the parable literally: 'If God show you a way in which you can lawfully get more than in another way (without wrong to your soul or any other), if you refuse this, and chose the less gainful way, you cross one of the ends of your call-ing, and you refuse to be God's steward.'[11]

Put together the new secular notion of vocation, the stress on dili-gence, the anxious need to avoid sin, the keenness to see success as a sign of election, and the parable of the good steward, and we can see the basis for a new character and a new attitude towards work and accumulation. In fact, we can see the spirit of capitalism.

## Weber's Critics

Despite the very widespread acceptance of Weber's thesis and the enormous literature of commentary that has developed, there are still some fundamental misunderstandings.[12] A very common response to Weber has been to show that Luther, Calvin, Zwingli, and other Protestant theologians were opposed to greed, to acquis-itiveness, and to being over concerned with wealth—which, of course, they were. Calvin can be seen as giving the conventional Christian view that only poor people can truly do the will of God. But this criticism rather misses the nature of Weber's causal con-nection. His argument is concerned not with the intentions of Calvin and Luther but with the later and unintended consequences of a combination of their ideas.

The case of Scotland is also offered as refutation of the Weber thesis. Unlike the situation in England, where the Reformation was only partial and more the product of political considerations than of popular sentiment, Protestantism in Scotland was popular and quickly conquered the Lowlands, where the majority of Scots lived. Furthermore, though Weber uses the English divine Richard Baxter for many of his illustrations, Scots Protestants were more influenced by the teachings of Calvin than were their English counterparts. Scotland had a lot of the Protestant ethic, so it should also have had a lot of capitalism. Yet its economic development was slow. Capitalist industrialization proceeded faster in England than it did in Scotland. Critics believe this refutes Weber's thesis.

Of course, it does no such thing. Weber believed that he had discovered the origins of the *spirit* of capitalism, not the origins of capitalism. It could be that Scotland was full of potential industrialists who were full of the spirit of capitalism and that the development of the full-blooded phenomenon was retarded by the absence of some other necessary conditions—such as a developed financial system, good communications and transport, advanced raw material extraction, and law and order. That is, Weber is not saying that the Protestant ethic on its own was enough for capitalism. If the other conditions had been absent, there would simply have been a lot of frustrated proto-capitalists. To put it in logical terms, Weber is not claiming that the Protestant ethic was a sufficient condition for capitalism.

Recent research suggests that such a defence of Weber is exactly right. Gordon Marshall has studied the coal-mining enterprise of Sir John Clerk of Penecuik and we find in Sir John the capitalist spirit in large doses. It was not for want of trying that his efforts and those of like-minded people did not produce capitalism.[13]

The obverse case is sometimes made with Japan. Here we have a very successful capitalist economy and not a Calvinist Protestant in sight. But, as with the Scotland case, this criticism misses the point. Weber is not suggesting as a universal proposition that only Calvinist Protestants can be capitalists. Indeed, he is not making any universal claims at all. He is trying to explain a particular historical event: the innovation, not the continued popularity, of the phenomenon. He does not argue that the Protestant ethic is a necessary condition for capitalism. A lot of practices and innovations quickly come free from their point of origin and are admired and adopted for their own merits, irrespective of the motives of the originators. In that sense, the Protestant ethic quickly becomes secularized.

Non-Calvinists, non-Protestants, and even non-Christians can be impressed by the merits of 'this-worldly asceticism' and the rationality it encourages, even though they do not share the religious basis which originally made these attractive.

Interestingly, the most telling criticism of Max Weber's thesis is the least often pursued and that is his shortage of evidence on a vital link in his thesis. Weber shows us that one Puritan divine—Richard Baxter—was imbued with the Protestant ethic. Weber also gives us the American Benjamin Franklin as a spokesman for the spirit of modern capitalism. But Franklin was writing in the late eighteenth century—two hundred years after the crucial time for this explanation. Weber does not present any evidence for the widespread distribution of the spirit of capitalism in the important time period. It is not enough to show us that the Puritan leaders had it; it is not even enough to show that they preached it. What matters is whether their congregations internalized such a spirit and acted on it. We might assume that they did because they listened to their ministers. We certainly know that Baxter and others were popular preachers whose sermons were very widely read. But assuming and knowing are not the same and we are unlikely to know because the letters and diaries of Puritan small businessmen have rarely been preserved.

A measured evaluation of the Weber thesis would be that it is plausible and fits what we know. Though there are gaps in the evidence, Weber appears to have made an important connection between the Reformation and the increased rationalization of the modern world.

In completing the foundations for the next chapter, I would like to draw out two further implications of the Reformation.

## The Reformation and Science

Modern science is not easy for cultures which believe that the world is pervaded by supernatural spirits or that the divinities are unpredictable. Systematic exploration of regularities in the behaviour of matter requires the assumption that the behaviour of matter is indeed regular. It is not impossible but it is hard to discover the laws of physics if one supposes that volume may be measured by the displacement of water one day but not the next. Such a culture may produce the odd Archimedes but it retards the development of a community of scholars directing sustained effort to the discovery of the ways of matter. In that simple sense the Judaeo-Christian tradition, by simplifying a supernatural menagerie to one God and supposing him distant from the material world, made way for modern science.

Just as the medieval Church retarded and temporarily reversed the ethical rationalization inherent in Judaism and early Christianity, so the development of science was retarded by the Church's imposition of orthodoxy on all fields of thought. The Church claimed to speak in an unchanging and authoritative fashion not only on matters of behaviour but also on the behaviour of matter. The Reformation, by breaking the power of the Church (albeit in many places replacing it with the power of a church), made way for a variety of thought and for the questioning of tradition which is so vital to natural science. The Protestant advantage in this sphere is noted by McMullin in his comments on the Catholic Church's intellectual stagnation.

In the early growth of this science, bishops like Grosseteste, Albert of Saxony and Oresme, as well as priests like Albertus Magnus, Bradwardine and Buridan had played a decisive part. . . . But within a generation all this had changed. Reactionism set in, and the intellectual forces of the Church gradually withdrew from the fields of secular learning which they had dominated for so long, back to the seemingly secure fortifications of a tried and true traditionalism.[14]

In his studies of the relationship between Puritanism and science, Robert Merton argues for a positive connection.[15] He ably demonstrates that a strong desire to demonstrate the glory of God by displaying the majesty of his Creation, the rational and systematic attitude of the Protestant ethic, and the Puritan's desire to control the corrupt world combined to produce in seventeenth-century England a great interest in natural science.

## Individualism and Fission

Finally in this chapter I want to draw attention to the most profound of all the consequences of the Reformation. David Martin put it succinctly when he wrote that 'The logic of Protestantism is clearly in favour of the voluntary principle, to a degree that eventually makes it sociologically unrealistic.'[16] It is perhaps an obvious point, but belief systems differ greatly in their propensity to fragment. Much of the variation can be explained by the theory of knowledge that lies at the heart of the beliefs.[17] Some belief systems claim a unique grasp of the truth while others allow that there are many ways to salvation. The Catholic Church claims that Christ's authority was passed to Peter, the first Bishop of Rome, and was then institutionalized in the office of Pope. The Church claims ultimate control of the means to salvation and the right finally to arbitrate all disputes about what is God's will. So long as that central claim is not disputed, the Catholic Church is immune to fission and schism.

In contrast, the religion created by the Reformation was extremely vulnerable to fragmentation because it removed the institution of the Church as a source of authority between God and man. If, by reading the Scriptures, we are all able to discern God's will, then how do we settle disputes between the various discernings that are produced? The Reformers, being theists who believed in one God, one Holy Spirit which dwelt in all of God's creation, and one Bible, could hope that the righteous would agree, but history proved that hope false. Tradition, habit, and respect for learning or piety all had the effect of restraining the schismatic tendencies but they could not prevent them. The consequence of the Reformation was not a Christian church strengthened because it had been purified but a large number of competing perspectives and institutions. As we will see in the next chapter, this fragmentation of the dominant religious culture was to have profound effects on the position of religion in the modern world.

## Conclusion

The Reformation was far more than a change in the dominant religious tradition in Europe. It did not arise out of nothing and I could have started this account at an earlier point to show the social, political, and economic changes that encouraged the Reformation. But if we take it as our starting-point, we can see the tremendous effects it had in laying the foundations for 'modernity'. In insisting that all people had a responsibility for their own spiritual state, the Reformation inadvertently added greatly to the growth of individualism. It created the need for ordinary people to become better informed about their religion, and by promoting printing, the use of the vernacular, and literacy it gave them the means to become so informed. It also contributed to the rationalization of the world, the growth of modern science, and the fragmentation of once dominant religious cultures, and thus, as we shall see in the next chapter, inadvertently contributed to the erosion of religion.

## Notes

1. For basic histories of the Reformation, see Steven Ozment, *Protestants: The Birth of a Revolution* (London: Fontana, 1993); R. W. Southern, *Western Society and the Church in the Middle Ages* (Harmondsworth, Middx.: Penguin, 1970); Clare Cross, *Church and People 1450–1660* (London: Fontana, 1970), and A. G. Dickens, *The English Reformation* (London: Fontana, 1967).
2. Peter L. Berger, *The Social Reality of Religion* (London: Faber & Faber, 1969).
3. Ibid. 115.
4. Although it is nowhere nearly as well expressed, this section draws heavily on Ernest Gellner, *Plough, Sword and Book: The Structure of Human History* (London: Paladin, 1991), 100–3.
5. Max Weber, *The Protestant Ethic and the Spirit of Capitalism* (London: George Allen & Unwin, 1976). Some of the misunderstandings of Weber's work stem from the piecemeal way in which his enormous output was translated into English and made widely known. We get a clearer understanding of what he was trying to do if we appreciate the order in which various essays were written, and their relationship to each other and to contemporary debates. See Gordon Marshall, *In Search of the Spirit of Capitalism: An Essay on Max Weber's Protestant Ethic Thesis* (London: Hutchinson, 1982).
6. Marshall Sahlins, *Stone Age Economics* (Chicago: Aldine, 1972).
7. S. J. Tambiah, 'The Ideology of Merit and the Social Correlates of Buddhism in a Thai Village', in Edmund R. Leach (ed.), *Dialectics in Popular Religion* (Cambridge: Cambridge University Press, 1968), 41–121.
8. Quoted in Michael Lessnoff, 'Protestant Ethic and Profit Motive in the Weber Thesis', *International Journal of Sociology and Social Policy*, 1 (1981), 5.
9. Some branches of the reformed faith (particularly in the Lutheran tradition) retained the institution of confession but regarded it not as a sacrament but merely as a useful spiritual exercise.
10. Matt. 25: 23.
11. Quoted in Lessnoff, 'Protestant Ethic', 4. See also his *The Spirit of Capitalism and the Protestant Ethic: An Enquiry into the Weber Thesis* (Cheltenham: Edward Elgar, 1994).
12. Much of the literature is ably discussed in Marshall, *In Search*.
13. Gordon Marshall, *Presbyteries and Profits: Calvinism and the Development of Capitalism in Scotland 1560–1707* (Oxford: Clarendon Press, 1980).
14. Ernan McMullin, 'Science and the Catholic Tradition', in Ian G. Barbour (ed.), *Science and Religion* (London: SCM Press, 1968), 30–42.
15. Robert K. Merton, *Science, Technology and Society in the 17th Century* (New York: Fertig, 1970).

16. David Martin, *The Dilemmas of Contemporary Religion* (Oxford: Blackwell, 1978), 9.

17. A general theory of factionalism and schism was presented by Roy Wallis, *Salvation and Protest: Studies of Social and Religious Movements* (London: Frances Pinter, 1979), ch. 10, 'A Theory of Propensity to Schism', and applied to traditions within Christianity in Steve Bruce, 'Authority and Fission: The Protestants' Divisions', *British Journal of Sociology*, 36 (1985), 592–603.

# 3

---

# THE EROSION OF THE SUPERNATURAL

........................................................................................................

TRADITIONAL worlds were religious places. Indeed some primitive societies were so thoroughly permeated by religion, superstition, and magic that it is hard to separate religion from other parts of those worlds. Things we would regard as mundane and this-worldly, such as hunting or fishing, were enmeshed with religious ritual. Unless the rituals were properly performed, the hunting or fishing would not be productive. Such societies simply did not divide the supernatural from the natural in the way we do.

The social institutions of modern societies have become sufficiently specialized for us to see religion as a distinct sphere of activity and it is thus possible to talk about its influence and popularity. The fundamental point of such talk is that the modern urban industrial societies of Western Europe, North America, and Australasia—and it is those that are the concern of this book—are considerably less religious than the formations that preceded them. This change—secularization—will be described and explained in this chapter. The examples will be drawn initially from Britain, but we can be confident, both from the evidence from other countries which I will add, and from the fact that many of the scholars on whose work I draw were themselves basing their conclusions on examples gathered more widely, that, though elements of the script are particular to Britain, the drama is one that was played out across the industrializing West.

First, two qualifications. As should be clear, this study is concerned with religion in so far as it is visible or 'empirically given'. That is, we are concerned with the changing popularity and place of certain beliefs and types of behaviour; we are not in the business of judging the quality of those beliefs and actions or the sincerity of those who adhere to them. In talking of a decline in religion, we want to avoid making any judgement about what is 'true religion'. It may well be that all that has changed has been the loss of a nominal adherence to churches, the performance of religious rites primarily for social reasons, a shallow acceptance of prevailing ideas, and an unnecessary entanglement of religious roles and institutions with secular matters. It is possible to argue that what those of us who remain attached to religion now possess is a purer, more 'religious' faith. But such judgements are not in the competence of the social scientist.

The second qualification: it should also be stressed that the social scientist is primarily concerned with the social significance of religion. What effect do religious beliefs have on the operation of the social system, on the lives of societies? Of course, that must be closely related to the importance of religion for individuals. While some nineteenth-century church adherence can be explained by the pressure to conform to the prevailing *mores*, it should be obvious that people only go to church because they feel that the community requires it of them if someone (and it must be either a majority of the someones or a majority of the important someones) actually believes. It is thus likely that a decline in the social significance of religion will be accompanied by a decline in the popularity and importance of religion *per se*. Or at least, if it is the case that religion is no longer important for a particular society but remains vital for many of the individuals who compose it, then there has been a highly significant change in the way that people live out their beliefs.

Secularization may be sought in the following three related changes: the decline of popular involvement with the churches; the decline in scope and influence of religious institutions; and the decline in the popularity and impact of religious beliefs. I will offer some evidence for those changes now and insert other data at relevant points in the rest of the book.

But first we should have an accurate sense of the major changes in context. There is no point in inappropriate cross-cultural comparisons. As I suggested in the explanation of this book's title in the Introduction, the relationship of the individual to the religious culture at the period where this study begins—in the medieval world—was very different from that which obtains in the modern world. Church membership itself is a modern idea. The unitary church of the pre-Reformation feudal society did not have members; it represented the entire people. It was financially supported primarily by the rental or produce from gifts of land given by the king and the gentry. Its offices were performed according to the calendar irrespective of popular attendance. They were thought to be effective in pleasing God even if, as in the case of the daily Masses said in most churches in the fifteenth century, none of the common people attended. That the religious activity of the Middle Ages did not rest on the involvement of individual members of the laity was clear from the very architecture of churches and the forms of the services. In small parish churches, away from the high ceremonial of the cathedral, 'frequently the priest read the entire service in a low and inaudible voice with his back to the congregation throughout'.[1] The laity were not discouraged from hearing Offices in places where they were publicly sung, but 'unless they understood Latin there was little inducement for them to do so'.[2] The remarkable point of contrast with our situation is that, with so little encouragement, so many people in the pre-Reformation world did regularly attend services, and attendance at church for rituals concerned with major life events—birth, marriage, and death—was almost universal. In some parts of England, the Puritan Reformers were highly critical of the ritual of 'churching' mothers a month after childbirth. One reformer listed it as 'No. 55' of the serious errors of the Church of England. Nevertheless, in late Elizabethan Salisbury more than three-quarters of mothers were 'churched'.[3]

Hamilton's judgement of the impact of Christianity seems sensible: 'The medieval world was Christian in the sense that everybody shared a common understanding of the world in which they lived based on Christian premises. Only the very learned had full and detailed knowledge of the whole world picture, but everybody understood some part of it.'[4] He goes on to note that 'Everybody knew the *Our Father*', that 'People in the Middle Ages were willing to spend considerable sums of money in payment for masses', that 'Everybody believed that man had an immortal soul', and that 'Most people seem to have accepted that it was necessary to make reparation to God for serious and wilful sins either in this life or the next.'[5]

However dimly comprehended, the Christian faith had enough impact on popular attitudes for the swearing of oaths on the Bible to be an effective form of social control and for people to go to great lengths to avoid blaspheming. In writing of the various sacraments, Keith Thomas says: 'Before a man died . . . he was extended . . . extreme unction, whereby the recipient was anointed with holy oil

and tendered the viaticum. In the eyes of everyone this was a dreadful ritual . . .'.[6] Rituals that are not widely believed in hardly inspire
dread.

Thomas also documents in fascinating detail the strength of popular belief in the supernatural, especially in malign spiritual forces.
Belief in the Devil was strong and widespread, as was the corresponding belief that the Christian Church had the power to protect
against evil. As Hamilton writes: 'People wanted their houses blessed,
their fields blessed, their food blessed, their weapons blessed.'[7]

The Reformation, by fragmenting Christendom and introducing
the voluntary principle, inadvertently created the notion of church
membership (though the practice of trying to count members
accurately dates from the Methodist movement). Each wave of
Protestant religious dissent brought an increase in individual knowledge of religion as the sectarians argued and proselytized and taught
their new beliefs, and as the established churches were obliged to
argue against the new heretics. In many European countries there
developed a division between the religious life of the towns and
cities, where the dissenters and sectarians prospered, and the rural
areas, which were slow to change from the pre-Reformation model.
A respected modern historian of Methodism has used Flora
Thompson's description of the religious life of the village of Lark
Rise to exemplify nineteenth-century rural religion, and, if one
removed the reference to anti-Catholicism and inserted mention of
an obsessive interest in supernatural powers, it could stand for most
pre-Reformation settings.

Thompson . . . estimates that nine out of ten Lark Rise inhabitants would
have declared themselves members of the Church of England, having been
christened and married in the parish church. In addition, they buried their
dead at church, attended festivals at Christmas, Easter and harvest time,
visited the rectory on May Day, qualified themselves for the valuable charities dispensed by clerical families, paraded their finery and singing voices
on Sundays, and could even be roused under certain circumstances to
exhibit half-hearted displays of anti-Catholic sentiment. The majority, of
course, never darkened the church's door outside festival time, unless
closely bound by deference to squire or clergyman, and most of them,
especially the men, resented clerical visits, particularly if the subject of religion was mentioned.[8]

The people of the towns and cities were more thoroughly divided
into the godly and the ungodly, with class emerging as an important
issue. With the exception of the Catholic Church, which in England

and Scotland retained the affections of the poor, religion was more appealing the higher one's status. Especially in the cities, the class division was often seen as an incentive to evangelistic activity. Turning the ungodly into the godly would also transform the dangerous masses into respectable honest artisans.[9]

## Modern Decline

Though there were still many places like Lark Rise, by the nineteenth century the voluntary principle had become so well established that individual church adherence was a matter of concern and attempts were made to assess it. There are considerable technical difficulties involved in making inferences from various records, but we are unlikely to be far wrong if we suppose that about 18 per cent of the adult population of England were church 'members' in 1800, that this rose to 27 per cent by 1850, declined slightly to 26 per cent in 1900, and then continued to decline so that the corresponding figure for 1990 would be about 14 per cent or less.[10] As the two extremes of personal enthusiasm and personal indifference to religion replaced simply living in a religious culture, the proportion of people who might be described as 'belonging' to a church or sect rose and then began a long decline which has not yet ended. Membership of the Protestant denominations—which until recently represented the vast bulk of British Christianity—fell from 22 per cent of the adult population in 1900 to just 7 per cent in 1990.[11]

It may require far less effort to have one's name on a church roll than to attend its services. A better sense of the penetration of formal religion might be gained from looking at the proportion of the people who were prepared to take part in public acts of commitment. As far back as we have records, the Church of England and the Church of Scotland have had far more people on their rolls than have attended church.[12] Nominal association is even greater for the Roman Catholic Church, which counts as Catholic anyone baptized as such. The proportion of baptized Roman Catholics who actually attend Mass has declined from 47 per cent in 1900 to 33 per cent in 1990. Generally only the small and more sectarian Protestant churches have had more people in their congregations than on their books. According to a major 1984 census of the Scottish churches, only the small Baptist Church was attended by more people than claimed membership.[13]

Although they vary greatly in the quality of the data they produced, there were many surveys of church attendance in the nineteenth century, often inspired by increasingly bitter arguments about the privileges of the state churches. Newspapers organized local surveys, the Churches themselves collected figures, and in 1851 there was the national Census of Religious Worship conducted by Horace Mann. There are technical problems in interpreting Mann's Census.[14] Especially for Scotland, where the returns were less complete than for England and Wales, there are doubts about some of the original figures. The Census enumerates attendances rather than attenders and many people attended more than once on any Sunday. Some scholars add together morning, afternoon, and evening attendances and make the point that the disappearance of multiple attendance is itself a significant mark of declining commitment that should be noted. Others take only the figures for the best-attended service, whichever that is for any particular congregation. Attendances at church represented 61 per cent of the Scottish population and 58 per cent of the population of England and Wales. One estimate put the number of church-goers at around half of the attendances; that is, it is assumed that most church-goers went twice on a Sunday.[15] Very few people would have attended three services, so we can guess that about one-third of the British people attended church on the census Sunday in 1851. By the 1980s 'double sitting' was confined to the very small evangelical Protestant sects and we can take the figure for attendances to be the same as the figure for attenders: in Scotland 17 per cent of the population, in Wales 13 per cent, and in England 9 per cent.[16]

Many of the technical problems with the 1851 Census data have been resolved by Gill, who has also brought together an impressive array of other local and church-based surveys. In noting the effects of weather, Gill says that 'total attendances on an exceedingly wet day in Cheltenham, 29 January 1882, amounted to 47.7% of the population, whereas those just a week later, but on a fine day, amounted to 61.4%'.[17] Not even bourgeois Cheltenham could now hope to exceed 12 per cent, no matter what the weather! Gill has studied the records of churches in rural Northumberland in particular detail. He notes that Anglican attendances peaked in 1866 and declined thereafter. The zenith for the Presbyterians was in the 1860s and 1870s. Roman Catholic attendances peaked earlier: 'Their combined Easter Mass attendances were 234 in 1849, 480 in 1855, but had declined to 297 in 1861, to 187 in 1892, and to just 109 in 1899.' Gill's own census of the remaining twenty-nine buildings in use in the area (out of a total of forty-five in 1901) found that only 9 per cent of the total population attended morning services.[18] The timing may have been slightly different for urban areas, but the general trajectory is the same: 'a careful analysis of London and Liverpool census data suggests that there has been a continuous process of declining Sunday attendances in the Church of England since the 1851 Religious Census.'[19] Gill adds: 'Free-Church attendances overall have declined since the 1880s. In Greater London they declined from 13 per cent in 1887, to 11 per cent in 1903, and to 4 per cent in 1979.'[20]

As we would expect, the changing vision of the place of religion and the competition that came with the proliferation of dissenting sects and denominations saw an increase in popular involvement with formal religion. Membership and attendance then peaked and began the steady decline which is so far unabated. Social historians of religion disagree about the precise shape of the curve and the placing of the peak, but, whatever objections they might raise to this or that measure, they are agreed that there are now far fewer church members and church-goers than there were in 1950, 1900, 1850, or 1800.[21]

The shrinking of the British churches can be seen as clearly in the number of clergy. In 1900 there were just over 20,000 Church of England clerics. By 1984 that had halved to just over 10,000. Across the Channel a very similar pattern emerges in the main church. France in 1948 had almost 43,000 Roman Catholic clergy; by 1987 this had declined to 28,000. Since 1975 there have been fewer than 100 ordinations a year.[22] Ordinations to the Catholic Church in England have also now fallen below replacement levels.[23] In Belgium in the 1950s it was normal to go to church; half the population did it. By 1990 only 18 per cent of Belgians attended Mass regularly.[24] To take an example from the other side of the globe, the percentage of Australians claiming 'no religion' in the decennial censuses has increased from eleven in 1961 to twenty-three in 1991.[25] Different countries show different rates of decline and different sorts of measures show different aspects of the change, but the direction of change in all indices of involvement in institutional religion is the same: downwards. Of all societies in the industrial West, only the United States is an exception to this pattern, and it will be discussed at length in Chapter 6.

What of the churches' involvement in the community? Calling on the churches to celebrate important social events certainly remains more popular than membership or attendance, but here too we see signs of decline. The ritual churching of women has completely gone. The relative size of the Church of England and its role as the national church means that we can take its baptismal records as a good index of Protestant baptism in England. In 1900, 65 per cent of live births were baptized in the Anglican Church. In 1927, it was 71 per cent; in 1960, 55 per cent, in 1970, 47 per cent, and in 1993, it was 27 per cent.[26] White weddings are still popular but less so than they were. At the start of the century almost 70 per cent of English couples marrying did so in the state church. By 1990, this had fallen to 53 per cent. In early Victorian Scotland almost all marriages were religious ceremonies; for example, in 1876, 98.9 per cent of weddings were solemnized in church. In 1990 it was 57 per cent.[27]

Church involvement is not the only expression of religious sentiment nor is it a necessary one. We cannot immediately assume that, because we are far less likely than our grandparents to be churchgoers, ours is a less religious society. However, it is not enough to assert that a significant number of those Britons who are not involved in any of the vast range of religious activities that are on offer are none the less 'religious'. Some evidence must be adduced. Unless people act on a certain belief or opinion, we can only discern what they think or feel by asking them. In order to ask a large enough number of people to be confident that the answers are representative of a large social group, we need to use the pre-structured question-and-answer format of the social survey and we are well aware of the weaknesses in data generated by such instruments. Even if we assume that survey respondents are really doing their best to give accurate and truthful answers to questions, we still have the problem of having to believe that all respondents interpret our questions in the same way and mean the same thing by their answers. Generally speaking, the more concrete the issue, the more reliable the response. Surveys are better at discovering the ownership of televisions than they are at discerning attitudes and the more abstract the matter in hand the less useful the data. Asking people if they agree with the government's privatization of the water supply will produce more reliable responses than asking if they believe in God. None the less, surveys have asked people if they believe in God, if they are religious, and so on, and, provided we are careful in the conclusions we draw from them, such data are worth reporting.

A consistent finding of such surveys is that a very high proportion of people in Europe assert some confessional or denominational identification. In Britain, generally less than a quarter of respondents in a variety of surveys claim 'no religion'. To be more specific, few people claim to be atheists or agnostics: in the 1991 British Social Attitudes (hereafter BSA) survey, 10 and 13 per cent respectively.[28] However, the unbelievers are now more numerous than a decade earlier, when only 4 per cent identified themselves as 'atheists'. In 1947 only 6 per cent said, to use the Gallup formula, that they 'Don't really think there is any sort of spirit / God or life force'; in 1968 it was 11 per cent.

Secondly, and this is not just a restatement of the previous point, most people say they believe in some sort of God. In the BSA survey, 72 per cent claimed to believe in some sort of supernatural power. When asked a differently worded question later in the same survey, only 50 per cent said they believed in God. Of those, only half felt close to God, and almost a quarter felt 'not close at all'. The BSA survey also asked about changes in belief: those who had once believed but no longer did outnumbered by two to one those who had become believers.

It requires something of an act of faith to take the results of surveys conducted years apart, even when they use an identical form of words for their questions, as evidence of the nature or extent of change. If we make that assumption, the traditional Christian view of God as a person is now less popular than a very wide range of non-theistic visions of the supernatural. Between 1947 and 1987 the proportion of respondents who agreed that 'There is a personal God' fell from 45 to 37 per cent, while those who choose the option 'There is some sort of spirit or vital force which controls life' increased from 39 to 42 per cent. The various agnostic and atheistic positions increased in popularity from 16 to 21 per cent. To take the central Christian claim, 71 per cent of Gallup respondents in 1951 agreed that 'Jesus Christ is the Son of God'. In 1965 it was 64 per cent and in 1982 it was only 43 per cent. In a 1957 survey 54 per cent said they believed in life after death. In the BSA survey only 27 per cent made the same claim. Other traditional beliefs were similarly unpopular. Only 24 per cent of respondents said they believed in the Devil or in hell.[29]

The BSA survey asked people if they were religious and gave them seven options. They could describe themselves as 'religious', 'very religious', and 'extremely religious', as 'neither religious nor non-religious', or as one of the corresponding three degrees of 'non-religious'. A large proportion—41 per cent—described themselves as religious, but almost all of them choose the weakest of the three positions. Taken together, the neutral category and the three non-religious ones outnumbered the religious. We do not have corresponding survey data from previous centuries, but, given everything we know from newspapers, diaries, letters, church statistics, and the political debates of the time, it seems inconceivable that, had such questions been asked in the eighteenth or nineteenth centuries, the 'religious' would have been outnumbered by the rest.

If it is the case that a large part of the unchurched retain a strong interest in religion despite losing interest in the churches, there ought to be some evidence of this apart from verbal assent to survey questions. To cite a parallel, we know that many people who very rarely attend football matches remain keen on football because they watch it on television and they subscribe to satellite services to watch foreigners play it. We know that the sales of newspapers can be affected by the amount and quality of their football coverage. It is very hard to find any similar mark of religious interest among the unchurched. Sales of religious books have declined.[30] The space given to church and spiritual matters in the popular press is now vestigial; only a sex scandal (for the tabloids) or a money scandal (for the broadsheets) will get the churches out of a bottom corner on an inside page. Although religious programmes on television commanded large audiences in the 1960s, this seems to have been largely a matter of supply. With only two television channels, an agreement to preserve a prime-time slot on Sunday evenings for religious programming and the willingness of a large part of the audience to watch whatever was on ensured that the church-goers who enjoyed the BBC's *Songs of Praise* or ITV's *Stars on Sunday* were boosted to a healthy audience share. Now that the 'God slot' has been abandoned and there are four terrestrial television channels and a plethora of others on satellite, the audience for religious programming has declined from three-quarters of the number of viewers of the most popular secular programmes to under a quarter. The conclusions of the third in a series of detailed studies of responses to religious programming are clear:

The 1968 survey showed that 40 per cent of respondents deliberately turned on to watch a religious programme and over half said they paid attention when a religious programme was on. By 1987, this was found to have changed, with only seven per cent of people saying they deliberately turned on when a religious programme was being shown.[31]

When we put these observations together with the evidence of decline in the popularity of the churches, we can see an increasingly secular people gradually losing faith in the specific teachings of the Christian tradition but retaining a nostalgic fondness for it—many of us want the great cathedrals to be preserved so that we can visit them for carol-singing at Christmas time—and continuing to make vague and weak religious affirmations.

A clue to explaining the apparent tension between the popularity of claiming to be religious and the unpopularity of every expression of religious beliefs and values can be found in Richard Hoggart's rich description of working-class life in northern towns in the first half of the twentieth century. Discussing attitudes to the churches, Hoggart wryly observes that the term 'Christian' was taken to mean decent, honest, and ethical.[32] Something similar seems to be the case with modern claims to be 'religious'. In Northern Ireland the working-class description for someone who becomes a committed Christian is 'good living'. In describing themselves as 'religious', survey respondents are asserting their continued commitment to the general social values that they take to be the consequences of Christianity rather than saying that they are Christian in the traditional sense.

It is important to note just how weak are the measures of 'religiosity' used in modern surveys. Let us recall the beliefs which historians of the Middle Ages readily describe as taken for granted: the existence of a real heaven and hell, the reality of the Mass as a repeat of Christ's real sacrifice for our sins, and the effectiveness of the Church's means of ensuring our salvation.[33] These are extremely 'religious' beliefs, quite at odds with the cosmology of the modern world. They were once common; they are now rare.

Talking of the content of religious belief systems brings us to an important point. The decline in popularity of the churches and the culture they promote is not the only evidence of the increasing implausibility of religious ideas. There are also important changes within the churches. Though they are interesting in their own right, I have in mind, not the sometimes spectacular rejection of orthodox beliefs by radical theologians but the more subtle and general sidelining of what were once taken to be central tenets of the faith. Much of the Thirty-nine Articles, the statement of faith of the

Church of England, would embarrass most contemporary Anglican clergymen, and the ideological centre of the Presbyterian churches has shifted so far from their origins that when new ordinands assent that they accept the Westminster Confession of Faith as the subordinate standard of their church (subordinate to the Bible, that is) they do so with considerable reservations. One senior Church of Scotland minister told me, only slightly facetiously, that he had recently reread the Confession and been surprised to find something there that he could agree with.

It is not much of an exaggeration to say that the main churches have themselves become secularized in the sense of reducing the specifically supernatural in their product. Major elements of the Christian faith—the miracles, the Virgin Birth, the bodily resurrection of Christ, the expectation of Christ's return, the reality of eternal damnation—have quietly been dropped from the teachings of the major Christian churches.

Along with the gradual disappearance of specific Christian tenets there has been a fundamental redirection of many doctrines. What used to be regarded as objective truths have been 'psychologized'. They are now held to apply only in so far as people choose to believe in them and then they apply only subjectively, for the psyche of the individual. What were previously taken to be true stories about the real world (there was actually a person called Christ who was the Son of God and who died for our sins) have been reoriented as propositions which become true when they have the desired effect on the mind of the believer. Essentially the faith has been relativized so that it is now just one of a range of belief systems which are to be judged not by how accurately they describe a single past, present, and future but by how useful are the effects they have on adherents.

The new understanding of the status of the faith allows a new attitude to other faiths. What were once competing convictions are now seen as being all, in some sense, equally valid. And that courtesy has been extended beyond the Christian churches so that they no longer divide the world into the saved and the damned, the righteous and the unregenerate; now, however unaware we may be of this fact, we are all God's children. The ecumenical movement began at the start of this century with evangelical Protestants discovering common interests. As it grew, it embraced first the less radical wings of the main Protestant churches and then the Orthodox churches and the Roman Catholic Church. The World Council of Churches now includes among its members various African churches (such as the Kimbanguist Church of Zaire and the Aladura Church of the Lord in Nigeria) which profess some, from a Christian standpoint, highly deviant views. It has even had its congresses attended by representatives of North American nativist religions.[34]

More will be said about the way in which the Christianity of the West has changed this century. At this point it is enough to note that it would be a blinkered vision that considered only the popularity of formal religious organizations and did not also note that the Churches themselves had changed.

As I shall show below, the religious cultures of different societies have developed in very different ways. However, as a starting-point, we may note that, with the partial exception of the USA (which will be discussed in detail in Chapter 6), the pattern of decline in the social significance and popularity of religion sketched above is common to most industrial societies and there is widespread agreement that such evolution is driven by common social forces and hence that a general explanation of secularization is possible.

## Explaining Secularization

Nothing as complex as a massive change in culture and social behaviour across a variety of very different societies is going to have a simple explanation. However, it is possible to distinguish the broad contours of an explanation and I will do that by sketching first the 'deep structure' and then adding the 'surface structure'.

First we must eliminate one persistent but misleading explanation of secularization. It is not the case that religion has declined because people have become better educated and less credulous.[35] Committed atheists—the sort of people who join rationalist and humanist associations—and some very liberal Christians believe that religion has lost its medieval dominance because modern people are too clever to believe in old superstitions. Some critics of religion like to portray it as an infantile delusion which societies have grown out of as science has replaced religious falsehood with secular truth. Auguste Comte, the nineteenth-century Frenchman who was one of the founding fathers of sociology, believed that the new science of sociology would replace the old myths.[36] Sigmund Freud declared his hand when he called one of his essays on religion *The Future of an Illusion*.[37]

Increasing knowledge and maturity cannot explain the decline of religion. There are too many examples of modern people believing the most dreadful nonsense to suppose that people change from one set of beliefs to another just because the second lot are better ideas. The history of the human ability to believe very strongly in things that turn out not to be true suggests that whether something is true and whether it becomes widely accepted are two very different questions. Whether any particular religion is true is a theological, not a sociological, question. Fortunately we can avoid such unprofitable terrain by recognizing that all beliefs—true ones as much as false ones—need explaining.[38] Hence we can ask what is it about our societies, other than our supposed greater maturity, that explains why religious beliefs are less plausible or credible than they once were.

Let us begin with 'modernization'. Clearly modernization has something to do with economic growth. Marion Levy has suggested that it be defined as the growing ratio between inanimate and animate source of power.[39] Men and animals built the pyramids. We build with machines driven by fossil fuels. As we shall see, technology brings with it major changes in social structures, social relations, and the ways that people think. Though Levy's definition raises some problems that we need not address, it has the useful consequence of reminding us that to talk of modern societies (with the implied contrast with 'pre-modern' societies) is actually a short cut for talking about a range of positions along an axis. It also reminds us that we are talking about stages in that process rather than a particular time in history. Hence this book is about religion in the First and Second Worlds rather than about religion 'now'. That Iran or Burma is unlike Britain or Norway goes without saying. Like the Weber thesis, the argument of this book is in the first instance an attempt to explain a set of changes that occurred at a particular time in a particular place. Again, like the Weber thesis, because my explanation involves a number of causes which are general rather than context-specific, there is the possibility that some of the processes described here will also occur in very different societies, but, prior to detailed study, it is only a possibility. A sensitive reading of my argument would allow us to identify those features of Iran and Burma that make it more and less likely that their religious cultures will develop in ways recognizably similar to those of Britain or Norway, but that is too great a work to be undertaken here.

Most sociologists believe that there are features of the modern societies which make them unconducive to religion. Three seem to be particularly salient: the fragmentation of societies and of social life, the disappearance of the community and the growth of the massive bureaucracies (national and international), and increasing rationalization.

## Fragmentation

One obvious feature of modernization is the division of single social institutions into smaller but more specialized units. The family was once a unit of economic production as well as the site for biological and cultural reproduction. It no longer is; production is now organized in factories. The family was once the site for all education and socialization. Now we have special places called schools to which people go to be educated by professional educators.

In this general process, religious institutions have been pushed out of, or have withdrawn from, many spheres of life. The first and most significant exclusion is from the economy. Ideas from the world of production and exchange—the need to increase efficiency, supply, and demand as the fixer of price, and so on—are so powerful in our culture that it is difficult to believe that the medieval Church made a valiant attempt to control such matters. In the fourteenth century, lending money for profit was regarded as sinful and the Church's own courts claimed jurisdiction over usurers. A century before, the craft guilds used church courts to enforce their restrictive practices. Breaches of contract were tried before church courts.

Modernization saw the freeing of economic activity from religiously sanctioned controls and the development of the world of work as a domain of human life driven only by its own values. Gradually other spheres went the same way. Consider the range of activities engaged in by the Church of Scotland in the eighteenth century. It provided education. The local minister was often also the school teacher and ran the school. If the parish was big enough to have a separate teacher, he was usually a trainee minister and was paid by the Church. It provided social welfare. Money was raised either in special collections or through taxes and given to the beggars of the parish, who were licensed to beg by the elders of the Church. It provided social control. One way of raising money for the beggars' fund was to fine parishioners who engaged in pre-marital sex or other morally unacceptable acts. They would be called before the Kirk session and 'tried'. If they were found guilty, the Church administered the punishment.

The pre-Reformation church was often also the government bureaucracy and the keeper of national records. When in 1291 King Edward I of England wanted to prove his claim to the vacant Scottish throne, he sent letters of enquiry to the English monasteries asking for relevant historical information to support his case.[40] At a specially convened meeting near the border, magnates of both realms presented their historical proofs, failed to agree, and returned to the more common form of settling such disputes: warfare. But the diplomatic battle continued and much of it was conducted through letters to the Pope. Even though he had secured the Scottish throne and repelled the English, Robert Bruce sought the Pope's blessing.[41] That example pointedly reminds us how constrained the authority of religion has become. It also shows the impact of individualism. The governments of the West no longer seek legitimacy from bishops or popes; they claim to represent the will of the people. What medieval monarchs sought from God's representative on earth, democratic governments seek from the ballot box.

The church was also involved in what we now call 'health care'. Many of the first hospitals and infirmaries were religious foundations or adjuncts to monasteries.[42]

The process by which specific areas of social life became distinguished from each other and dominated by a specialized institution proceeded slowly and unevenly. At first the new institutions continued to be dominated by religious professionals but in time they were eclipsed as ever more specialized professionals were trained, and new bodies of knowledge or skill were generated in which religious professionals were not routinely trained to the same advanced levels. There were valiant attempts to regain lost ground. In the second quarter of the nineteenth century, the leading Church of Scotland evangelical Thomas Chalmers tried to recreate in a Glasgow parish the all-encompassing institutions of the previous order.[43] Churches continued (and still continue) to supplement the provisions of secular institutions, but, even when they are a major provider of services, they operate within the logic of the secular world. The Church of Scotland's Board of Social Responsibility is now the largest voluntary social work agency in Scotland and is second only to Strathclyde Region's social work department, but religious affiliation plays no part in the selection or training of the personnel who provide its services, which are indistinguishable from those of local authorities. Although the Catholic Church maintains clerical control over appointments and promotions in its schools, the majority of its staff are secular professionals and in most countries there is little about Catholic schooling that now distinguishes it from secular alternatives. Indeed, at the level of higher education, there is almost nothing about such American Catholic academies as Notre Dame or Loyola which distinguishes them from secular universities.

The division of life into ever-more specialized areas was accompanied by the division of people into distinct classes and social groups. Economic growth led to the emergence of an ever greater range of occupation and life-situation. Feudal societies had considerable disparities of wealth, but most people lived similar lives and they lived cheek-by-jowl. In medieval tower houses and castles, the gentry and their servants often slept in the same room, separated only by curtains. They ate at the same table, with the salt dish marking the gentry from the riff-raff. Because there was a strong hierarchical social structure which was quite open and clear about differences in status, superiors did not feel threatened by the presence of their minions and could inhabit the same physical and mental space.

This physical closeness of different 'degrees' was destroyed by increasing prosperity and increasing egalitarianism. As people of differing status became more alike in principle, they moved further apart in practice. Innovation and economic expansion brought with them occupational mobility. People no longer did the job they had always done simply because their family had always done that job. Occupational change made it hard for people to internalise visions of themselves that supposed permanent inferiority. People cannot improve themselves and their class position at the same time as thinking of themselves as having a 'station' or a 'degree' in a fixed hierarchical world. Modern societies are thus inherently egalitarian.

Furthermore, economic growth brought more contact with strangers. Profound inequalities of status can only be tolerable and not to lead to constant friction if the ranking system is widely known and accepted. Soldiers can move from one regiment to another and still know their place because there is a uniform (in both senses) ranking system. In a complex and mobile society, there is no way of ensuring that we know whether we are superior or subordinate to this new person. Once people had trouble knowing who should bow first, they gave up bowing. Basic equality became the normal presumption.

Thirdly, the separation of work and home, of the public and the private, made for equality. One could not be a serf from sunrise to sunset and an autonomous individual for the evening and at weekends. A real serf had to be full-time. A temporary work-role is not a full identity, and, though work-roles are usually part of a hierarchy, they could no longer structure the whole world-view. In the absence of a shared belief system which sanctioned inequality and subjection (and the decline of religion usually removes that), egalitarianism became the default position.[44]

Democracy was slow to come, but the creation of a modern economy brought with it the general interactional presumption that we are 'much of a muchness'. The better off, now a little unsure about the legitimacy of their superiority, moved to safeguard their prerogatives by physically moving away from their subordinates. As towns and cities developed, they did so with clear class divisions. About 1775 the Edinburgh bourgeoisie began to abandon the old town, where judges and poor artisans had inhabited flats (of very different quality) in the same tenement building, for the social exclusiveness of the New Town.[45] As the world became more clearly separated into private and public spheres and the public realm became more egalitarian, those who could afford to used their privacy to distance themselves from the rest.

Economic growth deepened the division of labour and widened the gulf between classes. Especially with the shift to the cities and the growth of big 'manufactories', people spent more of their time with others in the same economic circumstances and less time with their superiors or subordinates. Different social groups began to see the world in different ways. The idea of a single moral universe in which all manner and condition of persons have a place in some single grand design became less and less plausible.[46] Traditional integrated organic conceptions of the moral and supernatural order fragmented into a welter of competing conceptions as different classes developed religious world-views which made sense of their lives and interests. The Church of England is an episcopalian church. At the top is God, who talks to the archbishop, who talks to the bishop (*episcopos* is the Greek for bishop), who talks to the dean, who talks to the clergy, who tell lay people what to believe and do. When, in the post-Reformation period, there was argument about the correct organizational form for the true church, most of the upper classes could be found arguing for episcopacy on the grounds that the hierarchy of this divinely ordained social institution would legitimate other hierarchies. James VI of Scotland put it succinctly when he said 'No bishop, no king'. To this day the landed classes tend to remain in the Church of England because they like the model of the world as an organic community built around a stable ordered structure of authority with people ranked in their proper stations and them at the top. And the gentry kept their peasants in line. So we have the pattern in England of the Episcopalian church being strongest among the gentry and their farm servants. The independent farmers and the emerging middle classes who broke away from aristocratic control in the late eighteenth century preferred a more democratic form of organization. They liked the idea that we are all equal in the eyes of God and they liked to run their own affairs. Hence the appeal to them of those forms of Protestantism that stressed the priesthood of *all* believers: Presbyterianism, Methodism, and Congregationalism. In Northern Ireland the pattern is very clear: the small farmers of County Down and County Antrim are Presbyterians but the landed gentry and their estate workers of Fermanagh and Tyrone are Episcopalians.

As societies grew and became more complex, they fragmented into distinct classes and regional groups, and, where the religious culture allowed it, the dominant tradition also split into competing churches. As we saw in the previous chapter, one of the great innovations of the Protestant Reformation was the idea that we are all able to discern God's will for ourselves. We do not need a professional cadre of priests to do that for us. An unintended consequence of that innovation was the possibility of schism.

The possibility, however, is not the reality. Where the religious culture did not allow it—in Roman Catholic countries—there was a more radical and abrupt division with some classes remaining faithful to the Church and others breaking off completely. Hence in Scotland and England, there are twenty denominations. In France, Italy, and Spain there is a smaller Catholic Church and a large secular anti-Catholic and Communist section.

## The Eclipse of Community

The general fragmentation of community and social life is accompanied by a matching phenomenon which Bryan Wilson has called 'societalization', the process by which 'life is increasingly enmeshed and organized, not locally but societally (that society being most evidently, but not uniquely, the nation state)'.[47] Close-knit, integrated, small-scale communities have disappeared, undermined by the growth of large-scale industrial and commercial enterprise; by the emergence of modern nation-states co-ordinated through massive, impersonal bureaucracies; and by the development of the anonymous city.

Religion, Wilson argues, has its source in, and draws strength from, the community. As the society rather than the community has increasingly become the locus of the individual's life, religion has lost many of its purposes. In his study of *The Elementary Forms of the Religious Life* Durkheim argued that religion was explained by its social functions. When traditional people worshipped their Gods, they were really worshipping their own commonality. The point of religion was to create and sustain a common sense of identity.[48] Even if one does not accept that religion came into being and persisted because of its role as social cement, one can readily recognize that religion traditionally ritualized and legitimated local life. When every birth, marriage, and death in generation after generation was celebrated and marked with the same rituals in the same building, then the religion that legitimated those rituals was powerful and persuasive because it was woven into the life of the village. When the total, all-embracing community, working and playing together, gives way to the dormitory town or suburb, there is less held in common to celebrate. The decline of the community and the previously mentioned process of social differentiation means that people are no longer raised in one shared set of values and can no longer be controlled by the 'conscience' placed in them by the community and reinforced by informal social controls. The societal system relies less on the inculcation of a moral order and more on the use of efficient technical means of eliciting and monitoring appropriate behaviour. Policing is now more important for controlling people than are appeals to conscience; surveillance video cameras a greater deterrent than the disapproval of neighbours.[49]

Governments and public figures may continue to talk about God (usually in the context of linking the fate of the nation and God's will), but in order to avoid offending large sections of the population of a culturally plural society, such talk has to be extremely vague. American politicians from Lincoln (with his famous Gettysburg address) through John F. Kennedy to Ronald Reagan have invoked the divinity but none has been able to commit himself even to a Christian God, let alone to any of the competing versions offered within Christianity.

The decline of the community and its replacement by a society (typically a nation-state) which contains within it a number of different cultures and religions not only has important public policy consequences for religious institutions. It also has serious consequences for the plausibility of religious beliefs.[50]

Imagine you are born into a small stable society—the anthropologist's tribe by the lagoon—in which everyone believes that the giant squid is God. Every important life-event (births, marriages, deaths, and so on) has attached to it Squid-worshipping events. Every day, in hundreds of small bits of interaction, the divinity of the Squid is evidenced by such things as explaining bad weather by the anger of the Squid and casually dropping 'The Squid be blessed' into conversation. In such a world, the idea that the Squid is God is not a belief; it is a fact. It is just how the world is and is nearly incontestable for anyone raised in that society. Now imagine that a sudden increase in population and in the ease of travel means that the Squid tribe comes into contact with three or four other civilizations, none of which worships the Squid. Suddenly the divinity of the Squid is not a fact; it is a belief and it is a belief that is earnestly contested. The Squid tribe may still have faith in the Squid and may even start missionary societies to convert the others to Squid worship, but they can never return to the earlier condition of a naïvely taken-for-granted world-view.

Modern societies are culturally diverse places. Anything approaching the innocence of the tribe by the lagoon with its shared single world-view is no longer possible. In some settings diversity was created by migration as peoples with different cultures mingled with one another. In others the expansion of the political unit brought a range of cultures into an emerging nation-state. A third source of cultural pluralism was the internal fragmentation of the dominant culture, and I want to dwell on this case because the social psychological impact seems greater than in the other two instances. This is a caricature, of course, but the cognitive threat from strangers is always less than that from one's own people. When the Roman Catholic Irish started to settle in large numbers in lowland Scotland in the late eighteenth and nineteenth centuries, the Presbyterian Scots did not conclude that Catholicism was a different but equally plausible religion. They turned to invidious stereotypes to reinforce their own beliefs and dismiss those of the Irish. Why should we take their religion seriously? After all, they are no-account, alcohol-soaked, priest-ridden illiterate beggars. Finding reasons not to take seriously the carriers of a competing religion is easy and commonplace. But it becomes less easy to protect beliefs in that way when the challenge is being posed by members of one's own people who have broken away from the true faith. Between the Reformation and the middle of the nineteenth century, Scotland went from having one national church to having three nationally distributed and large churches and some ten other popular churches, each claiming to have the truth. In those circumstances it becomes hard for people to hold their beliefs with the conviction shown by our hypothetical Squid worshippers. The nineteenth-century Scot, as well as knowing that, somewhere out there, were African pagans and Arab Muslims, and, closer to home, Irish Catholics and English Episcopalians, had to come to terms with the presence among his own people of divisions into Kirk, Free Church, Free Presbyterian Kirk, Old Seceders, United Seceders, Brethren, and Baptists. As Berger neatly puts it, the big change is that, however willingly we choose our religion, we know that we choose God rather than God choosing us.[51]

Religion is no longer a matter of necessity; it is a question of preference. We are forced to make a choice and, for the 'deep-structure' reasons being outlined here, we choose in circumstances that make it less and less important and likely that we will choose to believe in any religion. The very fact of being challenged means that those who do choose to believe will often do so with an intensity and enthusiasm which would have surprised those of early periods who simply took their faith for granted. As we see in the efforts of the Methodists or the Scottish Free Church evangelicals, the challenge to evangelize can inspire a powerful movement, but what is gained in individual intensity is lost in background affirmation. Becoming religious is attended by more dramatic behaviour consequences, but fewer people do it. There are now more zealots but fewer believers.

To summarize so far, differentiation and societalization reduce the plausibility of the idea of a single overarching moral and religious system to which we all belong. The single 'sacred canopy', to use Berger's phrase, is displaced by competing conceptions of the supernatural which have little to do with how we perform our social roles in what is now a largely anonymous and impersonal public domain and more to do with how we live our domestic lives.[52]

Religion may retain subjective plausibility, but it does so at the price of its objective taken-for-grantedness. Religion becomes privatized and is pushed to the margins and interstices of the social order. Its focus narrows to the individual. As a study of modern Catholicism in rural France shows:

> The notion of an atoning ordeal and sacrifice and the age-old and dominant problem of sin and redemption is disappearing. The contemporary emphasis on the close personal relationship with God as a source of fulfilment and on the riches of relationships with others, is shifting parochial Catholics towards a 'transcendent humanism', offering an 'ethico-affective' and predominantly this-worldly conception of salvation.[53]

To express the same point in terms of functions, the primary function of religion—the expression of the relationship between God and humankind, the natural and the supernatural—remains the same, but there is a shift in the secondary or latent functions from the social to the personal, from the life of the community to the life of the individual self.[54]

The fragmentation of society, the break-up of the religious culture, and the shrinking of the role of churches are closely related. A church could sensibly and reasonably exercise a wide range of social functions when everyone belonged to the same church and the parish structure mirrored the evolved boundaries of communities. When people are split into a variety of competing churches, maintaining a wide range of roles becomes difficult for any church—difficult to do effectively and difficult to justify against opposition. The first response of the dominant religious tradition to defections was to try to enforce conformity, to use the power of the law and the state to press people back into the state church, but, as more and more people broke away, the social costs of trying to coerce them into the parish church became too great and the state gave up.[55] Except in one or two trivial ways (such as having seats in the House of Lords), the Church of England now has to compete with all other denominations on an equal footing.

## Rationalization

The rise of rationality was discussed in the previous chapter. Here I want to look at its consequences for the plausibility of religion. By rationality, we mean a concern with routines and procedures, with predictability and order, with a search for ever-increasing efficiency. We could allow DHSS clerks to give as much money as they liked to claimants on the basis of their personnel prejudices, their religion, or their family connections. Those methods have all been used for allocating resources in previous societies. Yet we believe that the fairest and most efficient way of organizing anything on a large scale is to establish rules and procedures which constrain actions and decisions to the matter in hand. Bureaucratic organization replaces personal preference. Having created procedures, we do not view them as sacred and immutable. If someone can suggest a more efficient means of achieving the same end, we change our methods.

We can readily see how a world of rationality is less conducive to religion than a traditional society. Everything is seen as potentially improvable. Everything can be made more efficient. We find it very easy to talk about means and procedures but very difficult to discuss transcendental ends. *The Shorter Catechism*, that seventeenth-century distillation of the key points that was used to teach Scottish Presbyterians their faith, has as its first question: 'What is the chief end of man?'.[56] In our societies such a question is rarely asked because we know that we could not agree on an answer.

We also suppose predictability; that what worked yesterday will work today. We live in a world of timetables and calendars which allow us to record appointments for next year. Very few of us expect a sudden invasion of the supernatural. Very conservative Protestant churches still have on their notice boards 'Meeting 11 a.m. (DV)', but that 'God willing' is a residue. In practice almost no one expects that God will intervene to prevent the next service taking place.[57]

Thus far there has been no mention of science and that delay has been deliberate. When asked to explain the decline of religion, a lot of people mention the rise of Western science and the competition between scientific explanations and religious ones. They point out that many of the beliefs of the early Christians have been shown to be wrong. The earth is round and not flat. The earth moves round the sun and not the sun around the earth. The earth and human life are vastly older than the ages traditionally taken from biblical accounts. While scientists recognize that there are still huge gaps in our knowledge, there is a consensus that an evolutionary model along the lines of Darwinism offers a better explanation of the origins of species than does the account of divine creation in seven days given in the Old Testament book of Genesis.

For all that, I do not actually think that science has directly contributed much to secularization. The argument between Darwin and the Church of England Bishop Samuel Wilberforce was gripping for middle-class Victorians, but it hardly penetrated to ordinary people.[58] Anyway, to insist that one set of beliefs lost popularity because another proved them to be wrong is to miss the difference between truth and plausibility. There are all sorts of ways in which we can insulate our beliefs from apparently contradicting evidence if we want to. We can easily avoid hearing the troublesome evidence. We can dismiss it by blackening the character of those who bring the bad news. For example, many American fundamentalists who want to believe in Genesis diminish the threat from evolutionists by accusing them of being sexually promiscuous and left wing. But such strategies require social support. The person who stands against the consensus is a lunatic and will be treated as such. In order to maintain a shared belief system we need a social strategy which organizes shared defences against the cognitive threats. Where such resources are available, new ideas, no matter that they might be better supported by the evidence, can readily be ignored or rejected.

Although it would be hard to draw a single line between the two classes of ideas, it is useful to distinguish between specific propositions (for example, species evolved by natural selection) and more subtle assumptions about the nature of the world. My point is that, with the right social support and in the right social context, the threat to our beliefs from specific counter-propositions can be neutralized. It is far less easy to avoid being influenced by widespread and powerful but subtle assumptions about the nature of the world. Berger, Berger, and Kellner argue that, irrespective of the extent to which we are aware of it, modern technology brings with it a 'technological consciousness'.[59] An example of what they mean is 'componentiality'. The application of modern machines to production involves the assumption that the most complex entities can be broken down into their 'components' and that each of those components is replaceable. Any 1976 Vauxhall Viva radiator will fit any 1976 Vauxhall Viva. The relationship between the engine and one radiator is expected to be exactly the same as that between the engine and any other matching radiator. There is nothing sacred about any particular bond. Another fundamental assumption is 'reproducibility'. Technological production takes it for granted that any creative complex of actions can be subdivided into simple acts which can be repeated infinitely and always with the same consequence. While there is no obvious clash between these assumptions and the teachings of most major religions, there are serious incompatibilities of approach. There is little space for the eruption of the divine.

Science and technology have given us a notion of cause and effect that makes us look first for the natural causal explanation of an event. When an aeroplane crashes with the loss of many lives, we ask not what moral purpose the event had but what was its natural cause. And, in so far as we keep finding those causes (a loose engine nut or a terrorist bomb), we are subtly discouraged from seeking the moral significance.

Pluralism is also implicated in the primacy of scientific explanations in that it weakens the plausibility of alternatives. The rational basis of science, and the social structures of training, examination, and dissemination of results which protect that base, mean that there are fewer disagreements among scientists than there are among the clergy. Despite the recent and growing disillusionment with the authority of the secular professions, they still command the sort of respect enjoyed by the medieval Church. If the crash investigators say it was a bomb, almost all of us will agree it was a bomb. We may then wish to add a divine or supernatural additional explanation of why it was this bomb on this flight, but, because we do not share a religious culture, we will not be able to agree on whether it is even appropriate to search for such religious significance, let alone what the significance might be. Concentrating our explanations of life events on the material world brings more agreement than searching for religious messages. That the religious culture is badly fragmented weakens the ability of religious explanations to complement, let alone compete with, naturalistic ones.

Our attention is further concentrated on the natural world by the success of technology in delivering the goods. Technically efficient machinery and procedures reduce uncertainty and our need for the supernatural. There is simply no need to turn to the Gods for help with ringworm in cattle when you can buy a drench which has proved over and over again to be an excellent cure for the condition. Technology reduces the domain over which religion offers the most compelling explanations and the most predictable outcomes. The growth of technical rationality gradually displaces supernatural influence and moral considerations from ever wider areas of public life, replacing them by considerations of objective performance and practical expedience. When people had no idea what caused plague and no way of preventing it, shared rituals of repentance were a popular response. Now that we now what causes plague and how to prevent it, a whole series of occasions for a revival of religious interest has been removed.

There is a further subtle way in which science and technology reduce the place for religion and that is through the social power of the institutions that are based on scientific knowledge. Despite the recent interest of some parts of the middle class in 'natural' birth and death, these two crucial events in the lives of individuals, families, and communities are now mostly administered and arranged by doctors and medical technicians in hospitals.

In modern worlds, religion is most used for the dark recessive areas of human life over which control has not been established by technology: unhappiness, extreme stress, and the like. When we have tried every cure for cancer, we pray. When we have revised for our examinations, we pray. We do not pray instead of studying, and even committed believers suppose that a research programme is more likely than a mass prayer meeting to produce a cure for AIDS. Our notion of the scope of the divine is then much smaller than that of pre-industrial man.[60]

This is not to trivialize the events and problems which still cause many of us to turn to God. The unexpected death of a loved one or the injustice of some act of suffering may be enormously important to us. In that sense, the 'gaps' in our rational control and intellectual understanding of our world may loom very large. But they do so in an individualized manner. They are personal, not social problems.

To summarize, I am suggesting that the effect of science and technology on the plausibility of religious belief is often misunderstood. The clash of ideas between science and religion is far less significant than the more subtle impact of naturalistic ways of thinking about the world. Science and technology have not made us atheists. Rather, the fundamental assumptions underlying them which we can summarily describe as 'rationality'—the material world as an a-moral series of invariant relationships of cause and effect, the componentiality of objects, the reproducibility of actions, the expectation of constant change in our exploitation of the material world, the insistence on innovation—make it unlikely that we will often entertain the notion of the divine.

It is not an accident that most modern societies are largely secular. Industrialization brought with it a series of social changes—the fragmentation of the life-world, the decline of community, the rise of bureaucracy, technological consciousness—which together made religion less arresting and less plausible than it had been in pre-modern societies.

## Criticisms of the Secularization Thesis

Not everyone would accept either the general claim that modernization has been accompanied by secularization or all of the elements of the explanation of that process which I have offered. The bulk of the social-science community has no doubt that modern societies are less religious than traditional ones. Compare, for example, the attention given to religion by historians of nineteenth-century Britain, France, or Germany with the topic's absence from recent studies of class and power . Yet a number of American sociologists of religion have taken to resolutely denying secularization.[61] The place of religion in American society will be considered in detail later. Here I want to consider briefly some of the most commonly offered general objections to the secularization thesis.

The first and most easily dealt with is the claim that the secularization thesis is merely an ideology; that those of us who offer versions of the above are not trying to describe and explain reality but are instead pursuing the ideological agenda of getting rid of religion. One ready rejoinder is to point out that those sociologists who support aspects of the approach outlined above are not all unbelievers who welcome what they claim to observe. David Martin, who has questioned some elements of the above account but who has also formulated *A General Theory of Secularization*, is an ordained Church of England clergyman. Bryan Wilson is an atheist, but he is also a political conservative who thinks that shared religions are important for social cohesion and mourns their passing. Peter Berger is a committed Lutheran. Wallis was an atheist who shared many of Wilson's misgivings about the secular modern world.

A second rejoinder is to point out that why someone promotes a particular theory and the value of that theory are always separable issues. It may be fascinating as gossip to know what (other than a desire to discover the truth) motivates this or that scholar, but in the end such sociological explanation of the desire to see a certain case realized tells us little or nothing about its truth. Why Gallileo wanted the earth to rotate around the sun is neither here nor there for determining if he was right.

A more pressing criticism of the secularization thesis is that it mistakenly implies some earlier golden age of religious orthodoxy.[62] As I argued above in describing the changing notion of church membership, we need to be very careful not to view the distant past anachronistically through the expectations of the present. There is evidence that medieval people were not terribly attentive Christians, but this needs to be interpreted with more caution than is usually demonstrated. Studies of medieval court records show peasants being hauled up for playing cards and firing off shotguns in church, for failing to attend church, or for engaging in pagan rites and rituals,[63] but consider the nature of such records. The church courts were charged with enforcing religious discipline. To rest our estimate of the past on such records is as sensible as judging present attitudes to the law by citing only criminal court cases. Secondly, what is often being complained about in such records is not irreligion but the wrong religion.

Thirdly, in taking the modern enthusiast as our model of the religious person we fail to appreciate others ways of expressing commitment. A personal anecdote may illustrate the point. I once had to interview a Jewish businessman and we arranged to meet at the synagogue. I expected to see him before or after the service and was initially shocked to find us talking about mundane matters in the very doorway of the room in which the prayers were being said. While we talked, he stood with one foot inside the room. This, he explained, was because his presence was required to make the quorum necessary for prayers. My first reaction was to think that this was a man who did not take his religion seriously; where was the attentive posture redolent of piety? Later I realized that his attitude expressed absolute certainty, a conviction that there was a God, that God required ritual prayers, that for the prayers to be effective there had to be a quorum of male Jews, and that his toe in the door met those requirements and thus glorified God.

Let us go back to the apparent irreverence of medieval Christians. Because there were no seats in churches and most of the business was muttered in Latin by a priest facing away from the audience, people used to mill about and gossip with their neighbours. We might find that disrespectful and see it as evidence of a lack of personal piety but we would miss the more important point that people still felt obliged, by God as much as by social pressure, to be there even when there was so little for them to do. Furthermore, it is clear from the specific questions that lay people used to address to church authorities about which parts of the divine Offices they had to pay particular attention to, that they thought involvement in certain parts of the services was a matter of great importance. During the Elevation of the Host, which was signalled by the ringing of a bell, people stopped milling about and knelt in reverent silence.[64] When our present church leaders agonize about how they might make church services more interesting and exciting for young people, the fact that such large numbers of people in the Middle Ages attended church services which made almost no concessions to their presence suggests that, despite their failure to comport themselves in the manner that we now expect of church-goers, our medieval ancestors were religious people.

Studies of sixteenth-century wills show that it was common for money to be left to pay for religious services. In 1546 Gilbert Kirk of Exeter bequeathed 4d. to each householder in St Mary Arches parish 'to pray to Our Lord God to have mercy on my soul and all Christian souls'. Robert Hone donated 1d. to each spectator at his burial in return for their prayers and forgave his debtors on the condition that they prayed for him. He also left 12d. to each of his godchildren 'to say a *Pater Noster*, Ave and Creed, praying for my soul'.[65] Where it succeeded, the Reformation brought an end to prayers for the dead and may, as Whiting argues, have briefly blunted religious interest in some places, but the foremost historian of Elizabethan and Jacobean England, Patrick Collinson, demonstrates that the 'godly' people made up a considerably greater part of the population than they now do.[66]

Without wishing to concede its accuracy, I would add that the 'golden-age' criticism partly misses the point. The secularization thesis does not require that pre-modern people were all well-informed active participants in their local churches. There were parts of the country where religious services were rare. Many clerics were barely literate and could hardly preach at all, while others preached way above the heads of their congregations. None the less, the evidence shows that most medieval people believed in the supernatural and frequently called on its powers for assistance in this world. Even among the ungodly, a fundamental supernaturalism was more widespread than it is now. If one takes the notion broadly, Christian beliefs were obviously far more widespread and far more central to the lives of ordinary people. Contemporary Protestants may not be able to make provision in their wills for prayers for their souls, but they could leave money for ministerial training, or to fund missionary work or subsidize church building. Benefactors today, however, are far more likely to leave money to animal charities than to the promotion of religious activities.

It is no easy matter to judge the religious climate of an age so different from our own and so remote. Margaret Spufford wrote the following, initially as a reply to Keith Thomas's demonstration that superstition and magic were more important than orthodox Christianity:

The degree of importance that religion held in the lives of non-gentle parishioners in the sixteenth and seventeenth centuries will never be established. The beliefs of such people were not normally of interest even to the ecclesiastical authorities. . . . Genuine popular devotion of a humble kind leaves very little trace upon the records of any given time. The believer, especially the conforming believer, makes less impact than the dissentient. At no periods is it possible to distinguish the conforming believer from the apathetic church-goer who merely wished to stay out of trouble.

It is possible, therefore, for the historian to start from the very probable thesis that 'the hold of any kind of organized religion upon the Mass of the population was never more than partial', add the complaints of puritan reforming ministers about their flocks' performance of their uncongenial duties, support these with figures of the considerable minority who were presented for absenteeism in the church courts, and point the case further with the disrespectful remarks of a further minority, which was also presented in the church courts. If it is set against this background, the importance of astrology and magic . . . then seems very great. Yet the negative picture that emerges is based on the silence of the majority of witnesses.

An alternative picture, illustrating the convictions of the humble, also depends on the selection of examples which may be atypical. It runs from the demonstration of bequests to the church lights, altar and fabric normally made by every parishioner who left a will before the Reformation, through the remarkably concrete fact that over half the Marian martyrs listed by Foxe whose social status is known were agricultural labourers. It continues by showing that the rural laity were actively involved in the complaints against scandalous ministers and in the anti-Laudian petitions of the 1640s.[67]

In further remarks four years later, Spufford reminds us that complaints to church courts were themselves 'religious' acts of people trying to change the Church in this or that direction. In some places enthusiastic clergy and elders prevented people from taking communion because they were judged to be 'unregenerate' and then reported them for not communicating! This tells us a lot about struggles for the soul of the Church of England, but it means that such data as can be extracted from church court records and ecclesiastical correspondence cannot be taken as evidence of the extent or nature of lay church involvement without a degree of sophistication that is missing from most sociological uses of the historical literature. Spufford concludes: 'I have been searching for sources which permit me to quantify genuine religious conviction of all types for some fifteen years. Until I find more, I shall continue to feel that although measurement and its instruments . . . should all be used to their fullest sensible limit . . . there are areas beyond its reach.'[68]

Fortunately, those areas are not beyond the reach of the other skills of the historian, and, having no grounds to challenge their judgements, we have to be guided by the consensus among the experts. Despite the fuss made by a few sociologists keen to challenge the secularization thesis, that consensus is very clear: our medieval past was considerably more religious than our modern present. The challenge posed by Thomas, the only British historian cited by such revisionists as Stark and Iannaccone, is far more limited than they appreciate. In showing the extent to which pre-Christian superstitions and magical practices continued alongside the orthodox teachings of the Christian Church, Thomas amply illustrates the importance of those superstitions. Church officials may have despaired at the perversions of their teachings peddled by the laity, but, if we are to be impressed by the high proportion of our contemporaries who, despite having no church connection, now claim to be religious and to believe in God, how much more should we be impressed by the ordinary people of the sixteenth or seventeenth century who made offerings to the shrines of saints, took seriously oaths sworn on the Bible, left money to pay for Masses and for church decoration, attended church services that were a complete mystery to them, and sprinkled holy water on their houses, fields, and sheep.

The secularization approach can be challenged from the other end of the implied trajectory by arguing that it underestimates the present popularity of religion. The resurgence of Islamic fundamentalism in Iran and in parts of the Arab world is sometimes offered as evidence that religion is still of considerable social and political significance, which of course it is. Some confusion is caused here by using terms such as 'modernity' and the 'modern world' when what we mean is the 'First World': those societies which modernized in the eighteenth and nineteenth centuries.

More to the point, it can be argued that the First World is not as secular as it looks. It has been argued that the collapse of Christianity in, say, Britain or Holland reflects a lack of faith in the major religious institutions rather than a lack of faith in their beliefs. This point has already been addressed. Only a little facetiously, I will summarize the counter-argument by using again the case of someone who asserts that he is a keen football fan but when pressed admits that he has not been to a game since his father stopped taking him at the age of 5, never watches matches on the television, does not read the football sections of newspapers, does not support any team, does not encourage his son to attend matches, and cannot name any prominent footballer.

Put simply, the revision downwards of our estimate of how religious was the past and upwards of how religious is the present depends on making inappropriately light of signs of religiosity in the pre-modern period and making inappropriately much of weak rhetorical affirmations in the present. For example, the authors of a 1976 survey which asked a very large sample if they were 'aware of, or influenced by, a presence or power, whether referred to as God or not, which is different from their everyday lives' are impressed that 36 per cent of the sample claimed such an awareness.[69] However, that a much larger number (which interestingly included some church-goers!) asserted the very strong negative 'never in my life' seems more significant, as does the fact that, of those who reported some sort of spiritual experience, two-thirds claimed it only 'once or twice' and only a quarter were aware of a power or presence 'often' or 'all the time'. Furthermore, when the authors pursued those supernatural experiences, they found that they included such occurrences as surviving unharmed a violent motor accident that should have caused severe damage.[70]

In Chapters 7 and 8 I will look in detail at present-day interest in the supernatural as it is expressed outside the confines of traditional religions. Here I want to consider just what sort of challenge is offered to the secularization thesis by the evidence of assertions of religious interest and sentiment by the unchurched. First, as I have already suggested, before we interpret the results of such surveys we need to think about the nature of the research process and the likely bias it will produce. Peter Brierley, Britain's leading recorder of indices of religious belief and behaviour, explains the exaggerated claims for church attendance produced by surveys as follows: 'The reason is . . . that they ask people what their behaviour is, and their memory . . . [is] not always accurate, or they wish to please the interviewer by answering more positively than perhaps they might otherwise.'[71] Given that there are still strong residues of Christianity in the cultures of most Western societies, we should be a little cautious of self-descriptions as 'religious'.

The critics of the secularization approach want to present such residues as evidence of an enduring latent demand for religion. It might just be that, but there is a more obvious depiction. Like the house of a once-rich person who has fallen on hard times and has been forced gradually to sell off the family possessions, the culture of a once-Christian society still possesses a few remnants, a few reminders of its past. If we can take the results of a series of disparate surveys as evidence of a trend, that trend is clear. Those marks of an enduring interest in religion that persist outside the churches are themselves becoming weaker and more rare. If one wants to call those residues 'implicit religion', then one has to recognize that the implicit is decaying in the same way as the explicit. It is not a compensating alternative.

Secondly, it should be no surprise that, though there are more avowed atheists than there were twenty years ago, they remain rare. Self-conscious atheism and agnosticism are features of religious cultures and were at their height in the Victorian era.[72] They are postures adopted in a world where people are keenly interested in religion.

Thirdly, it should be accepted without reservation that people have not replaced a Christian world by the rational law-governed world of the caricatured scientist. The beneficiaries of twelve years of compulsory education and high technology can still believe that Granny spoke to them from the other side. This is good evidence against Comte's view of secularization as intellectual maturing, but, as I stressed at the start of this explanation of secularization, that is not my argument, nor is it that of Wilson, Martin, Berger, or any other modern sociologist. That the decline in the mainstream religious traditions allows space for people to entertain a very wide range of diffuse and privatized beliefs is precisely what we would expect. The point that needs to be made is that individual beliefs which are not regularly articulated and affirmed in a group, which are not refined and burnished by shared ceremonies, which are not the object of regular and systematic elaboration, and which are not taught to the next generation or to outsiders are unlikely to exert much influence on the actions of those who hold them and are even less likely to have significant social consequences.

The evidence of diffuse and ambiguous beliefs in some sort of supernatural sphere shows that this 'implicit religion' (if that phrase does not exaggerate its cohesion or salience) is declining in tandem with explicit religion. To see it as a counter to the collapse of institutional religion is wishful thinking. But, even if it were important, I see no reason why the shift from institutional religion to some amorphous supernaturalism should not be described as 'secularization'.

## The Surface Structures

Thus far I have sketched the major social forces that produced secularization and briefly responded to the most commonly offered criticisms of this approach. Though social scientists search for general patterns under the historical particulars, we are well aware of the very different careers of religious change in different cultures, and it is to those variations that I now turn. David Martin has suggested that the range of variations in societies' religious experiences can be understood in terms of a limited number of patterns which typically have to do with the date of the onset of industrialization and the nature of the dominant form of religion in that society.[73]

First, there are states in which the Reformation era left the Catholic Church dominant but which were greatly affected by the French Revolution. That period saw the Church ally itself with the old regime and the social élite against the forces of social reform. For the many who espoused the Revolution, the Church was discredited by its anti-revolutionary stance, and these countries have since the late eighteenth century been largely divided between believers—often the more rural people—and secularists, who were often concentrated in the more urbanized and industrialized areas. These secularists are also often overtly anti-clerical. Thus a traditional monolithic religious bloc is confronted by the equally monolithic organic ideology of Communism and socialism. Just such a radical division can be seen in France, Italy, Spain, and Portugal: on the one side, the traditional highly committed

Catholics; on the other, socialists and Communists. The Catholic states of Western and southern Europe fall into this category.

In a second type of society, where Protestantism became dominant, broad state churches, allied with national élites, were confronted by liberal and socialist movements which were able to draw upon dissenting strands within the Protestant faith. Because many of the radicals were also religious sectarians (usually Baptists or Methodists), religion itself did not become a central focus of conflict. The arguments concerned only the discriminatory way in which certain of types of religion were privileged. The masses found themselves little served by a state church which drew its professionals from the upper classes and advanced the ideological perspectives of the socially dominant, but they reacted towards it by withdrawal from anything more than a nominal attachment, rather than by overt hostility. Alternatively, they dropped away in the course of major social dislocations (in England, during the Civil War, the Restoration of the Stewart monarchy, the Industrial Revolution, the First and Second World Wars). The northern European states of Britain and Scandinavia fall into this category (with some of the Scandinavian countries drifting slightly towards the Catholic pattern, an outcome of the only partially reformed character of Lutheran Churches).

Thirdly, there are the Protestant migrant societies. These have been largely formed since the late eighteenth century by migration, initially of Protestants and only later of Catholics. What is significant about these societies is that, although they are dominated by Protestantism, they do not show the typical pattern of secularization seen in the second type just described. Rather, despite being highly modernised, they have rather high church attendance rates. The specific case of the USA will be looked at in detail in a separate chapter, but here I briefly note the following. First, migration itself gives religion an important additional significance as one of the few sources of cohesive identity for the migrating people. Secondly, urbanization came much later in these societies than it did in Britain and Western Europe.[74] Thirdly, the successive waves of migration brought a great deal of ethnic conflict and competition, especially between the first white Anglo-Saxon Protestant settlers and the later Irish and southern European Catholics. For reasons that will be discussed in Chapter 5, ethnic competition gave religious identity an importance it did not have in the old country. Finally, in many rural parts of the new world, each religious minority was able to construct for itself a society in which it was dominant to a degree reminiscent of the pre-Reformation world and was thus able to blunt many of the secularizing forces that come with pluralism. Thus, for example, while Canada as a whole might have shown a great deal of religious diversity, many parts of Canada were Catholic or Protestant strongholds.

The greater the plurality of religious expressions available (that is, the greater the variety of dissent), the stronger the continued involvement of the masses in religious institutions in Protestant-dominated settings. (The extreme case here is the USA, which, at the level of the nation-state, if not of every state, county, and town, represents the universalization of dissent.[75]) No one religious expression was uniquely identified with the social élite, and a multiplicity of forms were imported or invented to appeal to all manner and condition of persons. In this type of society, religious freedom represents a central value of the nation. Religious adherence is an aspect of commitment to the national identity, but religious expressions themselves tend to adapt to the secular values of the society.[76]

To return to the basic patterns, all the Protestant-dominated immigrant-based societies display (to a greater or lesser extent, depending on the degree of priority retained by the Anglican Church) the ability to combine a great variety of dissent with the continued involvement of the masses in religious institutions.

However, it is worth noting that the relative strength of religion in migrant-based societies might be expected to characterize only the early phase in the development of such societies. After a number of generations, the proportion of the population which has arrived by migration declines as native birth takes over and whatever peculiarities that came from migration disappear. As we would expect, the church attendance and membership rates for Australia, New Zealand, and Canada have been declining rapidly since the 1970s.[77]

The fourth pattern describes those societies which the Reformation era left fairly equally divided between Catholics and Protestants. Here 'pillarization' occurs: each confession encapsulates its own and provides distinctive institutions to serve their social and political needs. While religious attachments remain relatively high, Catholics and Protestants have increasingly to collaborate to retain a Christian character to the society in the face of liberal and secularist forces.[78] Such collaboration, however, can take place only where both sides have agreed on the issue of national sovereignty—

often in the course of securing freedom from imperialistic domination (as was the case in Switzerland, Holland, and, though it has a very small non-Catholic population, Belgium). Where the issue of national sovereignty is unresolved, religion is likely to be the basis of divergent national aspirations and thus a symbolic focus of dispute. The obvious case is that of Northern Ireland.[79]

Finally, to cover the broad territory of Western Europe, there is the case of Catholic states in which class formation and social differentiation did not produce widespread and sharp antagonism towards the Church, because the Church provided a central focus of cultural identity in opposition to an imperialistic neighbour which sought to impose an alien set of cultural values and identities upon a reluctant populace. Religious adherence remained strong as an expression of protest, of rejection of alien values and domination, and of cultural and social integrity. The obvious cases are Poland and the Irish Republic.

## Conclusion

Putting together the account of the deep structure of secularization and the surface variations in patterns of change suggests a very broad principle: modernization generates secularization except where religion finds or retains work to do other than relating individuals to the supernatural. This principle helps explain not only some of the patterns outlined above, but also some of those to be found within particular societies. We might say that religion diminishes in social significance except in two broad contexts which will be the subject of Chapter 5: cultural defence and cultural transition.

## Notes

1. Bernard Hamilton, *Religion in the Medieval West* (London: Edward Arnold, 1986), 55.
2. Ibid. 56.
3. David Cressy, 'Purification, Thanksgiving and the Churching of Women in Post-Reformation England', *Past and Present*, 141 (Nov. 1993), 115.
4. Hamilton, *Religion*, 87.
5. Ibid. 105–7.

6. Keith Thomas, *Religion and the Decline of Magic* (Harmondsworth, Middx.: Penguin, 1973), 41.

7. Hamilton, *Religion*, 106.

8. David Hempton, 'Popular Religion and Irreligion in Victorian Fiction', *Historical Studies*, 16 (1987), 185–6.

9. For various studies of religion and respectability, see T. W. Lacquer, *Religion and Respectability: Sunday Schools and Working Class Culture 1780–1850* (New Haven: Yale University Press, 1976); Robert Q. Gray, *The Labour Aristocracy in Victorian Edinburgh* (Oxford: Oxford University Press, 1976); and Hugh McLeod, 'White Collar Values and the Role of Religion', in Geoffrey Crossick (ed.), *The Lower Middle Class in Britain 1870–1914* (London: Croom Helm, 1977).

10. These data were calculated from the series in the appendices to Robert Currie, Alan D. Gilbert, and Lee Horsley, *Churches and Churchgoers: Patterns of Church Growth in the British Isles since 1700* (Oxford: Oxford University Press, 1977). So that the definition of 'membership' is rigorous, Anglican figures are of those who took communion on Easter Day rather than of those on the electoral rolls, which are generally twice as large. Catholic estimates have been derived by reducing the baptismal total in proportion to those attending Mass on an average Sunday.

11. Peter Brierley, *A Century of British Christianity: Historical Statistics 1900–1985 with Projections to 2000* (London: MARC Europe, 1989).

12. The parallel figures for membership and attendance in Currie, Gilbert, and Horsley, *Churches and Churchgoers*, show clearly that more people belong than attend, yet one recent attempt to persuade us that the present is not significantly more secular than the past follows a presentation of church-membership figures with the assertion: 'Moreover, the British may be far less inclined than are Americans or Canadians to actually see to it that they are signed up as church members, since a far larger percentage of the British population claims to attend church with some frequency than are counted on church rolls' (Rodney Stark and Laurence R. Iannaccone, 'A Supply-Side Reinterpretation of the "Secularization" of Europe', *Journal for the Scientific Study of Religion*, 33 (1994), 243).

13. Peter Bisset, 'Size and Growth', in Peter Brierley and Fergus Macdonald (eds.), *Prospects for Scotland: From a Census of the Churches in 1984* (London: MARC Europe, 1985), 17–25.

14. For discussions of the technical issues as well as the results, see Keith S. Inglis, 'Patterns of Religious Worship in 1851', *Journal of Ecclesiastical History*, 11 (1960), 74–87; Donald J. Withrington, 'The 1851 Census of Religious Worship and Education: With a Note on Church Accommodation in Mid-19th Century Scotland', *Records of the Scottish Church History Society*, 18 (1974), 133–48; and Robin Gill, *The Myth of the Empty Church* (London: SPCK, 1993).

15. Callum Brown, *The Social History of Religion in Scotland since 1730* (London: Methuen, 1987), 19, and *The People in the Pews: Religion and Society in Scotland since 1780* (Glasgow: Economic and Social History Society of Scotland, 1993), 7.

16. Fergus Macdonald, 'Introduction', in Brierley and Macdonald (eds.), *Prospects for Scotland*, 5.

17. Gill, *Myth*, 26.

18. Ibid. 35–8.

19. Ibid. 76.

20. Robin Gill, 'Secularization and Census Data', in Steve Bruce (ed.), *Religion and Modernization: Sociologists and Historians Debate the Secularization Thesis* (Oxford: Oxford University Press, 1992), 109.
21. It is worth noting that even Callum Brown, who is cited by Stark and Iannaccone as an opponent of the secularization thesis, says: 'Scotland, like both England and Wales and the United States showed strong growth in church adherence *per capita* from 1840 to 1905 . . . to be followed by very slow and erratic decline until 1956 when rapid and sustained decline commenced' (*The People in the Pews*, 30). In case the meaning of the repeated word 'decline' is in doubt, he later says: 'It was only after 1956, and especially after 1963, when church adherence started its presently unstoppable plummet' (p. 44).
22. Danièle Hervieu-Léger, 'Religion and Modernity in the French Context: For a New Approach to Secularization', *Sociological Analysis*, 51 (1990), S15–25.
23. Michael P. Hornsby-Smith, *The Changing Parish: A Study of Parishes, Priests and Parishioners after Vatican II* (London: Routledge, 1989), 37.
24. Anne Van Meerback, 'The Importance of a Religious Service at Birth: the Persistent Demand for Baptism in Flanders', *Social Compass*, 42 (1995), 47–58. See also Karel Dobbelaere and Lilianne Voyé, 'From Pillar to Postmodernity: The Changing Situation of Religion in Belgium', *Sociological Analysis*, 51 (1990), S1–S13.
25. Phillip J. Hughes, *Religion: A View from the Australian Census* (Sydney: Christian Research Association, 1993).
26. Brierley, *A Century of British Christianity*, and Andrew Brown, 'Birth Celebration Without Religion Offered', *Independent*, 23 July 1994.
27. Phillip Rose (ed.), *Social Trends 23* (London: Her Majesty's Stationery Office, 1993), table 11.7.
28. The reports on the 1991 British Social Attitudes survey are from my own analysis of the original data sets, which are available from the Economic and Social Research Council's Data Archive at the University of Essex.
29. The 1947, 1951, 1957, and 1965 figures are from George H. Gallup, *The Gallup International Public Opinion Polls: Great Britain 1937–1975* (New York: Random House, 1976). The 1981 data are from David Gerard, 'Religious Attitudes and Values', in Mark Abrams, David Gerard, and Noel Timms (eds.), *Values and Social Change in Britain* (London: Macmillan, 1985), 50–92. The 1987 data are from Michael Svennevig, Ian Haldane, Sharon Speirs, and Barrie Gunter, *Godwatching: Viewers, Religion and Television* (London: John Libbey/Independent Broadcasting Authority, 1989).
30. Brierley, *A Century of British Christianity*.
31. Barrie Gunter and Rachel Viney, *Seeing is Believing: Religion and Television in the 1990s* (London: John Libbey/Independent Television Commission, 1994), 53.
32. Richard Hoggart, *The Uses of Literacy* (Harmondsworth, Middx.: Penguin, 1962), 113.
33. Hamilton, *Religion*, 87–108.
34. For a history of the ecumenical movement, see W. H. T. Gairdner, '*Edinburgh 1910*': *An Account and Interpretation of the World Missionary Conference* (Edinburgh: Oliphant, Anderson & Ferrier, 1910), and Barry Till, *The Churches Search for Unity* (Harmondsworth, Middx.: Penguin, 1972).
35. Stark and Iannaccone ('A Supply-Side Re-interpretation') assert that the secu-

larization thesis supposes that enlightenment has eroded religious belief. They offer no evidence that Berger, Wilson, Martin, or any other modern sociologist of secularization holds this view.

36. Ronald Fletcher, *The Making of Sociology*, i. *Beginnings and Foundation* (London: Nelson, 1971).

37. *The Future of an Illusion* is now available in *Civilization, Society and Religion etc.* (Pelican Freud Library, 12; Harmondsworth, Middx.: Penguin, 1986).

38. Here I am explicitly endorsing the sociology-of-knowledge perspective of Peter Berger, which argues that all 'knowledge' needs to be similarly explained. This is a radical departure from the common notion that ideas divide into 'truth' and 'ideology' and that, while the former requires no explanation, we need to explain people's mistakes in accepting falsehood. The most dramatic example of such 'explanatory dualism' is the Marxist treatment of ideology but it is also common in non-Marxist forms; see e.g. Karl Mannheim, *Essays on the Sociology of Knowledge* (London: Routledge & Kegan Paul, 1952).

39. See Peter L. Berger, Brigitte Berger, and Hansfried Kellner, *The Homeless Mind* (Harmondsworth, Middx.: Penguin, 1974), 15.

40. E. L. G. Stone, 'The Appeal to History in Anglo-Scottish Relations between 1291 and 1401: Part 1', *Archives*, 9 (1969–70), 11–21.

41. Grant Simpson, 'The Declaration of Arbroath Revitalised', *Scottish Historical Review*, 56 (1977), 11–34.

42. Many monastery 'infirmaries' cared only for their own monks but others took in the lay ill.

43. On Chalmers in Glasgow, see Andrew L. Drummond and James Bulloch, *The Scottish Church 1688–1843* (Edinburgh: St Andrew Press, 1973).

44. This account is taken from Gellner's theory of nationalism. See Ernest Gellner, *Nations and Nationalism* (Oxford: Blackwell, 1983).

45. H. G. Graham, *The Social Life of Scotland in the Eighteenth Century* (London: A. & C. Black, 1937), 263.

46. This point is made in a number of places by Bryan R. Wilson: see *Religion in Secular Society* (London: C. A. Watts, 1966), and *Contemporary Transformations of Religion* (Oxford: Oxford University Press, 1976).

47. Bryan R. Wilson, *Religion in Sociological Perspective* (Oxford: Oxford University Press, 1982), 154.

48. Emile Durkheim, *The Elementary Forms of the Religious Life* (London: George Allen & Unwin, 1971). For an account of Durkheim's ideas, see Kenneth Thompson, *Emile Durkheim* (London: Tavistock, 1982).

49. This case is argued persuasively in Bryan R. Wilson, 'Morality in the Evolution of the Modern Social System', *British Journal of Sociology*, 36 (1985), 315–32.

50. This section is heavily influenced by Peter Berger's synthesis of the phenomenology of Alfred Schutz and the American tradition of symbolic interactionism; see Peter L. Berger, *The Social Reality of Religion* (London: Faber & Faber, 1969), and Peter L. Berger and Thomas Luckmann, *The Social Construction of Reality* (Harmondsworth, Middx.: Penguin, 1973).

51. Peter L. Berger, *The Heretical Imperative: Contemporary Possibilities of Religious Affirmation* (London: Collins, 1980).

52. *The Sacred Canopy: Elements of a Sociological Theory of Religion* (New York: Doubleday, 1967) was the American title of the book published in Britain as *The Social Reality of Religion* (see n. 50).

53. Hornsby-Smith, *The Changing Parish*, 60, summarizing the conclusions of Danièle Hervieu-Léger, *Vers un nouveau christianisme: Introduction à la sociologie du christianisme* (Paris: Cerf, 1986).

54. Bryan R. Wilson, 'The Functions of Religion: A Reappraisal', *Religion*, 18 (1988), 199–210.

55. This point is argued at length with illustrations in Steve Bruce, *A House Divided: Protestantism, Schism and Secularization* (London: Routledge, 1990).

56. Thomas Vincent, *The Shorter Catechism Explained from Scripture* (1674; Edinburgh: Banner of Truth Trust, 1980).

57. The extent to which belief in the imminence of the supernatural has become attenuated, even among conservative Christians, is clear in the extent to which even conservative Protestant churches accept secular definitions of mental illness.

58. A. Symondson, *The Victorian Crisis of Faith* (London: SPCK, 1970).

59. Berger, Berger, and Kellner, *Homeless Mind*.

60. It is worth adding here that a sociologist who spent thirteen years in detailed study of an Australian outback community doubts that religion serves even this attenuated role. He concludes that his study 'fails to confirm the claims of Berger, Mol and Wallace that church-oriented religion has the potential for at least partially meeting a wider range of fundamental socio-psychological needs' (Ken Dempsey, 'Is Religion Still Relevant in the Private Sphere? The State of Organized Religion in an Australian Rural Community', *Sociological Analysis*, 50 (1989), 247–63).

61. In one of the least plausible but best-known examples of such arguments (it was reprinted in a collection of readings which accompanies a best-selling introductory sociology textbook), Hadden shows a complete misunderstanding of the scope of most secularization theories by offering Iranian fundamentalism as strong counter-evidence; see Jeffrey K. Hadden, 'Toward Desacralizing Secularization Theory', *Social Forces*, 65 (1987), 587–611; repr. in slightly abridged form as Reading 48 in Anthony Giddens (ed.), *Human Societies: A Reader* (Cambridge: Polity Press, 1992), 230–7. The matter is frequently confused by scholars using the secularization thesis as a peg on which to hang arguments and observations that have little or nothing to do with the secularization arguments as presented by Wilson, Martin, Berger, and others. For example, Liebman situates his observations on religious extremism by saying in the abstract of a journal article that 'contrary to prevailing paradigms of modernization and secularization . . . extremism is the religious norm' (Charles S. Liebman, 'Extremism as a Religious Norm', *Journal for the Scientific Study of Religion*, 22 (1983), 75). See also R. Stephen Warner, 'Work in Progress towards a New Paradigm for the Sociological Study of Religion in the United States', *American Journal of Sociology*, 98 (1993), 1044–93.

62. R. Martin Goodridge, 'The Ages of Faith: Romance or Reality', *Sociological Review*, 23 (1975), 381–96.

63. Much of this sort of material can be found in Thomas, *Religion and the Decline of Magic*.

64. Hamilton, *Religion*, 115–18.

65. Robert Whiting, *The Blind Devotion of the People: Popular Religion in the English Reformation* (Cambridge: Cambridge University Press, 1989), 70.

66. Patrick Collinson, *The Religion of Protestants: The Church in English Society*

*1559–1625* (Oxford: Oxford University Press, 1982), and *Godly People: Essays on English Protestantism and Puritanism* (London: Hambledon Press, 1983).
67. Margaret Spufford, *Small Books and Pleasant Histories* (London: Methuen, 1981), 194–5.
68. Margaret Spufford, 'Can We Count the "Godly" and the "Conformable" in the Seventeenth Century?', *Journal of Ecclesiastical History*, 36 (1985), 437–8.
69. David Hay and Ann Morisy, 'Reports of Ecstatic, Paranormal or Religious Experience in Great Britain and the United States: A Comparison of Trends', *Journal for the Scientific Study of Religion*, 17 (1978), 255. It is worth noting that Hay and Morisy's data show a very strong connection between conventional indices of religiosity and the experiences they document and measure, which hardly supports the general claim that 'implicit' religion is an alternative to, and compensation for the absence of, conventional religion. Bibby tried and failed to find evidence of implicit religion in Canadian survey data. He concluded 'lack of empirically identifiable invisible religion is further evident in the answers posed to the so-called ultimate questions. Only the theme of traditional religious commitment is consistently associated with clear-cut answers to such questions' (Reginald Bibby, 'Searching for Invisible Thread: Meaning Systems in Contemporary Canada', *Journal for the Scientific Study of Religion*, 22 (1983), 117). For an introductory discussion of implicit religion, see Edward Bailey, 'The Implicit Religion of Contemporary Society: An Orientation and a Plea for its Study', *Religion*, 13 (1983), 69–83.
70. David Hay and Ann Morisy, 'Secular Society/Religious Meaning: A Contemporary Paradox', unpublished paper, 1981.
71. Private communication, 6 July 1994.
72. Susan Budd, *Varieties of Unbelief: Atheists and Agnostics in English Society 1850–1960* (London: Heinemann, 1977).
73. The following is in effect a summary of David Martin, *A General Theory of Secularization* (Oxford: Blackwell, 1978). For an empirical elaboration, see Liana Giorgi, 'Religious Involvement in a Secularized Society: An Empirical Confirmation of Martin's General Theory of Secularisation', *British Journal of Sociology*, 43 (1992), 639–56.
74. The specific question of the supposed relationship between urbanization, pluralism, and secularization has been much debated. Often the arguments are highly technical and concern the relative merits of different statistical techniques for measuring each variable. The more general disagreements concern the already mentioned (and I believe mistaken) assumption of the critics of the secularization approach that it requires steady and unrelieved decline in institutional religion. As I have argued in this chapter, it is quite possible to accept (a) that elements of urbanization encouraged greater personal commitment, deepened individual religious knowledge, and strengthened social ties to fellow-believers in voluntary associations *and* (b) that industrialization and urbanization promoted social, political, and cultural changes that made the general environment less fertile for religious belief. For recent contributions to the arguments, see Callum Brown, 'Did Urbanization Secularize Britain?', *Urban History Yearbook* (1988), 1–14; Steve Bruce, 'Pluralism and Religious Vitality', in Bruce (ed.), *Religion and Modernization*, 170–94; Roger Finke and Rodney Stark, 'Religious Economies and Sacred Canopies: Religious Mobilization in American Cities, 1906', *American Sociological Review*, 53 (1988), 41–9; and Kevin

D. Breault, 'New Evidence on Religious Pluralism, Urbanism and Religious Participation', *American Sociological Review*, 54 (1989), 1048–53.

75. David Martin, *General Theory*, 30.

76. This case is argued at length in Will Herberg, *Protestant–Catholic–Jew: An Essay in American Religious Sociology* (Chicago: University of Chicago Press, 1983), and Bryan R. Wilson, 'Religion and the Churches in America', in William G. McLoughlin and Robert N. Bellah (eds.), *Religion in America* (Boston: Houghton Mifflin, 1968), 73–110.

77. For data on declining church attendance in Australia, New Zealand, and Canada, see notes to Chapter 4. For a comprehensive review of religion in those countries, North America, and Western Europe up to the 1970s, see Hans Mol (ed.), *Western Religion: A Country by Country Sociological Inquiry* (The Hague: Mouton, 1972).

78. G. A. Irwin and J. J. M. Van Holsteyn, 'Decline of the Structured Model of Electoral Competition', *Western European Politics*, 12 (1989), 21–41.

79. Steve Bruce, *God Save Ulster! The Religion and Politics of Paisleyism* (Oxford: Oxford University Press, 1986), and John Fulton, *The Tragedy of Belief: Division, Politics and Religion in Ireland* (Oxford: Oxford University Press, 1991).

# 4

---

# STRUCTURING RELIGION

..........................................................................................................

Aᴛᴛᴇᴍᴘᴛs to understand secularization can no more be reduced to counting bodies in pews than political science can be reduced to comparing numbers of voters. We should be as interested in the nature and quality of religion, and, in order to make comparisons across cultures and ages, we need a consistent vocabulary. Just as biologists need to classify species, the comparative student of religion needs a way of consistently and economically describing types of religious organization. The main purpose of this chapter is to go over the same historical terrain as the last chapter, this time concentrating on the internal dynamics of churches, sects, denominations, and cults.

It is important to appreciate the wide variety of ways in which expressions of religious belief and behaviour can be structured. To give some sense of that variety I will briefly describe two very different types of religious structure, both within the Christian tradition. The Catholic Church is a world-wide organization with a highly centralized bureaucratic structure. At the top of the pyramid is the Pope and his Vatican officials. They control appointments to senior positions in every part of the world where the Church is active and they further maintain control by having emissaries appointed to link the Vatican direct to the various national churches. Within each area, there is a clear hierarchy so that every official from the lowest curate to the highest bishop is placed in a chain of command. Central control is further strengthened by having promising junior officials brought to Rome for periods of further training.

The top of the hierarchy controls every aspect of the Church's life from liturgies and doctrines to its responses to pressing social and political events. In the Vatican there are offices for foreign affairs, banking, and the organization of education and training of clergy. Most important there is an office for correct belief: a body which has the task of determining what is truth and what is heresy. The decisions of the Second Vatican Council (1962–5) resulted in some loosening of central control.[1] Services are now conducted in local languages rather than in Latin, for example. However, the pontificate of the Polish John Paul II has seen a return to centralization and a more authoritarian Catholicism.

There could be no greater contrast with high Catholicism than a small evangelical Protestant sect called the Cooneyites.[2] Around 1900 William Irvine, an itinerant evangelist working for the Faith Mission in Ireland, came to the conclusion that the Christian Churches were offending God by having formal structures and paying their functionaries. His reading of the New Testament led him to conclude that Christ wanted an unpaid ministry of itinerant preachers, like the early disciples. He left the Faith Mission and took to walking the countryside with a companion, preaching wherever people would listen and holding Bible study classes in receptive homes. He gradually recruited a large number of followers to his vision of primitive Christianity. In 1907 over 600 followers attended a convention on the banks of Lough Erne in County Fermanagh.

The sect continues to this day despite an almost complete lack of formal organization beyond its annual conventions. Preachers, appointed in no more formal sense than that they feel called, start preaching and people listen to them. They are not paid but must subsist on the spontaneous gifts of their audience. There is no system for training, licensing, or disciplining preachers. The only control is that informally exercised by the audience: those who teach doctrines unacceptable to the hearers are not supported.

The contrast of the Roman Church and the 'Two-by-Twos' shows us the considerable range of organizational shapes that can be taken by the same tradition of beliefs. It also shows us that even those groups which do not actively encourage organization still have some. After all, the Cooneyites do meet. They do have enough in common to distinguish them from their neighbours, so that, though they may disclaim any label other than 'Christian', they do recognize each other.

A difficulty in talking sensibly about religious organizations is that we use words like church, sect, denomination, and cult loosely and inconsistently. The prominent American archivist of new religious movements J. Gordon Melton, for example, follows journalistic usage in describing any new religion as a 'cult'.[3] As well as being used promiscuously, such terms are also used to endorse or condemn. I belong to a church: you belong to a sect. No one ever describes themselves as members of a cult.

Clearly what is needed for any sensible comparison is a standardized set of categories and one of the purposes of this chapter is to present a typology of religious organizations that can be used, not only to describe changes in Christianity in the modern world, but also to give us purchase on religious changes outside our tradition.[4] I will begin by looking at the use of the terms 'church' and 'sect' in the history of the Christian tradition in Europe.

## The Church and the Sect

The notion of the church derives its force from the growth of Christianity and the historic forms of Catholic, Orthodox, and Coptic churches. These bodies sought to be co-extensive with their societies. They were inclusive in that they offered their ministries and offices to all members of the society (even to those who were unwilling to accept them!). They were typically closely aligned with the secular social order and fitted into its hierarchy of power and status. When churches were wealthy bodies with extensive powers and lands, their leaders possessed the rights, prerogatives, and influence of secular princes and nobles.

Because churches and societies were largely co-extensive, people were born into the church as they were born into the society; membership was a status ascribed at birth. The church offered its salvational services through a professional clergy who performed a prescribed, calendrical rota of rituals. Attendance at the most important of these was usually compulsory. The clergy were a separate order, or 'estate', living a distinctive form of life (for example, by being celibate). Being closely allied with the society and the prevailing social order, the church was typically conservative in character and tended to identify more closely with the comfortable classes than with the poor and deprived. While the professional clergy might have to live a distinctive mode of life entailing purity and devotion, the church made relatively few demands on the ordinary members beyond periodic attendance, financial support, and verbal commitment to its creed.

Such a body found itself from time to time faced with dissent or revolt. There were those who protested against ecclesiastical pomp and wealth or sought to live out or practise a more radical form of the faith. Unless these dissidents rejected the authority of the church and its pontiff, they could often be incorporated within the church as a separate unit—for example, as a religious order. Such orders might have adopted a more demanding, more ascetic mode of life and religious practice, siding, at least at first, with the poor and oppressed. Of course, such exemplary piety often attracted the support of the wealthy, seeking to secure some element of religious virtue or grace by providing buildings or land to support the monks. In time such orders became wealthy, complacent, and exploitative of those they were originally founded to serve, which in turn provoked new dissent and the foundation of new orders of religious virtuosi.

But not all the dissidents accepted the authority of the church or the pontiff. Worse still, some advanced radically new interpretations of the doctrine, permitting them to be identified as heretic. Such groups and movements were viewed as sects, as schismatic bodies which had separated from the 'true church'. The sect was thus a form of religious deviation or protest. Some radical movements began as a largely secular form of protest but the close identity between the church and the state often meant that the church would 'anathematize' as heresy and dissent, protests against the secular order which it legitimated. Similarly religious protest called forth the wrath, not only of the church but also of the state which rushed to defend the church which certified and sustained its legitimacy.

Religious deviation in the form of sects was thus normally met with repression. Crusades were launched against the Albingensians. The Lollards, the Brotherhood of the Spirit, and other medieval heresies were subjected to harsh persecution. For this, if for no other reason, sects were normally small bodies. One was not normally born into a sect but became a member through choice; membership was an achieved status. Sectarians were enthusiasts who subjected themselves to a demanding moral regime. Commitment and moral standing were tested before the novice was allowed to become a full member. Such groups often appealed more to the poor than to the comfortable because they focused on the eschatological themes of the Christian tradition—the imminent return of Christ (or second 'advent') and the coming Millennium (the thousand years of righteousness when the first would be last and the meek would inherit the earth). These adventist doctrines were socially subversive, as was the rejection of a professional clergy in favour of the practice of the priesthood of all believers.

The state persecution of subversive teachings ensured that many sectarian groups were short-lived; members were brought to recant or eradicated. Some survived by migrating to more tolerant or emptier parts of Europe. Others kept their beliefs and practices secret from outsiders, carefully excluding unbelievers and screening those who wished to join.

The upheaval of the Reformation generated many new sects. The flourishing of dissent against the Church and the emergence of many different interpretations of the Christian tradition led to dozens of small groups of enthusiasts pursuing widely different theologies. Quakers and Shakers, Amish and Hutterites, Sixth Monarchy Men and 101 sects emerged, along with the Baptists, Lutherans, Presbyterians, and other Protestant bodies that came to prominence in those states which seceded from the Catholic world. The more extreme sectarian groups were persecuted by Catholic and dominant Protestant churches alike and often escaped only by taking the perilous route to the Americas, where, outside the Puritan states of New England, they might live unmolested.

The pre-modern Christian world then was dominated by the 'church'. With the Reformation came the flourishing of sects. As they proliferated and as some of them grew to supersede the churches, the state had to change its attitude towards religious monopoly and religious conformity.

## The Rise of Toleration

Most human action is profoundly ironic in its consequence and the rise of religious toleration is a very good example of such irony; I shall illustrate it from the Scottish case.[5] From the Reformation, Scotland had a national Protestant church which encompassed most of the population, and significant but geographically constrained Catholic and Episcopalian minorities. In theory the reformed kirk, like its predecessor, claimed the right to enforce conformity to its standards and it expected the 'civil magistrate' (or, to use the modern term, 'the state') to do the enforcing. The first dissent from the reformed Church came, not from liberals opposed to the idea that people should be prodded with bayonets into the true church, but from zealots of enforced orthodoxy who objected to the composition of this particular state church and to the terms of the offered relationship between church and state. As Calvinist Presbyterians, the Covenanters believed that the state had an obligation to promote the 'true religion' and they were willing to wage war for that principle.

The first major split from the Kirk came in 1733 and concerned the failure of the Church to protect its Presbyterian nature against 'patronage': the principle that the landlords who funded the Church should be able to nominate parish ministers. The Seceders, as they were known, shared with the Covenanters the Calvinist principles of a state-supported church. Indeed, they were so keen on enforcing orthodoxy that they regularly opposed changes to the law from which they themselves would have benefited.

Only the third Presbyterian dissenting church owed anything to the principle of toleration. That occurred in 1761 when Thomas Gillespie was expelled from the Kirk for refusing to take part in the imposition of an unpopular minister on the congregation of Inverkeithing. His stand against the rights of patrons should have made him a recruit for the Secession Church, but he could not accept their view of church–state relations and he formed the Relief Presbytery. We can appreciate the relative unpopularity of liberalism by noting that the Relief grew far more slowly than the Calvinist Secession Church.

The fourth and largest division occurred in 1843 when about a third of the ministers, elders, and members of the Church of Scotland left to form the 'Church of Scotland Free'. Again, the defectors were not critical of the principle of a state-supported and enforced religion. The Free Churchmen departed because, as evangelicals, they objected to the reign of the 'Moderates' in the Kirk and to patronage. And even that point of principle rested on a large amount of self-interest: generally it was moderate clergymen who were imposed on evangelical congregations by patrons. Had it been the other way round, patronage might not have been so unpopular. As they were at pains to stress, the founders of the Free Church were establishment men; they objected only to the state supporting this particular generation of theologically moderate clergy.

Despite having begun as firm believers in religious coercion, the Secession and the Free Church gradually came to argue for religious freedom, in defence first of their own rights, and then of the rights of dissenters generally; finally they came to see the value of the general principle of religious toleration. But the evolution was a slow and painful process, often scarred by the expulsion of those clergymen who promoted the cause of toleration ten years too early, before the majority of their colleagues recognized its inevitability. There is no mystery about the circumstance which led to the reluctant acceptance of pluralism: their own failure to win over the majority of the Church of Scotland. Only when each wave of dissent realized that it could not succeed in taking over the instruments of state coercion did it begin to find the use of such instruments offensive.

Fission created a plurality of organizations and the divisions of the people of God meant that the price of enforcing conformity was too high for a modern democratic state. The consequence, quite undesired by most of those who brought it about, was religious toleration and the rise of the secular state.

Toleration allowed the sects to grow and recruit a following, largely free from civil and political discrimination. Thus the Christian world in the early modern era became divided into churches (which claimed exclusive jurisdiction), sects (which were minority and often persecuted groups), and a growing band of mutually tolerant respectable religious bodies which certainly sought to bring in as many people as possible, often had a professional clergy, and typically imposed few substantial demands on their members—and yet were clearly not 'churches' in the classic sense. It is these bodies which we normally call 'denominations'.

## The Denomination

Denominations differ from sects in that they are not exclusive (that is, there is no real test of merit or grace before one is permitted to join) and they are relatively undemanding. People may choose to join, but many people are members because they were born into the group. Like the church, the denomination has a professional ministry, it is large, and it is often associated with the comfortable classes. It thus represents a position intermediate between the sect and the church. However, it differs from both sect and church in one particularly important respect—namely, that both the sect and the church think they have a monopoly of the truth. They claim that only by embracing their path can we hope to reach salvation. Each says that it and only it has the path to heaven. The denomination does not claim such exclusive access to the truth that saves. Rather it says that it has a particularly clear vision of the Christian message and its purest organizational form but allows that there are other religious bodies which also have much of the truth. The Congregationalists do not believe that Methodists are going to hell because they are not Congregationalists. Instead they concede that Methodists have got much right and can be partners in such common enterprises as foreign mission, evangelistic crusades, and social-welfare efforts.

For the reasons discussed in Chapter 2, the historic churches have also become more denominational. In the United States and in Holland, the Catholic Church is relatively tolerant and willing to collaborate with other churches. The Church of England, though it retains some formal advantages over the bodies it once dismissed as 'nonconformists' (such as the right of some bishops to sit in the upper chamber of the legislature), accepts and works with other organizations. When all, or almost all, of the population belong to one religious organization, it can think and act like a church. But when a population becomes divided between a number of organizations, the conditions for the church form are undermined in two ways.

First, there is what one might call the politics of the new circumstance. The state has to become neutral and abandon support of any particular form of religion. The US constitution is a classic statement of this position in that it both guarantees individual religious liberty and prevents the state from supporting any particular religion. The major religious organizations then have to reduce their claims and recognize that they are in the same boat as their competitors. Gradually competition between organizations is reduced and there is an increase in interdenominational co-operation.

The realism brought on by pluralism can be illustrated from the structure of religious broadcasting in England. If the English all belonged to the Church of England it would be quite possible for the publicly funded British Broadcasting Corporation (BBC) to allow the Church of England to organize all religious broadcasting. All the morning services, all the Prayers for Today and Thoughts for the Day, and so on, would be delivered by Anglicans and would present Anglicanism as the one true faith. The broadcasts could even openly criticize alternative faiths. However, with only a small proportion of the population members of that organization and perhaps three-quarters supporting no organized religion, there is no justification of such a monopoly over religious broadcasting. So the churches have to co-operate. Indeed, with each denomination being small, it is only by co-operating that they can present a respectable claim to have any access to the air waves. Hence most religious broadcasting units of the BBC have on their staff a Catholic, an Anglican, and a Nonconformist, and the work they produce is deliberately ecumenical and uncontroversial.[6] Opportunities to broadcast church services are rotated around the various denominations in proportion to their size. Each organization scales down its claims, stresses what it has in common with the others, and reduces what is distinctive. There is a general agreement not to criticize each other. This is the necessary accommodation to pluralism.

Secondly, there is the social psychology of the pluralistic culture. It is easy to believe that one's religion is absolutely right in every detail when there is no competition. Every increase in competition makes that certainty, that dogmatism, more and more difficult to maintain. If the competing faith belongs to some subordinate social minority, it can be dismissed as only fitting for that kind of people, but when small communities of socially similar people start to fragment, so that some stay in the Church of Scotland and some go to the Free Church down the road and some attend a Baptist meeting around the corner, and you live and work with these people, it becomes more and more difficult to insist that your own link with God is unique and that the others are all wrong. Gradually the way in which people hold their beliefs changes so that absolute certainty and intolerance diminish; the result is the denominational position of supposing that all these organizations, in their different ways, are doing God's work.

To recap, because, both in relations between the religious organization and the state, and in the way believers view their own faith, the fragmentation of the dominant tradition makes the church form more and more difficult to sustain, there is a marked shift to a series of attitudes that we call denominationalism.

If the compromise of the church is one route to denominationalism, the other is the compromise of the once-radical sect.

## The Decline of Radicalism

The decline of sect radicalism is fascinating for the insight it gives us into both the changing nature of society and the internal dynamics of organizations. Although he was more concerned with denouncing the fragmentation of Christianity than with explaining the shift from sect to denomination, the American theologian and historian H. R. Niebuhr built on the work of Ernst Troeltsch to produce an extremely influential set of observations in *The Social Sources of Denominationalism*.[7] He notes that time and again what begins life as a radical sect critical of the mundane world evolves into a comfortable denomination, at peace with the world around it. There are a number of reasons why this should happen.

The first generation of members deliberately and voluntarily accepted the demands of the sect. They made sacrifices for their beliefs. The people who broke away from the state churches in England and Scotland in the eighteenth and early nineteenth centuries sometimes suffered political, social, and financial penalties. The state could confiscate their property, exclude them from holding political office or military rank, and remove their children to have them raised as good Anglicans. How vigorously such powers were used depended on local magistrates. The diaries of George Fox, the founder of the Quaker movement, make his England appear as a bizarre snakes-and-ladders board. In some villages he was welcomed by the local squire, wined and dined, and invited to preach. The following week and only twenty miles away he was thrown into a dungeon and beaten and starved.[8] Overall those charged with applying the laws behaved with more charity and flexibility than those who framed and passed them.[9] None the less, religious dissent did incur a loss, if only the loss of social esteem. In so far as they made sacrifices for their beliefs, the founding generation of sectarians invested more than just their hopes in their new faith, and their commitment, thus tested, was all the greater. But the second generation, the children of the sect founders, did not join voluntarily. They were born into it and, even when the greatest effort was put into socializing the children into the sect's ideology, it was inevitable that their commitment would be less than that of their parents.[10]

This was especially the case if the sectarians, by working diligently to glorify God and avoiding expensive and wasteful luxuries, had achieved a status and standard of living considerably more comfortable than that of their own parents. The children of most first-generation Methodists were moving up in the world and hence had more to lose by remaining so much at odds with it. They mixed with others of more elevated status than their parents. They were a little embarrassed at the roughness and lack of sophistication of their place of worship, their uneducated minister, their rough folk hymns and liturgies. They began to press for small adaptations towards a more respectable format, more comparable to that of the Church of England.

Furthermore, many sects were adventist or millenarian. Part of the spur for the initial enthusiasm of the sect was the idea that the end of the world was nigh and the saints had to prepare themselves for the millennium. Some added the idea that, by getting saved, making sacrifices, and promoting the new beliefs, they would hasten the end of the world. Either way, there was no expectation that the very high levels of commitment displayed at the start would have to be maintained for long. Once a few years had gone by and the world had failed to end, the sect had to get used to the idea of a long future.

In particular, and this takes us back to the first point, there was the difficulty of the status of the sect's children. The sect began with a radical distinction between itself and the rest of the world. It had the truth; everyone else was the heathen. Usually the sect was highly critical of those religious organizations that accepted children, because it believed that only a conscious, voluntary, informed, and hence adult conversion experience guaranteed salvation. But the sect's own children threatened that demarcation. After all, it was a little hard for the sectarians to believe that their own children, who had been raised in the true faith, immersed in the Word since they were babies, and surrounded by examples of pious living, were as fully excluded as the offspring of outsiders. Gradually the very strict membership criteria were relaxed until they were indistinguishable from those of the corrupt church so bitterly denounced at the sect's formation.

There is a further point that the German political scientist Robert Michels elaborated in his studies of change in left-wing political organizations and that concerns the development of organizational structure and the interests of officials.[11] Although most sects began as primitive democracies, with the equality of all believers and little or no formal organization, gradually a professional leadership cadre emerged. Especially after the founding charismatic leader died, there was a need to educate and train the preachers and teachers who would sustain the movement. There was a need to co-ordinate the growing organization. There were assets to be safeguarded and books to be published and distributed. With organization came paid officials, and such people had a vested interest in reducing the degree of conflict between the sect and the surrounding society. They could also compare themselves to the clergy of other churches and wanted the same status and levels of education, training, and reward that they enjoyed.

Unless the sect follows the path of such communitarians as the Amish, the Hutterites, and the Doukhobors and succeeds in isolating itself from the surrounding environment, its members will be in frequent contact with unbelievers. Sectarians may have various strategies for dismissing such people as of no consequence, but if they have frequent and positive and rewarding relationships with outsiders, then the idea that they possess a monopoly of the truth is bound to become more difficult to sustain. The simple fact of human sociability will cause a gradual reduction of the claims that the sectarians make for their sect.

Niebuhr saw the sect as a short-lived form of religious organization, gradually becoming more tolerant, lax, and upwardly mobile, and eventually becoming a denomination. This pattern can readily be found. It often takes more than one generation, but the development of the Methodists in the three generations after Wesley's death fits the picture, as do the changes among the Quakers in the late eighteenth and nineteenth centuries. The austere commitment of early followers, with their distinctive mode of plain dress (with wide-brimmed hats for the men who conspicuously refused to doff them for the king) and distinctive forms of speech, gave way among those who came to be called 'Gay Quakers' to more conventional styles. The early Quakers would not have read a novel or attended the theatre, but the Gay Quakers (usually the offspring of wealthy merchants, manufacturers, and bankers) became more and more like the Church of England neighbours with whom they mixed as social equals. By the middle of the nineteenth century one finds them crossing over into first the evangelical wing and then the mainstream of the Church of England.[12]

As a sect compromised, so the cycle began again. Not everyone had shared in the prosperity that had seen the sect rise. Some were still poor and dispossessed. They broke away to find again a pristine and radical expression of Christianity. They founded new sects. These in turn grew, produced further generations, created a professional clergy, and so on. In the English-speaking world one sees the phases, like sedimentary layers of rock: Anglicanism gave way to Methodism and a rejuvenated Baptist movement. That wave was followed by the Salvation Army and the Holiness Movement. That wave was in turn followed by Pentecostalism.

The Niebuhr pattern captures an important truth but it needs certain qualifications. Niebuhr tends to concentrate on the internal dynamics of change and rather underestimates the influence of changes in the external world of the sect. For example, in the periods under discussion the economy was growing rapidly and standards of living were generally rising. For the reasons which form the basis for Weber's Protestant-ethic thesis, the 'this-worldly asceticism' promoted by Protestant sects should have meant that the sectarians prospered faster than the average, but none the less we can imagine that the temptations to compromise would be considerably fewer and weaker in an economy with very slow growth.[13] Secondly, the rise of a professional clergy and a bureaucratic structure are often described as though they followed from moral weakness on the part of the sectarians when they are in large part thrust upon any group in the modern world by the expectations of the rest of the society. Professionalism and bureaucracy are just how modern societies organize things and many sectarians find themselves obliged by the need to negotiate various forms of recognition from the state (the right to be conscientious objectors, for example) to become more organized.

Further, Niebuhr exaggerates the extent to which Protestant sects are much of a muchness. As Bryan Wilson has argued in detail, doctrinal differences between sects make them variously susceptible to the sort of accommodation Niebuhr describes.[14] We need not pursue the differences further than noting that sects can organize themselves and their relations with their surrounding society so as to remain sectarian for many generations. The drift towards the denominational compromise is a common career but it is not inevitable.

## The Cult

Finally we might briefly consider the fourth major form of religious organization. Ernst Troeltsch identified a distinct element of the Christian tradition which he called 'mysticism'.[15] Unlike the other forms, this was a highly individualistic expression, varying with personal experiences and interpretations. The organizational form that corresponds to Troeltsch's idea is that of the *cult*: a small loosely knit group organized around some common themes and interests but lacking a sharply defined and exclusive belief system. Each individual member is the final authority as to what constitutes the truth or the path to salvation. The cult, like the denomination, is tolerant and understanding of its own members (indeed it is so tolerant that it hardly has 'members'; instead it has consumers who pick and choose those bits of its product that suit them). Such groups are often short-lived, splitting over divergent opinions or unable to command the obedience of members.

## Refining the Distinctions

The above brief review of the major organizational forms of Christianity has attempted to pick out the common strands from an extremely complex history. As we saw with the criticisms of the Niebuhr thesis, scholars have argued about just how far we can generalize from particular parts of the history of Christianity to general models of religious organizations. I will not review the vast literature on the use of such terms as 'church' and 'sect'[16] but offer just one principle which explains why I adopt the following approach.

Typologies and definitions are neither true nor false. They are intellectual instruments, spanners and wrenches that are only more and less useful. Their use lies is in helping us compare and explain. The sorting principles most likely to be of value are those which best strike the balance between two competing imperatives. They should lift us above the peculiar and particular features of the specific cases (and here that means freeing the concepts of church, sect, and denomination from their Christian history) and towards the general sociological work we want to do with such concepts. Yet, and this is an important caution, they should not too firmly insert in their terms any explanations we might want to offer; that would make the whole process circular and mislead us into thinking we had found causal connections in the real world when all we had done was rename things. This was my reason for rejecting functional definitions of religion. We cannot demonstrate that religion has this or that purpose or consequence if we have already defined religion in terms of the purpose or consequence.

Wallis suggests an extremely economical way of thinking about all ideological organizations (see Fig. 4.1). He notes that most of the differences that interest us in how people organize their religious lives can be identified if we look at just two simple questions concerning external perceptions and self-image: (a) is the religion seen as respectable or deviant and (b) does it see itself as having a unique grasp of salvational knowledge. Most Mormons believe that their organization offers the only way to God. Hence they try to persuade people to join the Mormons. For Mormons, the Church of Jesus Christ of Latter-Day Saints is *uniquely legitimate*. The Roman Catholic Church has traditionally taken the same view, although in some settings it is now moderating its claims. The Exclusive Brethren also take the view that they and they alone have the Way. But there is considerable difference in the popularity, acceptability, and prestige of the Catholic Church, the Mormons, and the Exclusive Brethren. We can see the difference in the way the media treat them. It is common for documentaries to criticize the way in which the Brethren socialize their children to become the next

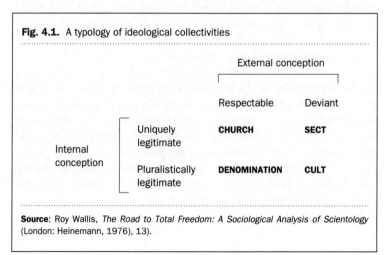

**Fig. 4.1.** A typology of ideological collectivities

External conception

|  |  | Respectable | Deviant |
|---|---|---|---|
| Internal conception | Uniquely legitimate | **CHURCH** | **SECT** |
|  | Pluralistically legitimate | **DENOMINATION** | **CULT** |

**Source**: Roy Wallis, *The Road to Total Freedom: A Sociological Analysis of Scientology* (London: Heinemann, 1976), 13).

generation of the Brethren. It is rare to see similar arguments being put about Catholic schooling or about the Catholic Church's insistence that the children of mixed marriages be raised as Catholics. Hence we would say the Catholics are a 'church' but the Brethren are a 'sect'. The position of the Mormons is interesting and allows me to introduce a crucial theme of the Wallis model: its social relativity. He is looking not for the unchanging essence of any phenomenon but the reality of its life in this or that place. The Mormons began as a highly deviant (and much persecuted) sect. In many parts of the world they remain a deviant sect. But in Utah they have achieved such numerical superiority as to be able to act as if they formed a 'church'.

Consider the bottom half of the figure. What the denomination—the Methodists would be an example—and the cult have in common is that they do not claim a unique possession of the truth. They think that they have something to offer, that you might be better off being a Methodist than a Baptist, but they recognize other organizations as being every bit as valid as themselves. Again what separates them is the top line—the extent to which they have succeeded in establishing themselves. The Methodists are a respectable part of our social and cultural landscape; cults are not.

The difference in self-image between the church and sect on the one hand and the denomination and cult on the other produces a considerable difference in vulnerability. Because they are so demanding and make such exclusive claims for their own product, churches and sects tend to be brittle. Their strength is of the sort that can, when subjected to the right sort of pressure, lead to large cracks and splintering. The denomination and the cult are vulnerable to change in a very different way. Denominations and cults are relatively weak institutions in that their beliefs and practices are barely distinguishable from those of a large number of similar groups. It is very easy to move from the Church of England (now a denomination despite its title) to the Methodists to the Baptists and back again. Similarly, cults find that their members are selective in their acceptance of the doctrines. They pick this or that bit and synthesize it with what they have acquired from other cults. For the top line, the danger is factionalism and schism; for the bottom line, it is low levels of commitment and drifting.

## The Fate of Religion in the Modern World

With the exceptions to be discussed in the next chapter, the fragmentation of most modern societies makes the church form of religion untenable. Those people who wish to remain religious in modern societies are likely to organize themselves in one of the other three.

I want now to pursue the consequences of the inclusivity and permeability of the denomination. What is often not sufficiently noticed is that the decline of church membership and attendance in the Western world has not affected all religious organizations equally. Unlike the rain which falls on the just and the unjust, secularization has born most heavily on the mainstream liberal Christian churches, those which by and large have the denominational form. Evangelical Protestantism—the sectarian alternative—has shown far greater resilience.

Consider the pattern of change in American religion. Almost all the major US Christian religious organizations grew between 1955 and 1965. The greatest percentage growth was shown by the more conservative Protestant churches such as the Assemblies of God, the Missouri Synod Lutherans, the Church of the Nazarene, and the Southern Baptists. That period also saw the first net decline in a major organization: the liberal United Church of Christ.

In the other major liberal denominations the rate of growth slowed, while the conservative bodies, large and small, continued to grow at a more rapid rate. It was in the latter half of the 1960s, continuing into the middle 1970s, that all of the theologically liberal denominations began to experience membership decline.[17]

Presenting the same data in another way, the highest growth rates between 1950 and 1975 were sustained by the two most conservative major denominations: the Southern Baptist Convention (80 per cent) and the Lutheran Church–Missouri Synod (60 per cent). The two lowest growth rates were recorded by the two most liberal denominations: the United Methodist Church (3 per cent) and the United Church of Christ (−7 per cent).

Bibby's extensive Canadian research shows a similar pattern. Some conservative churches have shown no growth relative to the total population, while others, in particular the Pentecostalists, the Christian and Missionary Alliance, and the Salvation Army, have grown faster than the population. But, although conservative Protestantism's 'cumulative proportional population gain over the century has been negligible', liberal and broad Protestantism has shown a considerable and marked decline.[18] The extent of the difference between conservative and liberal denominations can be illustrated with information about church attendance. In one of his surveys Bibby asked people to compare how often they went to church when they were children with how often they went now. The 'fall-out' rate clearly matched theology. The greatest decline was among the Presbyterians (53 per cent), the United Church (42 per cent), and the Anglican Church (42 per cent). Lutherans had a fall-out rate of 23 per cent, the Baptists came next with only 15 per cent, and a variety of evangelical denominations lost just 10 per cent of their attenders.[19]

We see much the same with British Protestantism. The extremely tolerant Unitarian Universalists have declined drastically. In 1943 there were 30,000. By 1980, there were 11,000 and in the last decade this has fallen to under 9,000.[20] The mainstream Church of England has seen steady decline. Within the 'Nonconformist' or 'Free Church' tradition, the broad and liberal churches such as the Methodists have declined, while the Independent sector (which includes the 'Open' Brethren, independent evangelical churches, and those charismatic groups known collectively as the House Church Movement) has grown. Brierley's church-attendance data show that, while the liberal wing of the Free Church sector lost 2 per cent of its church-goers between 1975 and 1989, the conservative evangelical Independents gained 14 per cent.[21] The United Reformed Church (URC) was formed in 1972 from the merger of the Presbyterian Church of England and the majority of congregations in the Congregational Union of England and Wales. The URC has shown a faster rate of decay than did any of its component before the merger. The Congregationalists who stayed out, largely because they were more evangelical then they expected the new body to be, have retained roughly the number of congregations and members they had in 1972. The URC has lost half of its 1972 membership.

Scotland offers a good setting to compare conservative and liberal varieties of Protestantism because the overwhelming majority of Protestants adhere to some form of Presbyterianism. Much of their history, liturgy, and doctrine is so similar that we can treat the variants as being distinguished primarily by the theological 'spin' they put on their doctrines. Between 1956 and 1986 the liberal United Free Church declined by more than 50 per cent. The mainstream Church of Scotland declined by 36 per cent and the two conservative Presbyterian churches—the Free Church and the Free Presbyterian Church—remained stable, and that stability has been achieved despite recruiting primarily from the Highlands and Islands, where the total population declined considerably faster than the Scottish average.[22]

Many Protestant churches are theologically broad and contain within them liberals and conservatives. Changes in the popularity of positions within an organization are extremely difficult to measure, but two studies of Baptist congregations suggest that within that denomination liberal Protestantism was waning. The first study showed that smaller congregations were growing and that smaller congregations were generally the conservative ones.[23] The second study was controlled for size by looking at only congregations larger than fifty people. Radical and middle-of-the-road ministers tended to have declining congregations. Evangelical ministers had growing congregations.[24]

In Australia, too, one finds the same pattern of conservative stability and liberal and mainstream decline. In the twenty years from 1966 to 1986, the number of Australians in the census identifying themselves with the Anglican Church fell from 3.9 million to 3.7 million. The numbers identifying with the Congregational, Presbyterian, Methodist, and Uniting churches declined from 2.2 million to 1.7 million. And that was against the background of a population growth of over a third. Surveys also showed a dramatic fall in the proportion of those identifiers who attended church.[25] In

**Table 4.1.** Monthly church attendance by denomination, Australia, 1960–1987 (%)

| Denomination | 1960 | 1983 | 1987 |
|---|---|---|---|
| Anglican | 31 | 14 | 15 |
| Catholic | 69 | 44 | 42 |
| Methodist ⎤ | | | |
| Presbyterian | 44 | 22 | 20 |
| Uniting Church ⎦ | | | |

Source: Phillip J. Hughes, 'Types of Faith', in Alan W. Black (ed.), Religion in Australia (Sydney: Allen & Unwin, 1991), 93.

contrast, though they still lag behind population growth, the Baptists grew from just over 166,000 to almost 200,000 between 1966 and 1986. In 1966 there were too few Pentecostalists to be listed in the census. In 1986 they were 0.7 per cent of the population and, as Hughes notes, nominalism is almost unknown in these two groups; almost all of those who describe themselves in the census as Baptists or Pentecostalists are active members.[26]

An almost identical pattern can be found in New Zealand. Hill and Bowman summarize their analyses of three decades of census data from 1951 to 1981 as follows: 'a decline in adherence to and an ageing within the larger religious bodies; a selective increase in sectarian and cultic adherence; the tendency of religious groups to attract more specialized social constituencies; [and] a growth in irreligion.'[27]

That the same pattern is to be found in so many different countries suggests that the special vulnerability to secularization of the most denominational form of Protestantism is not an accident and is not to be explained by particular features of this or that liberal Protestant organization. How then is it to be explained? It is worth being clear about where we should be looking. It would be a mistake to concentrate on the greater appeal to the same market of conservative alternatives. A large number of studies agree that the growth of conservative Protestantism owes little to the recruitment of people who were previously atheists or even liberal Christians.[28] The real difference lies in the retention of children. Typical is Bibby's data on Canadian evangelicals. A survey of twenty evangelical churches showed that 72 per cent of those who joined in a four-year period were moving from other evangelical churches. Only 28 per cent were 'converts' and almost three-quarters of these were the children of evangelicals.[29] This suggests that the explanation for the differing fate of the denominational and sectarian versions of Protestantism has more to do with the ability to retain children rather than attractiveness to outsiders.

Wallis and I have written at length on the problems of maintaining diffuse belief systems.[30] Here I want to mention those that relate closely to retaining members and socializing children. Because liberal Protestantism is extremely diffuse, it is often difficult for liberals to unite around a common theme or course of action. They are thus always potentially vulnerable to defection as members leave to join other narrower organizations, which, because they enjoy greater cohesion, are more likely to achieve their goals. This is especially a problem in a largely secular society where the clergy may seek increased relevance by finding new goals to pursue. In so far as liberal Protestants become involved in various forms of community work or therapy or politics, they are liable to be attracted by other organizations already working in these fields which, because they are more focused on the goals in question and have better track records of work in that area, are more likely to succeed. To extend the slogan popular with liberal clergymen, 'building bridges' to the secular world may simply encourage church members to drive across them and not return.

Secondly, liberal Protestants are tolerant to the point of being almost universalist. The enthusiasm for embracing diversity means that the fragmentation that comes with individualism is not a problem. Unlike the conservative Protestant tradition, liberal Protestantism is not racked by schism. But it crucially lacks any motive to proselytize and recruit. There is no pressing need to persuade others, even one's own children, to follow in the faith, because the liberal Protestant does not believe that there are no dire consequences that follow from getting it wrong. There is no hell. But even if they could agree that it was important to promote their faith, on what cardinal points of doctrine could they agree?

I have already suggested that the denomination is often the product of a sect or a church moderating the claims it makes for the uniqueness of its product. One can see this general historical process repeated in the decision-making of individuals. Many liberal Protestants (and, increasingly, liberal Catholics) came to their faith as a liberation from the authoritarianism of either the church or the sect form of religion. What those bodies that have been most influenced by liberalism cannot do is give any pressing reason why an atheist should accept their religious beliefs. There may be peripheral advantages in the company or the social activities offered by a church, but, so long as the mainstream churches tend to the universalism of endorsing secular beliefs as being pretty well equally valid and seek new roles for themselves by becoming involved in secular activities, they are offering little or no challenge to those presently outside the churches.

To summarize so far, I am suggesting that the denominational form of religion has declined more rapidly than the sect because of the diffuseness of its beliefs. Diffuseness also creates structural difficulties for the fourth type of religious organization: the cult. Indeed, the cult generally has a greater problem because it does not have the history and tradition of the once-sectarian or once-churchly denomination to give it stability. Methodists or Presbyterians may continue to support their denomination, despite the knowledge that what it offers is neither essential to salvation nor that different from what they could get anywhere else, simply because they have always done so. It may require some major change either in their own circumstances (moving town, for example) or in the nature of the denomination (a merger, for example) for them to leave. Inertia is a powerful social force, which is why denominational unions have generally backfired as each party to the merger loses those whose commitment is too weak to survive the need for change. Furthermore, the generous giving of previous generations of members, either during their lifetimes or in their wills, provides the denominations with a large amount of capital which, if wisely invested, allows the employment of a body of clergy larger than could be sustained by the donations of present members.[31] Most cults begin life as cults and hence gain no inertial benefit from the more strenuous commitment found in a more coherent form of religious organization from which they have evolved. The practical difficulties of the cultic form of religion will be examined in the discussion of New Age religion in Chapter 8.

## Conclusion

This chapter has introduced a vocabulary that allows us concisely to describe major changes in the type of religious expression common in certain sorts of society. I am not suggesting that sects, denominations, and cults were unknown prior to the Reformation; would that history were so simple as to allow only one sort of religion in any one epoch. What I am suggesting is that, for analytical purposes, the enormous range of ways in which people can organize their religious lives can be simplified to the four types of the Wallis model. Those terms then allow us economically to describe a fundamental change in the place of religion in society.

Modernization made the church form of religion impossible and churches became denominations. Religious dissent, accelerated by the social changes of the early modern period, created a profusion of sects, most of which became denominations (if they survived beyond one generation). The denominational form of religious expression, though it neatly solved the problem of peaceful coexistence in a pluralistic culture, was vulnerable because, by conceding that what it offered could readily be found elsewhere (including outside religion altogether), it removed many of the reasons why anyone should work hard to maintain it. The sectarian form of religion is demanding and it is potentially disruptive because it challenges other belief systems and modes of behaviour (religious and secular). To the extent that a nation-state or a society is prepared to allow its people social space in which to create their own subcultures, the sect form can prosper (as we will see in the discussion of fundamentalism in the USA). However, the distance between its beliefs and the cultural mainstream is so great that few outsiders will be attracted and its success will depend on socializing its children in the faith. Finally, we have the cult, which tends to succeed and fail at the same time. Its ideas and practices find an audience and even, in a diluted form, infuse the general cultural climate (as, for example, with the many holistic healing cults and alternative medical practices), but it is unable to elicit or maintain the commitment of those people interested in its innovations.

## Notes

1.  For an account of post-Vatican II Catholicism in Britain, see Michael P. Hornsby-Smith, *The Changing Parish: A Study of Parishes, Priests and Parishioners after Vatican II* (London: Routledge, 1989).
2.  D. Parker and H. Parker, *The Secret Sect* (Pendle Hill, NSW: The Parkers, 1982).
3.  J. Gordon Melton, *Encyclopedic Handbook of Cults in America* (New York: Garland Publishing, 1986).
4.  Because the typology is constructed around sociological rather than theological categories, it is also readily applicable to non-religious ideological organizations. See the essays in Roy Wallis (ed.), *Sectarianism: Analyses of Religious and Non-Religious Sects* (London: Peter Owen, 1975).
5.  This interpretation of Scottish church history is based on, among other sources, Andrew L. Drummond and James Bulloch, *The Scottish Church 1688–1843* (Edinburgh: St Andrew Press, 1973); *The Church in Victorian Scotland 1843–1874* (Edinburgh: St Andrew Press, 1975); and *The Church in Late Victorian Scotland 1874–1900* (Edinburgh: St Andrew Press, 1978); J. H. Burleigh, *A Church History of Scotland* (Oxford: Oxford University Press, 1973); and Callum Brown, *The Social History of Religion in Scotland since 1730* (London: Methuen, 1987).
6.  For a history of religious broadcasting in Britain, see Kenneth Wolfe, *The Churches and the British Broadcasting Corporation 1922–1956* (London: SCM Press, 1984). For a sociologically informed comparison of British and American

systems of religious broadcasting, see Steve Bruce, *Pray TV: Televangelism in America* (London: Routledge, 1990).

7. H. Richard Niebuhr, *The Social Sources of Denominationalism* (New York: Meridian, 1962).

8. Donald A. Rooksby, *The Quakers in North-West England*, i. *The Man in Leather Breeches* (Colwyn Bay, Clwyd: The Author, 1994).

9. An eminent historian says of the early nineteenth century: 'By contemporary standards, however, Britain enjoyed a large measure of religious freedom. Minority churches were neither suppressed nor expelled, as still sometimes happened on the continent and enforcement of the law was often lax' (James Obelkevitch, 'Religion', in F. M. L. Thompson (ed.), *The Cambridge Social History of Britain 1750–1950*, iii. *Social Agencies and Institutions* (Cambridge: Cambridge University Press, 1990), 315–16).

10. The 'supply-side' approach to religious change takes the US case to argue that a lack of state interference and hence 'low start-up costs' for new religions explain the success of the US religious 'economy'; see Roger Finke, 'Religious Deregulation: Origins and Consequences', *Journal of Church and State*, 32 (1990), 609–26. While it is certainly possible for the state to eradicate religious innovations, persecution may strengthen the commitment of members and boost the movement. The most obvious example is Christianity itself.

11. Robert Michels, *Political Parties: A Sociological Study of the Oligarchic Tendencies of Modern Democracy* (New York: Free Press, 1962).

12. Many of Britain's richest tea merchants, brewers, and bankers (for example, the Barclays, Buxtons, Gurneys, and Trittons, whose separate houses were gradually formed into Barclays Bank) began as strict Quakers, moderated and for a time were known as 'Gay Quakers', then joined the evangelical wing of the Church of England, and now show no particular religious attachment. See Hubert F. Barclay and A. W. Fox, *A History of the Barclay Family with Pedigrees from 1067 to 1933* (London: St Catherines Press, 1934); Augustus J. C. Hare, *The Gurneys of Earlham* (London: George Allen, 1897); Elizabeth Isichei, *Victorian Quakers* (Oxford: Oxford University Press, 1970); Arthur Raistrick, *Quakers in Science and Industry* (London: David & Charles, 1968); and Janet Whitney, *Elizabeth Fry: Quaker Heroine* (London: Harrap, 1951).

13. Another important exception is where the prosperity of the sectarians is vested in and derived from the sect itself, as is the case with the Seventh Day Adventists. Then increasing affluence depends on continued adherence to the sect and can act as a source of increased rather than diminishing commitment. See Malcolm Bull and Keith Lockhart, *Seeking a Sanctuary: Seventh-Day Adventism and the American Dream* (New York: Harper & Row, 1989).

14. Bryan R. Wilson, 'How Sects Evolve: Issues and Inferences', in his *The Social Dimensions of Sectarianism: Sects and New Religious Movements in Contemporary Society* (Oxford: Oxford University Press, 1990), and 'The Persistence of Sects', *Diskus*, 1 (1993), 1–12.

15. Ernst Troeltsch, *The Social Teaching of the Christian Churches* (Chicago: University of Chicago Press / Midway reprints, 1976), ii. 729–805. See also Colin Campbell, 'The Cult, the Cultic Milieu and Secularization', in Michael Hill (ed.), *A Sociological Yearbook of Religion in Britain—5* (London: SCM Press, 1972), 119–36, and 'The Secret Religion of the Educated Classes', *Sociological Analysis*, 39 (1978), 146–56.

16. For reviews of the literature and alternative conceptions, see Bryan Wilson, 'An Analysis of Sect Development', *American Sociological Review*, 24 (1959), 3–15; John A. Coleman, 'Church–Sect Typology and Organizational Precariousness', *Sociological Analysis*, 29 (1968), 550–66; James A. Beckford, 'New Wine in New Bottles: A Departure from Church–Sect Conceptual Tradition', *Social Compass*, 23 (1976), 71–85; Geoffrey K. Nelson, 'The Concept of Cult', *Sociological Review* 16 (1968), 351–62; David Martin, 'Sect, Order and Cult', in his *Pacifism* (London: Routledge & Kegan Paul, 1965); Benton Johnson, 'A Critical Appraisal of the Church–Sect Typology', *American Sociological Review*, 22 (1957), 88–92; 'On Church and Sect', *American Sociological Review*, 28 (1963), 539–59; 'Church and Sect Revisited', *Journal for the Scientific Study of Religion*, 10 (1971), 124–37; Rodney Stark and William S. Bainbridge, 'Of Churches, Sects and Cults', in their *The Future of Religion: Secularization, Revival and Cult Formation* (Berkeley and Los Angeles: University of California Press, 1985), 19–37.

17. David A. Roozen and Jackson W. Carroll, 'Recent Trends in Church Membership and Participation: An Introduction', in Dean R. Hoge and David A. Roozen (eds.), *Understanding Church Growth and Decline, 1950–1978* (New York: The Pilgrim Press, 1979), 13.

18. Reginald Bibby, 'Religious Encasement in Canada', *Social Compass*, 32 (1985), 288.

19. Reginald Bibby, 'The State of Collective Religiosity in Canada: an Empirical Analysis', *Canadian Review of Sociology and Anthropology*, 16 (1979), 105–16.

20. The most recent estimate of membership is from Peter Brierley and Val Hiscock, *UK Christian Handbook 1994/95 Edition* (London: Christian Research Association, 1993). The 1943 figure is in Hugh Martin and E. A. Payne, *A Christian Yearbook* (London: SCM Press, 1943). According to Robert Currie, Alan Gilbert, and Lee Horsley, *Churches and Churchgoers: Patterns of Church Growth in the British Isles since 1700* (Oxford: Oxford University Press, 1977), between 1850 and 1918 there were some 350 Unitarian congregations. By the late 1960s, there were fewer than 200 and the 1989 *Annual Report of the General Assembly of Unitarian and Free Christian Churches* shows 180 active congregations, many of them very small.

21. Peter Brierley, *'Christian' England: What the English Church Census Reveals* (London: MARC Europe, 1991), 43.

22. Steve Bruce, *A House Divided: Protestant, Schism and Secularization* (London: Routledge, 1990), 125–6.

23. John Briggs, 'Report of the Denominational Enquiry Group to the Baptist Union Council' (unpublished paper, 1979).

24. P. Beasley-Murray and A. Wilkinson, *Turning the Tide: An Assessment of Baptist Church Growth in England* (London: Bible Society, 1981).

25. Phillip J. Hughes, 'Types of Faith and the Decline of Mainline Churches', in Alan W. Black (ed.), *Religion in Australia: Sociological Perspectives* (Sydney: Allen & Unwin, 1991), 92–105.

26. Ibid. 94. See also Gary D. Bouma, 'Australian Religiosity: Some Trends since 1966', in Alan W. Black and Peter E. Glasner (eds.), *Practice and Belief: Studies in the Sociology of Australian Religion* (Sydney: Allen & Unwin, 1983), 15–24; Gary D. Bouma and Beverly R. Dixon, *The Religious Factor in Australian Life* (Melbourne: MARC Australia, 1991).

27. Michael Hill and Richard Bowman, 'Religious Adherence and Religious Practice in Contemporary New Zealand: Census and Survey Evidence', *Archives de sciences sociales des religions*, 59 (1985), 91–112.

28. Wade Clark Roof and William McKinney, *American Mainline Religion: Its Changing Shape and Future* (New Brunswick, NJ: Rutgers University Press, 1987), shows that 40 per cent of Americans have switched denomination at least once, but this is generally within a fairly narrow band of similar denominations. Dean Kelley's essay on conservative resilience—*Why the Conservative Churches are Growing* (New York: Harper & Row, 1972)—initiated a considerable debate over the relative importance of the doctrines of conservative Protestantism and the organizational structures common in sectarian organizations but rather muddied the waters by failing to distinguish clearly between the intrinsic appeals of religious beliefs and the structural consequences of certain beliefs. As I have argued at length, concentration on theological beliefs isolated from the organizational practices which they encourage or discourage is unhelpful in that it implies that liberal Protestant churches could adopt many of the successful socialization and recruitment practices of their conservative rivals. It thus misses the central point that the very nature of liberal Protestantism prevents it adopting such practices. The structural features have an affinity with the doctrines. See Bruce, *A House Divided*, 130–45. This may seem a small point, but it has major consequences for how we judge a functional theory of religion such as that of Stark and Bainbridge, which explains the decline of liberal Protestantism by the failure of its beliefs to satisfy 'needs'.

29. Reginald Bibby and Martin Brinkerhoff, 'When Proselytizing Fails: An Organizational Analysis', *Sociological Analysis*, 35 (1974), 189–200. See also their 'The Circulation of the Saints: A Study of People who Join Conservative Churches', *Journal for the Scientific Study of Religion*, 112 (1973), 273–85. See also Gary D. Bouma, 'The Real Reason One Conservative Church Grew', *Review of Religious Research*, 20 (1979), 127–37. Almost a decade later, Bibby and Brinkerhoff returned to the same issue and concluded that, even after the assumed evangelical growth of the later 1970s, 'most [recruits to evangelical churches] continue to be young people, recruited through friendship and family ties' (Reginald Bibby and Martin Brinkerhoff, 'Circulation of the Saints Revisited: A Longitudinal Look at Conservative Church Growth', *Journal for the Scientific Study of Religion*, 22 (1983), 253–62).

30. Steve Bruce, 'The Student Christian Movement: A Nineteenth Century New Religious Movement and its Vicissitudes', *International Journal of Sociology and Social Policy*, 2 (1982), 67–82; Roy Wallis, 'Sociological Reflections on the Demise of the Irish Humanist Association', *Scottish Journal of Sociology*, 4 (1980), 125–39.

31. However, the wisdom of investment policy is crucial. In the circumstances of high inflation found in most economies in the 1970s and 1980s, it became ever more difficult to conserve capital. In the 1990s denominations such as the Church of Scotland and the Methodists are finding it increasingly difficult to subsidize their present operations from interest on accumulated capital. A series of spectacularly bad investment decisions by the Church of England in the late 1980s saw the Church's capital eroded by almost a third and forced radical retrenchment. For over two centuries its historic assets have allowed it to maintain the structure and presence of a national parish church serving the

whole people despite religious dissent and indifference reducing it to being just one voluntary association among others. It is ironic that a fundamental reconsideration of its mission should now be forced on it by such a mundane matter as a bad investment portfolio. See Steve Bruce, 'Funding the Lord's Work: A Typology of Religious Resourcing', *Social Compass*, 39 (1992), 93–101, and John N. Wolfe and M. Pickford, *The Church of Scotland: An Economic Survey* (London: Geoffrey Chapman, 1980).

# 5

# RELIGION, ETHNICITY, AND SOCIAL CHANGE

THE main theme of the previous two chapters can be summarized in this proposition: modernity undermines religion except when it finds some major social role to play other than mediating the natural and supernatural worlds. Most of those social roles can be grouped under the two headings of cultural defence and cultural transition.

The role of religion in cultural defence can be described like this. Where there are two (or more) communities in conflict and they are of different religions (for example, Protestants and Catholics in Ulster, or Serbs, Croats, and Bosnian Muslims in what used to be Yugoslavia), then the religious identity of each can acquire a new significance and call forth a new loyalty as religious identity becomes a way of asserting ethnic pride and laying claim to what Max Weber called 'ethnic honour': the sense of 'the excellence of one's own customs and the inferiority of alien ones'.[1] Similarly when there is a people with a common religion dominated by an external force (of either a different religion or none at all), then religious institutions acquire an additional purpose as defenders of the culture and identity of the people.

The role of religion in cultural transition involves religion acquiring an enhanced importance because of the assistance it can give in helping people to cope with the shift from one world to another. It might be that the people in question have migrated; it might be that they remain in the same place while that place changes under their feet.

## The Ethnic Church

Some religions are straightforwardly ethnic in that their God is the God of a single people: Judaism is an example. In contrast, the major world religions claim a universal mission to all humankind. None the less, there are common features of the spread of religions and of the way in which they are structured which encourage the universal vision to be narrowed.

Religions tend to spread either with an ethnic or linguistic group which is the carrier, or within the boundaries of a particular political unit (which itself may be defined by shared ethnic identity). Often the initial conversion of a large population is no more than the conversion of the political élite which dominates it. Hence the diffusion of the new religion proceeds, not gradually, but in leaps and bounds, as whole territories are nominally converted. Imperial powers governing a multitude of peoples are often reluctant to challenge the religions over which they hold sway. In the early days of British rule in India, the East India Company was loath to allow Christian missionaries to operate, preferring stability and the pragmatic option of ruling through local leaders and established hierarchies to the missionary impulse towards cultural homogeneity.[2] But even where imperialism is cultural as well as political or economic, ethnic groups within the empire may resist acculturation or develop their own variant of the new orthodoxy.

Furthermore, even a single imperial religion requires local organization, and, as local structures will tend to follow the boundaries of existing political divisions, which in turn will often reflect ethnic divisions, a single church may find its subordinate units developing conflicting interests. Winning and keeping the hearts and minds of their people may force church officials to take sides against some other people. Hence it is common for even those religions with a universal mission to become guardians of an ethnic or national group. For example, although Montenegrins and Macedonians are Orthodox like their more powerful Serbian neighbours, the Macedonian Orthodox Church declared its independence in the 1960s, and in 1993 a Montenegrin cleric set himself at the front of an anti-Serbian movement by allowing his supporters to declare him the Bishop of Montenegro and thus challenge the existing Serbian bishop.[3]

Ethnicity may shape religion but a shared religion may also be vital in maintaining or developing a shared ethnic identity. For centuries, the Poles have found themselves under foreign rule of one sort or another. At the end of the eighteenth century the Polish kingdom was partitioned by its powerful neighbours.

The Catholic Church gave the Poles a distinctive character, different from the Germans and Russians. The Prussian Germans were Lutheran and the Russians were Orthodox. Both denominations, at that time, were instruments of absolute power for the kaiser and tsar, and hostile towards Catholicism. The administration of the Catholic Church embraced the old Polish territories and so unified the divided Polish kingdom. The old places of pilgrimage were venerated and visited with no regard for the tripartite division [between Prussia, Russia and Austria] and there the pilgrims were as one nation. They prayed together and discussed common problems, encouraging each other to be loyal to God and the nation. The often misinterpreted saying 'Polak-katolik'—to be a Pole is to be a Catholic—was at that time well understood.[4]

Hitler wanted nothing less than the eradication of the Poles. For the two years following the Ribbentrop–Molotov pact of 1939, which cynically divided Poland between Germany and the USSR, Stalin agreed that Europe could do very well without a sovereign Poland.[5] From 1946 until 1989, Poland was ruled by the Communist Soviet Union and its lackeys, the Polish Communist Party. Poles were denied the freedom of political association—other than the freedom to join the Communist Party, that is. They were denied the right to complain publicly about Soviet imperialism or about Communism. The Catholic Church acquired an important place in the thinking of most Poles, because it was a link with the pre-Communist past, it was largely independent of the state, and it was run by Poles. Moreover, as its concerns where at least superficially with the next world and not with this one, the Church could often subtly criticize the state and the party. What Tomka says of the Catholic Church in Hungary applies in Poland and elsewhere in the Communist world:

Religion happened to be the only source of counter-culture in the Communist era which had an effect on every social strata (in contrast to the explicit political opposition which was restricted to the narrow circle of intellectuals in the field of human and social sciences). Since that time there has been no other agency of comparable size undertaking the role of preserving and transmitting national cultures and basic values.[6]

To say this is not to suggest a cynical *pretence* of being religious. Nationalist Poles who were atheists did not pretend to be Catholics in order to do what was in effect politics. Something more subtle is being said. Being a staunch Catholic was one of the ways in which a Pole could assert his or her Polishness against the international Communism which the USSR wished to force on Poles. The attitude of the Church towards the State was always complex. It rarely engaged in outright defiance. To have done so would have brought down state oppression. Instead, it offered measured criticism and allowed itself to become associated in the mind of the people with a nationalism that was independent of the Communist Party. Although it is too early to be confident of the statistics, it is interesting to note that recent research shows that the success of Solidarity, the collapse of the Soviet Union, and the creation of a genuinely autonomous Polish state has been followed by a marked decline in the popularity of the Catholic Church.[7]

The same things could be said about the attractions of Catholicism in Ireland. Until the creation of the Irish Free State (later the Republic of Ireland) in 1921, the Catholic Church was the one institution which provided a source of national identity. Although it rarely engaged in open conflict with the UK government, it represented the interests of its people and provided an alternative leadership. Anyone who had problems with a landlord or with state officials would enlist the help of the local priest.[8] A third example is offered by the example of Catholicism in Lithuania, where again the Church has long acted as a guarantor of identity *vis-à-vis* Soviet imperialism.[9]

## Afrikaners and Ulster Protestants: The Threatened Elect

It is generally the all-encompassing 'church' form of religion that best serves as the legitimator and guarantor of ethnic identity, but there are examples of Protestantism becoming an important part of ethnic identity and cultural defence and I will discuss two in some detail: South Africa and Northern Ireland.

The first 'Afrikaners' were Dutch settlers brought to the Cape of Good Hope by the Dutch East India Company to run what was intended to be a refuelling station on the way to the East. The interests of the settlers and the Company soon diverged and the settlers trekked inland, where they started to come into contact with tribes foraging southwards. When the British replaced the Dutch as the main power in the Cape, the Afrikaners found themselves in a sandwich, dominated by the British but dominating the Bantu, as the natives were then called.[10]

The ability of the Boers to solve their problems with British and Bantu by trekking further inland slowed down the development of a strong sense of shared identity, but the treks also laid the foundations for the future myths. In 1835, about 6,000 Boers decided to move north, away from British control. In searching for their new promised land, they were frequently attacked by the Xhosa and defeated many times but also gained many impressive victories against superior numbers. At one battle in 1839, just under 500 Afrikaners made camp on the Ncome River. There they promised that, if God would grant them a victory, a church would be built on the spot. Ten thousand Zulus attacked and 3,000 were killed. Only three Boers were wounded. The Boers had rifles. The river was renamed Blood River.

And, as the Boers trekked and fought, so the references to being like the Children of Israel wandering in the desert *en route* to the Promised Land became more frequent. The leaders began to talk of a covenant between God and the Afrikaners. The Afrikaners were Calvinist Presbyterians, god-fearing people who kept the Sabbath and read their Bibles. The Xhosa were heathen and the British, mostly nominal Anglicans or Methodists, were little better.

A strong sense of Afrikaner identity was slow in coming. Even after the Boers had created their own 'statelets' of the Orange Free State and the South African Republic, there was difficulty in getting either military service or taxes out of the very independent-minded Boer farmers. But continued conflict with natives and with the British, which culminated in the Boer wars and the fixing of boundaries so that trekking-off could no longer be a solution, gradually heightened the sense of common purpose. An important symbolic point was the first commemoration in 1938 of the Great Trek. Greatly assisted by Dutch Reformed Church theologians and clergy, an Afrikaner nationalist movement developed which was elected to power in 1948 and established the apartheid state. A vital element of that state was the Afrikaner's sense of divine mission: a choosen people who had been persecuted and tested in the fire but delivered and given the promised land because they had been true to the Lord.[11]

Like the parties to the conflict in southern Africa, Protestants and Catholics in Ireland came into contact and conflict at a time when people still took religion seriously. The people who came from

Scotland were Calvinist Presbyterians. The natives were Catholics. Unlike those implicated in the southern African situation, these are not members of any two different religions; these religions are essentially antithetical. The Reformation was anti-Catholic and the Counter Reformation was anti-Protestant. The settler and native support of competing religions was an important reason for the two populations remaining distinct, and it was used by both sides in theodicies of success and failure. The settlers were able to explain and justify their privileges by seeing these as the natural result of having the true religion. Catholics were poor because they had not been saved and were kept in bondage by their priests. Religion also provided consolation for the subordinate population and the Catholic Church acted as the main repository of Irish identity.

Nothing that has happened since settlement, since the rise of the movement for independence from Britain in the nineteenth century, or since partition in 1921 has reduced the importance of religion. Far from it. Once the South was established as a Catholic country, with a constitution which explicitly defined the ethos of the country as Catholic, Protestants were bound to find the idea of a united Ireland abhorrent. In the 1980s a sizeable part of the Republic made it clear that it wished it to remain a Catholic country. Referenda that were intended to liberalize the Republic's moral legislation and thus make it more acceptable to the North backfired. The people voted to remain the only European country that does not permit divorce. Abortion was always illegal but the 1983 referendum made it unconstitutional as well as illegal. In 1992 the judiciary stepped in to close the loophole that had for years allowed a solution to the problem by making it illegal for Irish women to travel to Britain for abortions.

The place of cultural (and more specifically religious) differences in situations of ethnic conflict is always contested. There is a popular school of thought, generally informed by Marxism, that sees material advantages and disadvantages as being the main motive for such conflict and views references by the protagonists to cultural or religious differences as being window-dressing, a polite rhetoric put up to disguise the baser but real source of motivation. In the case of Northern Ireland, this form of analysis usually demonstrates that Protestants are privileged and Catholics discriminated against in Northern Ireland and then asserts that it is the desire to maintain that happy state of affairs which explains the reluctance of Protestants to accept a united Ireland. There is a problem with this sort of argument. Social scientists may well divide the material from the cultural but lay people often do not. In so far as they sometimes see themselves as being privileged, Protestants understand this as the consequence of having the right attitudes to the state, to law and order, to industry, and to personal discipline, and in turn they see these civic virtues as being the result of having the correct religion.

Furthermore, what is usually important in explaining behaviour is not objective but perceived reality, and, far from feeling privileged, many Protestants manage to feel that they are relatively deprived—a paradox which is readily explained if one understands the bitter zero-sum logic that always develops around ethnic conflict. One of the Catholic Church's reasons for maintaining its own institutions, schools, hospitals, and colleges is that state institutions in Northern Ireland are not genuinely secular. Some Protestants have seen the institutions of the state as Protestant, as they ought to be, given that Catholics refused to embrace them. But many Protestants felt a strong sense of betrayal when the state proclaimed (however disingenuously) that its institutions were open to all. Catholics had already been given most of the island. They were also given their own institutions in Northern Ireland. And then they had the right to enter the state's institutions. Catholic teachers had Catholic schools and could work in the state schools: two bites of the cherry to the one of the Protestants. Similarly in health care. Catholics had the Mater Hospital in Belfast, where Catholic religious activity was permitted, and Catholics could also use state hospitals, but Protestants were not allowed to hold prayer meetings or have gospel choirs in state hospitals, because that might offend Catholics. That is how the world looked to many Protestants. It may have been a distorted view but it was common and goes some way to explaining why Protestants do not see themselves as having been massively advantaged by the Stormont state which ruled Northern Ireland from 1921 until the British government intervened directly in the province's running in 1972.

Most commentators are happy to believe that evangelicals regard the conflict as religious but point out that such people form only a small proportion of Ulster Protestants (just as they are only a small part of Afrikanerdom). This entirely misses the nature of ethnic religion. What matters is not any individual's religiosity but the individual's incorporation in an ethnic group defined by a particular religion. I want to suggest that religion has a considerable influence even on those who are not themselves evangelicals and I will demonstrate the point with the example of Ian Paisley's Democratic Unionist party (DUP).

Since its foundation by dissident unionists (so-called because they want to maintain the union with Great Britain) in 1971, the DUP has come to rival the Ulster Unionist Party that governed Northern Ireland since its inception. The DUP founder and leader, Ian Paisley, is easily the most popular politician in Ulster. In each of the elections for the three Northern Ireland seats in the parliament of the European Community (later the European Union)—1984, 1989 and 1994—Paisley has come first with at least 29 per cent of the votes cast. In 1994 the Ulster Unionist Party candidate had to wait for the distribution of Paisley's surplus votes to be elected. Although the Ulster Unionists had ten Westminster seats to the DUP's three, the overall vote in Westminster and in local-government elections through the 1980s showed them to enjoy comparable levels of support.

The remarkable thing about the DUP is its reliance for activists on Paisley's small Free Presbyterian Church. Only some 1 per cent of Northern Ireland's Protestants are Free Presbyterian but 59 per cent of some 400 DUP activists were Free Presbyterians. Most of the others belonged to small evangelical sects and those candidates who were members of the mainstream Protestant denominations often distanced themselves in their election literature by having some reference to being 'involved in mission work', 'a keen evangelistic outreach speaker', or some such.[12]

Yet we know from the sheer size of the DUP vote that the majority of the people who vote for the DUP are not themselves evangelicals. This may have nothing to do with religion. It could be that non-believers support evangelicals because they believe them to be dogmatic and uncompromising and hence most likely to maintain an extreme unionist position. There is doubtless an element of this, but unionists have in the past been presented with non-evangelical politicians who were every bit as resolute in their unionism as the Paisleyites, yet they have preferred the evangelicals. That Paisley has triumphed over secular right-wing unionists suggests that his popularity cannot completely or even largely be explained by his political extremism.

The point should not be laboured, but there are also evangelical influences in Ulster Unionism beyond Paisleyism. To offer just one example, a leading figure of the Ulster Unionist Party is the Revd Martin Smyth, an Irish Presbyterian clergyman, who before entering politics, was Grandmaster of the Orange Order and a leading figure in evangelical pressure groups within his church.

One might suppose that people who support Paisley in some sense overlook his religion and his role as a minister and leader of a church. There are other politicians who are also clergymen but who play down their clerical role; a number of US senators and congressman are ordained clergymen (but none of them actually leads a congregation). But Paisley is not in the business of playing down his religion. Indeed, he has been willing to sacrifice political interests to religion on many occasions.[13] Compare Paisley's public persona with that of Pat Robertson, the televangelist and 'new Christian right' leader who in the late 1980s contested the Republican Party nomination for the presidency of the United States with the incumbent George Bush. Whereas Paisley stresses that his primary motivation is religious, Robertson went to great lengths to shed the designation 'televangelist' and to present himself as a successful businessman whose business just happened to be running a Christian broadcasting network.

Why 'secular' unionists should wish to be represented by evangelicals can be understood if we recall that voters vote not for people who are like them but for people who represent the things they like. Many secular Protestants want to support evangelical Protestants, not because they themselves are evangelicals, but because they recognize that evangelicals, although they may be spoil-sports with their sabbatarianism and total abstinence, embody what it means to be a unionist and a Protestant.

How have evangelicals acquired this position of symbolizing Protestant identity? In the first place there is the history of the people. Just as with the Afrikaners, the first Ulster Protestants were evangelicals and in their letters and speeches (which now form part of the canon of the Ulster Protestant's mythical history) they made frequent references to their faith. Secondly, evangelicalism was one of the few things that could transcend class, language, and ethnicity to unite Church of Ireland Protestants descended from English settlers and Presbyterians descended from the Scots.

Evangelicalism had the further resonance that it proponents had a long history of criticizing liberal Protestants. Liberal Protestantism, with its toleration and relativism, threatens to erode the differences between Protestants and Catholics. The ecumenical movement outside Northern Ireland may have been intended purely to bridge religious divisions, but in Ulster such a *rapproche-*

*ment* threatens the existence of the Protestant ethnos. Similarly in South Africa liberal theologians were often also politically liberal. At the start of the present round of conflict in 1970, those leaders such as Paisley who had a history of criticizing the religion of liberal Protestantism were seen as being also politically correct.

Furthermore, though a variety of non-religious ideologies are available, they have the major defect of reducing what separates Protestants and Catholics. Any version of socialism is suspect because it talks of the unity of the working-class. In periods of relative calm in Northern Ireland, Protestant working-class voters have supported socialists, but, as soon as the constitutional issue is raised, they revert to their traditional politics. Simply being 'British' has a similar problem. The British mainland and its politics are now thoroughly secular: divisions between Protestants and Catholics do not figure in British thinking. The Britain that attracts the Ulster Unionist is the Protestant Imperial Britain of the Victorian era. The present version has no appeal.

To summarize, evangelical Protestantism was a key part of the identity of the early Protestant settlers and it remains so for many Ulster Protestants, whose constant competition with Catholics has given them good reason to remain attached to their faith and its institutions. The distinguishing feature of ethnic religion is that it remains a powerful emblem, even for those members of the ethnos who do not personally share the faith. Thus one has the working-class Ulster Protestant who, though now not terribly pious, was raised in Sunday school, listens to the familiar prayers and Bible readings at the start and end of his Orange Lodge meeting, encourages his children to go to church, and is proud of his wife who is church-going and 'good living'. When stung to swear by some atrocity committed by the other side, he may refer to them by their political antecedents as 'Fenian bastards' but he is equally likely to call them 'bloody papists'. When confronted with a photograph of a priest giving the last rites to the Catholic victim of a Protestant outrage, he may well think 'It's those bloody priests who have caused all this trouble'. With very few changes the same picture could be painted of the typical Afrikaner. That interweaving of religious beliefs, traditions, and images of the superiority of one's own people is the essence of ethnic religion.

## Revivalism in America

Another example of the use of religion in cultural defence can be found in the religious revivals that swept nineteenth-century USA. Detailed studies of church attendance have shown that there is a strong correlation between the percentage of Catholics in cities of north-east America in the last century and the amount of church-going. But this is not because Catholics are better church-goers than Protestants. Quite the opposite. While immigration increased the religious pluralism of the USA, it also increased the conflict with native 'white Anglo-Saxon Protestants', which in turn increased the strength of religious commitment as the WASPs drew on their religion to buttress their ethnic identity. Finke and Stark explain the late-nineteenth-century increase in church membership as a result of Sunday school activity and note: 'while Catholics did not develop a strong Sunday school program, their presence stimulated the growth of Protestant Sunday schools'.[14] What seems to have happened is that the WASPs, who had been settled for fifty or sixty years, felt their status and culture to be threatened by the arrival of waves of poor, ill-educated immigrants from the poorer parts of Europe. They saw their own bourgeois Protestantism as a bulwark against social disorder and were keen to see the ill-disciplined newcomers converted, but the greatest impact of the 1831 Rochester, New York, revival was not on the unchurched but on the already churched and those just beyond their influence.[15] The already established and respectable used their religious identity as a way of stressing their superiority to the new immigrants. They become better Methodists and Baptists to separate themselves and to defend their culture against these alien hordes. The same point could be made about the deployment of religion in 'class defence', where the feared newcomers are social subordinates with dangerous habits and potentially more dangerous politics. The evangelistic activity engaged in by Thomas Chalmers in Glasgow in the first quarter of the nineteenth century was overtly directed to converting the rough working class, but its major consequence was in strengthening the faith (and social superiority) of those members of the middle-class and the 'respectable' working-class who devoted their energies to the city missions.

## Explaining Religion's Role in Ethnicity

One good reason why religion should be linked to ethnic identity is that, prior to the rise of nationalism as an idea and to the formation of the secular state as a social institution, religion was often the only thing people had in common bar a language, and, given that literacy was often a characteristic only of the clergy and lay religious leaders, even language often led back to religion. Prior to the formation of successful states, the church often provided the only social network that spread beyond the local community. To go back to the Irish example, in eighteenth-century Ireland the church was the only supra-local institution and the clergy the only source of social leadership other than the disliked English landlords and their state.

But religions also provide a series of ideas and images which people can draw on to explain their fortunes; it can explain why they are suffering these tribulations and it can promise some future end to their suffering.[16] The Afrikaners could explain their own success as a consequence of having the right religion (rather than the right weapons) and justify their oppression of the Xhosa and the Zulu by saying that these people were not God's chosen people; hence their opposition to the English missionaries who converted the blacks and so blurred the boundaries. Secular nationalist philosophies can perform a similar function, but religion does it better because there is no more comforting and reassuring thought than that one has God on one's side. Then what is desired becomes even more persuasive because it is also God's will and hence must come to pass.

In the previous chapter I contrasted the inclusive 'church' form of religion with the 'exclusive' sect. One enters the church simply by being born into the society but membership of the sect is *achieved* by displaying the proper beliefs, sentiments, and actions. Obviously the 'church' will be best suited to the task of legitimating ethnic interests—which are, after all, inherited. Many religions fall somewhere between these extremes, but we can think of them as being either communal or individualistic. Catholicism, Orthodoxy, Judaism, Islam—indeed all of the major religious traditions except Protestantism—are communal or churchly and have no trouble becoming linked with ethnic identity because all the people belong to the same religion. There is always a slight awkwardness in that, with the exception of Judaism, they are also universalistic. Islam would like the whole world to become Islamic, which creates a tension with local demands that it become identified with a particular people. Pope John Paul II, when he moved from being a Polish Catholic bishop to being the Bishop of Rome, had to abandon some of his allegiances. But in practice this is no obstacle to the lay people and the bulk of the clergy, who, until their Catholic country becomes involved in a conflict with another Catholic people, can happily keep their universal mission and their national mission in separate mental compartments.

Protestantism is primarily individualistic and thus sits less well in ethnic defence than does Catholicism or Orthodoxy or Islam, but, as we have seen, there is one strain which allows itself to be adapted in this way: the Calvinist Presbyterianism of the Afrikaners in South Africa and the Ulster evangelicals. The Calvinist belief in predestination means that, strictly speaking, membership cannot be achieved. Whatever one does to please God is not enough if one is not already choosen as one of the elect, but it only requires the right sort of conflict for Calvinists to shift those views slightly so that the members of the threatened ethnos are supposed all to be part of the elect and the enemy (which after all has shown its true colours by attacking the people of God) is taken to be outside the circle of the saved. What in other circumstances would be a 'sect' redefines itself as an ethnic 'church'.

## Religion in Cultural Transition: Migration and Social Change

Where identity is threatened in the course of major cultural transitions, religion may provide resources for negotiating such transitions. I want to look first at migration. Then I will consider the part religion can play in mobility that is primarily social rather than geographical.

Migration is always stressful. People do not normally leave their own land unless some major dislocation has made their previous way of life impossible or very unattractive. Secondly, the host country is often an unwelcoming place. For the waves of migrants to nineteenth-century USA, ethnic religious groups provided a mechanism for easing the transition between homeland and the new identity in the USA, a supportive group which spoke their language and shared their assumptions and values, but which also had experience of the new world and contacts within the new social and cultural milieu.

A similar pattern is evident among Asian immigrants to Britain. They congregate where others have gone before. They establish a religious community and its appropriate institutions and roles as soon as they can, and within that community they can reassert their cultural integrity, their commitment to its values, and a sense of the worth of the identity which it has created in them. They may often fall away from observance before they reconstruct their families, but they often become more observant (perhaps even more observant than they were in the home country) when these are established.[17]

## The New World

The importance of religion in migration is well demonstrated in Will Herberg's classic study *Protestant–Catholic–Jew*.[18] Herberg begins with the great American conundrum. Americans are apparently very religious: since 1926 there has been a fairly stable pattern of something like 60 per cent of Americans claiming some church membership. In 1953, 80 per cent of Americans said they believed the Bible to be the revealed word of God, but when these same respondents were asked to 'name the first four books of the New Testament, that is the four gospels', 53 per cent could not name one. For Herberg, this is the paradox:

The people who join the churches, take part in church activities, send their children to church schools and gladly identify themselves in religious terms are not fools or hypocrites. They are honest, intelligent people who take their religion quite seriously. [Yet] . . . the religion which actually prevails among Americans has today lost most of its authentic Christian (or Jewish) content. Even when they are thinking, feeling or acting religiously, their thinking, feeling and acting do not bear an unequivocal relation to the faiths they profess. Americans think feel and act in terms quite obviously secularist at the very time they exhibit every sign of a widespread religious revival. It is this secularism of a religious people, this religiousness in a secularist framework, that constitutes the problem posed by the contemporary religious situation in America.[19]

Herberg finds the answer to his question in the social functions of American religion and especially in the roles the churches played in easing the transition for wave after wave of immigrants.

It is an axiom of sociology that our sense of who we are is a profoundly social matter. Our identity depends on being able to locate ourselves in relation to others, preferably in some structure stable enough to be understandable. Migration usually involves abandoning the social structures that gave a sense of place; it always involves leaving the village, the community, the physical place with which one identified. Migrating to the USA not only raised the question of identity but also provided a new answer. Where in the old country people had divided themselves by dialect, in the new country they were grouped together by language. They became Poles, Russians, Slovaks, and Hungarians. The experience of being migrants to the same foreign country turned thousands of Polish-speakers who in their own country would not have seen themselves as a community into a distinct ethnic group united by their language. They only became Poles by migrating.

Central to the development of that group identity was the building and funding of an ethnic church. Although they were all Lutherans, Germans, Swedes, Norwegians, and Finns each created their own language-group Lutheran churches. Although the Roman Catholic Church managed to prevent overt fragmentation into ethnic churches, most parishes developed a clear identity as Irish, Italian, Lithuanian, and so on.

For the first generation of migrants, the ethnic church was a vital resource. Here they could meet people from the old country and reminisce in their mother tongue. As Herberg puts it:

The church and religion were for the parents the one element of real continuity between the old life and the new. It was for most of them a matter of deepest concern that their children remain true to the faith. In their anxiety, perhaps not only for their children but also for themselves, they tended even to make their pattern of religion more rigid than it had been before the great migration: 'what could be taken for granted at home had zealously to be fought for here'.[20]

The second generation were faced with very different circumstances. They were Americans. Although they might speak the mother tongue at home, they spoke English everywhere else. Their only contact with the old world was the nostalgia of their parents. They could respond in one of two ways. Some became leaders of the ethnic community and became zealous in their adoption of all things ethnic. Others drifted away from it, determined to become Americans.

The third generation have a more balanced attitude—neither in favour of ethnic segregation nor in favour of the complete assimilation in what American social scientists used to call the 'melting-pot'. The compromise was to become American in the major public things, the world of the economy and politics, but to retain some vestige of difference in life-style and leisure activity and especially in the private culture of religion. Herberg refers to 'Hansen's law': what the son wishes to forget, the grandson wishes to remember. What he can remember is obviously not his grandfather's language or even his grandfather's culture—they would be too much of a hindrance in the new world—but he can remember his grandfather's religion. The USA does not demand that he give up his ancestral religion as it demands that he give up the ancestral language and culture. Indeed, almost the opposite is the case. The strength of religious identification is so strong that not to be a Protestant–Catholic or Jew is to be un-American. Through church attachment, one displays ethnic origins; one becomes a German American, an Irish American, an Italian American. In the process, the religious traditions themselves become denuded of their distinctive features and reshaped in a more democratic, denominational form so that in the USA even the Catholic Church acts like just one denomination among others. By and large the major religious traditions have stopped arguing with each other and come together to form what many Americans call 'our shared Judaeo-Christian tradition': a common culture which in political myths is held to have been the basis for the USA's success as a world power.

Thus for Herberg the popularity of religion in the USA is explained not by its primary roles but by its secondary consequences, especially in aiding immigrant groups to maintain an element of their ethnic background while in public matters becoming thoroughly Americanized. It is interesting to note that the explanation does not depend heavily on the specifically 'religious' elements of ethnic religions. It rests rather on the shared or solidaristic nature of the shared religious culture and one could imagine a more secular shared culture—Kemal Ataturk's secular Turkish nationalism, for example—performing a similar role, although the fact that a religion tends to be inclusive and has the added legitimacy of supernatural origins makes it more effective than secular alternatives. I now want to turn to examples of the use of religion in cultural transition where specific teachings play a more important part.

## Afro-Caribbean Christianity in Britain

Most blacks in Britain have not been there for the three or more generations necessary for the Herberg thesis to be played out. Furthermore, the extent of racism is such that the rapid assimilation of blacks into an English 'melting-pot' is not the option that Herberg suggests it was for European migrants to America. None the less we can see religion playing a distinctive role both in helping blacks come to terms with their subordinate position and in helping them to improve their socio-economic position.

That religion is doing something for blacks in Britain that it is not doing for the white natives is clear from recent data on church involvement. Brierley estimates the Afro-Caribbean population of England as being around 600,000. Of these, 17 per cent or one in six were in a Christian church in October 1989, the date of Brierley's census, which is much higher than the English norm of under 10 per cent.[21] What is also significant is that this religious culture still draws evenly from the whole age range, which is a contrast with the pattern for the other Christian Churches, which are heavily dependent on older people and on older women especially.

Pryce's *Endless Pressure* offers an excellent description of the world of black Pentecostalists in Bristol. Pryce describes the church as a 'religion of the oppressed' in the sense that the Saints (as they were known) are reinterpreting Christianity to suit their position as working-class blacks in a white society. As Pryce puts it: 'If one cannot accept society or be aggressive towards it with a view to reforming it, then one can devalue the significance of this world by withdrawing from it in a community of like-minded individuals and projecting one's hopes into a supernatural and otherworldly Kingdom.'[22] Part of the appeal is to be welcomed among friends. In that sense the closed world of the Saints is a form of cultural defence. But it is also clear that, whether or not they intend to do this, the Saints are also providing themselves and their children with a set of values appropriate to the new world in which they find themselves; that is, their religion in assisting them in cultural transition. Saints believe that God's grace and spirit cannot enter an unclean body. Hence they do not drink alcohol and they do not smoke. Swearing, dancing, and mixing with sinners are also prohibited. The church prohibits flashy dressing and encourages modesty. As Pryce says, this means that the Saints dress very conventionally. The men, for example, wear dark suits, white shirts, and ties. Sexual relations are permitted only within a traditional marriage. As one preacher said:

And one more thing before I stop. You don't go around giving your bodies to immorality either. Sexual relations outside marriage is an abominable and horrifying sin! Our bodies are the receptacles of the Holy Ghost and they are not to be pampered and petted, kissed and rubbed and inflamed in the erotic regions, to the point where you are afraid to stand up![23]

Puritanism prevents the Saints falling into the behaviour patterns that make it so difficult for the poor to stop being poor. The sanctity of the family is vital. Rich people can afford the break-up of the home but being a single parent (and usually that means a mother) is one of the major causes of poverty and for those already in deep water the collapse of the family is often enough to push them below the surface. Drinking, drug-taking, and sexual promiscuity are doubly costly; they are themselves expensive and they often lead to the loss of reputation, and with it, the loss of a chance of retaining a well-paying job.

As well as prohibiting the negative, Pentecostalism also encourages the positive. Like the Boy Scouts, the Saints are instructed and encouraged to develop and maintain a wholesome character and a cheery disposition. A Saint does not get depressed or angry. A Saint is trustworthy and diligent. A Saint combines personal autonomy and self-reliance with a willingness to play an active and supportive part in the community of Saints. That community is itself important, not just because it controls deviance but also because it provides members with the positive benefit of mutual support.

In short, Pentecostalism not only reconciles subordinate people to their position but offers an ethical code and a model character which offers some hope of improving that position and a supportive environment in which to face the trials of everyday life. That is, Pentecostalism is highly adaptive.

## The Halévy Thesis and Latin America

As the name suggests, 'Latin' America has since the days of the Spanish conquest been Hispanic in language and Roman Catholic in religion. In the nineteenth century all the major Protestant denominations ran missions to Latin America. Most were not terribly successful. But in the last thirty years there has been an enormous growth in the membership of fundamentalist, evangelical, and

Pentecostal churches. One estimate suggests that between 12 and 15 per cent of the population are now 'born-again' Christians.[24]

As one would expect, the spread of evangelical Protestantism has not been even. The most fertile grounds seem to be those societies which remain religious in culture and ethos but where the Catholic Church is institutionally weakest. Argentina, Paraguay, Uruguay, and Mexico have the fewest Protestants: only about 2 per cent of the population. In Chile they are between 10 and 15 per cent. The highs are Costa Rica (16), Nicaragua (20), Brazil (20), and Guatemala (about 25 per cent). It is also likely that these figures underestimate evangelical numbers. Catholics count anyone who has ever been a Catholic. Protestant churches count only those who have voluntarily joined. Thus, while Brazil is nominally 70 per cent Catholic, there are actually more Protestant ministers than Catholic priests.

Such simplification is, of course, an exaggeration, but we can think of two radically contrasting approaches to such cultural change. Both identify social needs or social functions that are served by the new culture and thus explain the conversion but they identify a different group which is supposedly benefiting. The *false-consciousness* model supposes that the people who are becoming fundamentalists, evangelicals, and Pentecostalists are being misled into acting against their own interests by some other group, either the ruling classes of their own society, or international capitalism, or both. That is, the converts are being 'had'. The *personal-adjustment* view is that, whatever benefits other groups might derive from the spread of Pentecostalism, the core of the explanation must assume that the people who are converting do so because, however dimly, they perceive it as being good for them. That is, they must have some good reasons for conversion and those reasons have something to do with the requirements of the new social order.

As David Martin points out in his excellent study of Pentecostalism in Latin America, we have been here before. These two approaches to explaining a major cultural change have both been thoroughly aired in studies of the rise of Methodism in Britain and I want to go back to examine that movement before returning to Latin America.

Methodism can be dated from 1739, which was the year that John Wesley, a cleric in the Church of England, began his revival preaching. Challenged by the moribund condition of the Church, he revived the classic Protestant doctrine of justification by faith.

Unlike the Calvinists, Wesley believed that Christ had died for the sins of all of us and that we needed only to have faith in that fact to be saved. In technical terms, he was an Arminian: not a person from Armenia but a follower of Jacobus Arminius.[25]

Wesley placed far more weight on moral and ethical behaviour than on correct belief; he went so far in arguing against theological systems that he discouraged people from reading anything other than the Bible. He also differed from many Anglican clergy in the style of his preaching. Rather than read long and turgid argumentative sermons that picked over theological disputes, he extemporized and preached to the hearts of his listeners, stressing the evils of hell and damnation and the benefits of salvation. His was a call to religious action and many working-class people responded.

At first Wesley and his followers worked within the Church of England, but quickly bishop after bishop banned the Methodists from church pulpits. They then took to preaching in the open air and in public halls and in houses, which further offended the Church of England, which took the view that religion was something for the hierarchically organized church to deliver in tightly controlled settings. Worse, the Methodists were willing to let people who had not been ordained preach and gave important roles in the growing movement to lay people. Worse still, many of those lay people were women.

The result was that they were expelled from the Church of England and developed into a distinct sect (or, more exactly, a number of distinct sects). As such they grew rapidly. By 1767 there were 23,000 Methodists. By the end of the century there were almost 100,000. By 1850 there were 518,000 and in 1900 there were 770,000.[26]

To understand this growth of religious dissent, we need to look at the general social and political context. The assumption of most modern historians is that by the end of the eighteenth and start of the nineteenth centuries Western Europe was ready for revolution, for the rapid shift from the remnants of an old feudal order to the new modern industrial democracy. In France there was the Revolution in 1789 and the American colonies had declared their independence from Britain in 1776, but Britain was the dog that did not bark. As Semmel describes the rise of democracy in Britain:

this explosion of the energies of the masses was accompanied by a minimum of physical violence and bloodshed. Certainly among the more important reasons for this happy transition to the modern world . . . was the Methodist Revival which incorporated an attenuated, spiritual version of the new democratic faith in its Arminian Christianity, mobilizing popular energies in pursuit of personal salvation, while strengthening the motives for obedience and subordination.[27]

This is a restatement of a thesis first advanced in 1912 by the French historian Élie Halévy.[28] Britain, by virtue of its state of urbanization and industrialization, was ready for a radical restructuring of social relations. But there was no revolution. Instead the radical energy was expended in a movement of religious revival.

It is worth noting that the dissent of this period differed in one important respect from that produced in the middle of the seventeenth century by the English Civil War. As Niebuhr noted: 'the difference lay in the substitution of individualism and philanthropism for social ethics and millenarianism.'[29] The Civil War sectarians— the Ranters, the Levellers, the Sixth Monarchy Men—believed that they lived in the end times and that the millennium was about to occur, hastened by their own efforts in bringing down the established social and religious order. They were also community focused; they wanted political rather than personal change. In contrast, the Methodists offered salvation, not to a society, but to individuals. And, in so far as they criticized the dominant social arrangements, they did so in terms of encouraging individual changes of heart. Though the gentry may have been offended by being reminded that their souls were no better than those of the generality of the people and that their personal conduct could be much improved, they were not also threatened by any challenge to the institution of the gentry. The Methodists believed that the manifest social problems of industrializing Britain would be cured by individuals becoming moral and ethical in their behaviour and then practising personal philanthropy. While some local magistrates tried to suppress the dissenters, others appreciated the positive social consequences of their religion and tacitly encouraged them.

The supposed relationship between the appeal of the new religion and its supposed social effects is quite complex and requires some examination. Halévy is making a claim about the effects of Methodism: it prevented a violent revolution and was a major force in helping Britain move from old world to new democracy without the upheavals seen in most other European countries. But the irreversibility of time means that a *consequence* cannot be the cause of an action and hence cannot on its own explain why that action occurred. Avoiding revolution could only explain Methodism if those people who became Methodists were aware that social stability would be the consequence of their conversion and actively sought that end. Clearly they did not. Or at least most did not.

No doubt there were aristocrats and bourgeois who saw the potential of evangelical religion for diffusing social protest and conflict and who thought it important to clean up the masses and make them respectable. Taking an example from a slightly later period, Hannah More, a leading Anglican evangelical, formed a network of Sunday schools in the Mendips in which the lower classes were taught to read but not to write. She believed that allowing them to read the Bible and the uplifting and intensely conservative religious tracts which she penned would be good for them, but that if they were allowed to write they might start writing their own not-so-conservative tracts.[30] But this only tells us that some members of the upper classes were willing to encourage evangelicalism because they thought it would be a conservative force. It does not tell us why anyone else believed it.

To explain that, I want to start with an observation which is vital for the general argument of this book: most of the people who became Methodists were already Christians. If not regular adherents, at the very least they had grown up in a culture heavily informed by the basic Christian tenets and would have taken for granted the central propositions of the faith. For most we are explaining only why they preferred Methodism to what they had previously been getting in the other churches (usually the Church of England). The new belief system was entirely compatible both with many of the specifics of the old ('Christ was the Son of God' and 'the Bible is a holy book', for example) and with the most abstract assumptions ('There is a God').

Secondly, we need to explain why they were available for a new religion. Or, to put it another way, we can recognize that there are a whole range of pressures, many of them social, that discourage change. One important such pressure was the economic and social power of the landlord. Studies of the spread of Methodism show that the movement was most popular among those sections of the population that were freest to determine their own beliefs: independent small farmers with tenure in Lancashire and the north of England; independent tradesmen and craftsmen living in what were called 'free villages' (as opposed to those villages built on the land of one estate and hence under gentry control); and the new working-class of the towns and cities.[31] So this is our first consideration: what changes were freeing people from social domination so that they could choose their own religion?

One should also consider the strength and health of the previously dominant religion. Where the Church of England was well organized and funded, with conscientious vicars in parishes and a well organized network of lay workers to involve people in the Church, then the defections to Methodism were slight. Where the vicar took his stipend and went to live in Italy, paying an ill-educated curate a fraction of the income to do the job for him, defections were greater.

But this explains only why people were in the market for a new religion. It explains opportunity but not why the opportunity was taken. To do that, we must consider the social side-effects of Methodism.

Like all 'religions of the oppressed'[32] the new Puritanism of the Methodists offered a comforting critique of the upper classes. As Christ says in the New Testament, it is easier for a camel to pass through the eye of a needle than it is for a rich man to enter the kingdom of heaven. The meek shall inherit the earth. Which is terribly comforting to those who inherit nothing in this life. It also turns present privations into virtues. Not being able to afford to drink alcohol, eat rich foods, dress in expensive clothes, or gamble is a loss until one adopts a faith that says that all these things are sinful, an impediment to salvation.

Hinduism has this quality of reconciling poor people to their fate. It explains that one's present position is the earned consequence of actions in previous incarnations. Methodism did not just encourage passive acceptance of social injustice but also offered ways out in this life.[33] The newly born-again person stops drinking, smoking, gambling, and womanizing and becomes a better worker. He becomes trusted and so earns more. As one sees with Pryce's black Pentecostalists, the ascetic life-style means that wages are not frittered away.

Because it was led and organized by lay people and was democratic in structure, Methodism gave unprecedented opportunities for ordinary people to take charge of a part of their lives and thus gave them the sense that they could affect their own destinies. It also gave them opportunities to take leadership positions and to acquire organizational skills. It encouraged literacy and public speaking. Finally, although it was thoroughly individualistic in that it presented both salvation and self-improvement as tasks for the individual rather

than for the community and made social change dependent on individual reform, Methodism offered a solution to the alienation and
anomie of the new urban mass society because it provided a strong
fellowship for the converted.

If we consider the class position of those attracted to the
Methodist movement, we can see the appeal of these properties.
The Methodist church for the first time gave the upper working-
class and the lower middle-classes positions of authority and responsibility. Here was something which they were not excluded from by
virtue of birth. Personal merits and aptitude were enough to allow
a good man to rise in the movement, and, until the movement
shifted to denominational respectability, it gave women similar
opportunities. The moral discipline was also important. Members
of the respectable working-class were in an awkward position.
Increased wealth was making the temptations of the flesh a possibility for the first time. They could drink, eat too much, and spend
their money on clothes and gaming, but they could not compete
with the upper classes in conspicuous consumption and it would
have been silly to try. Further, their social and economic positions
were highly precarious. Newly acquired, they could be lost easily,
and there was a persistent dread of sliding back down into the not
respectable working-class, the lumpenproleteriat which crawled
around the slums of the cities. Their good living and religious conversion were immensely important to the Methodists because they
created a clear barrier between themselves and the undeserving
poor below. And they had the additional virtue of justifying criticism
of the upper classes.

In summary, I am suggesting that Methodism succeeded because
its ideology had a number of secondary qualities that made it appropriate to the age. It produced the right character for the industrial
democracy: self-disciplined, autonomous, hard-working, and puritanical.

As with the earlier example of the appeal of Catholicism to the
Polish nationalist, we need to be careful about implying a cynical
and utilitarian pretence of piety. I have written about the social
benefits or functions of religious change as though it was those
things that primarily attracted people. That is, I have rather implied
that a typical practising Church of England agricultural worker who
migrated to the town in 1790 thought 'I want to see myself as superior to my masters, I want to learn public speaking, and I want a bit
of puritanical discipline so that I can improve my standard of living.

I will therefore become a Methodist.' It did not work like that. The people who became Methodists did so because they believed Wesley and his followers to be right. That is, the conversions were genuine. The various beneficial social consequences might have been openly perceived. The preacher may have overtly made the point that giving up drink would save money. They might have been implicitly sensed. The potential convert might have noticed that the born-again Christians were better dressed, had tidier houses, had cleaner children, and seemed more self-confident. But he become a Methodist, not because he wanted those things (though he did), but because he saw those things as evidence that Methodism was right. That is, the beneficial side products were not the primary goal but were taken as circumstantial evidence that the new beliefs should be seriously entertained. The new behavioural patterns were adopted, initially with a degree of 'role distance', and only as the novice felt the new life to be working was the belief system which legitimated it fully accepted. The latent social functions or the good social consequences were not desired separately from the religion but added to the plausibility of the religion.[34]

If we follow the parallel with the rise of Methodism, we can understand what is happening in Latin America. First, most Latin American societies are going through all the changes that Britain experienced in the shift from a feudal agricultural economy to an urban industrial economy but with the difference that the timetable has been vastly shortened. Seventy-five per cent of the population of Brazil now live in urban areas. São Paulo now has a population of over 10 million. Seventy per cent of Mexico's population now live in urban areas; Mexico City has a population of over 10 million if one defines the city boundaries narrowly, and almost 30 million if one takes the equivalent of Greater London.

The destruction of the old agricultural and communal life has brought many advantages—liberation from feudal domination, the possibility of political democracy—but it has also brought all the problems of modern urban living, including poverty. It is not so much that many of the residents of São Paulo are poorer than they were when they were peasants; it is more that they are poor without the social solidarity and psychological support of a tight community and without the comforting inertia of a traditional world-view in which one expected nothing better. Just as the Church of England in the English industrial revolution, the Catholic Church has failed to move with the people and the times, and, in many places, it is discredited by its associations with the old ruling classes.

Some radical Catholic priests have gone down the road of the Levellers and Diggers of the English Civil War period and tried to create a radical and communal response to social change. The liberation-theology priests have attempted to turn the Catholic Church into an organization that campaigns against the exploitation of the poor and have promoted what they call 'base communities': mobilizations of all the people in the parish to both self-help and radical politics.[35] However, it has to be said that liberation theology has been much more popular with European and North American middle-class intellectuals than it has been with the poor people of Latin America.

Into the gap created by rapid social change and the collapse of the old world has flowed a pentecostal version of evangelical Protestantism which stresses the role of the Holy Spirit in providing such gifts as prophecy, healing, and speaking in the tongues of men and angels. As in the case of Methodism, the above story can be told in two versions: false consciousness and personal adjustment. The false-consciousness story is favoured by Marxists, Roman Catholics, and critics of American imperialism, and all three when they come together in liberation theology. They note that Pentecostalism has been heavily promoted by American and European missionaries, funded to work in Latin America by their home congregations in the Western capitalist world. American televangelists have spent a lot of money broadcasting their religious programmes to Latin America and other parts of the Third World. Liberation theologians believe it is in the foreign-policy interests of the United States, the main supplier of missionaries, to have Latin American countries become Western-style capitalist democracies (and, if that is not possible, into capitalist dictatorships). It is not in the interest of the Yankee dollar for radical priests to lead the people into creating alternative Marxist regimes. These two things are put together to suggest that Pentecostalism has succeeded in the Third World because it is in the American interest for it to succeed. The people who become Pentecostalists are suffering from false consciousness and are blinded to their own real interests. In Nicaragua, the Sandinistas referred to Pentecostalists dismissively as 'the Reagan cults' as though they existed only because the then President Reagan supported them.

There is an element of truth in this. Standing back and viewing the big picture of the last 400 years, we can see that the communal Hispanic culture of pre-Reformation Europe has been displaced by the individualism of Western capitalism, an individualism which both gave rise to and was promoted by the voluntaristic religious culture of Protestant Western Europe, led first by Britain and the British Empire and then by the United States. Less grandly, there is no doubt that Western missionaries acquired a degree of plausibility simply by coming from affluent and powerful countries.

But there are problems with the liberation-theology explanation of the spread of Pentecostalism. The first is that it supposes a curious model of human motivation and credulity. The personal adjustment explanation I have just offered for the appeal of Methodism has a big enough problem in implying that people were attracted to the new religion because it might serve their material interests. In the false-consciousness model we have the even stranger claim that people are attracted to a religion because it might serve the material interests of someone else. Secondly, it misses the point that Pentecostalism, like Methodism, is very much a lay movement. The external resources of foreign missionaries and some money to build a church were initially useful but they were not vital and they are not enough to explain the continued growth of Pentecostal churches past their first foundation. Only a small part of the Pentecostal leadership in the Third World is professional and only a small part of that is foreign.

Martin's conclusion, and it seems the right one, is that Pentecostalism has spread in Latin America because rapid social change has made the old culture and character of *hacienda* Catholicism obsolete and created new 'needs' which Pentecostalism is better able to address. Because it is seen as more appropriate and better suited, it also appears to be more plausible and thus attracts converts.

## Consequences and Plausibility

At the end of Chapter 3 I offered my general principle—modernity erodes religion except where it finds important work other than relating man and God—and I suggested that most of the examples of such work could be grouped under the headings of cultural defence and cultural transition. This chapter has sought to illustrate those two major patterns. I would like now to fit these observations into the general secularization thesis.

The ethnic religion we see in the cultural-defence examples is the 'church' form of religion. Thinking about the places in which it survives or flourishes allows us to see more clearly the conditions of the secularization thesis. The fragmentation of the people into classes, the differentiation of social life into distinct spheres governed by their own values, the replacement of community by the distant bureaucratic universalizing 'society', the increasing rationalization of all spheres of life, the fragmentation of the religious culture into competing sects: these processes—all key elements of the modernization of the Western world—are not inevitable. Some of them have such considerable 'functionality' that it is hard to imagine them away. For example, it is hard to see how widespread industrialization can fail to produce what Berger calls a 'technological consciousness' and it is hard to see how such ways of thinking can be confined to the compartment of work and not spill into other spheres. It thus seems highly likely that the adoption of technology will be accompanied by the rationalization of public administration and an increasing rational attitude towards the self. But other aspects of modernization are clearly linked by a more contingent and variable relationship. When a people finds itself under considerable external threat, the centrifugal forces of fragmentation can be retarded and cohesion maintained. Ethnicity can remain more important than class, region, or gender as a source of identity. However, timing is everything. Once a religious culture has become fragmented, and the close ties between religion and ethnicity lost, then no amount of external pressure will recreate a shared religion and restore it to a central place in cultural defence. Instead, as we see with the example of South African whites who in the 1990s remained opposed to majority rule, attempts will be made to mobilize a movement based on the secular ideology of racism, not the religio-ethnic basis of a choosen people.

If we consider the recent history of Roman Catholicism in England and Scotland, we see clearly the effects of social assimilation on the religious culture of a once distinct people. Most English and Scottish Catholics are the descendants of the Irish who settled in large numbers in the late eighteenth and nineteenth centuries. The Church drew its strength largely from serving the social needs of a dispossessed minority: 'their parishes were all-embracing social enclaves which provided them with fortress-like defences against the real or perceived attacks of a hostile, secular society.'[36] As the migrants and their children and grandchildren prospered, so the once-strong expectations of marital endogamy were disappointed. As Hornsby-Smith documents in detail, Catholics increasingly found spouses and close friends from outside the ghetto. Social success and acceptance brought declining conformity and declining church involvement: 'the upwardly mobile have in large measure jettisoned the conformity to an institutional "Catholic" identity which is strongest among the stable working-class.'[37] It is an obvious point but it should be clearly stated: the strength that a religion acquires through its role as the focus for the communal identity of a beleaguered minority will decline if and as that minority is integrated into the host society.[38]

The cases of religion assisting people to come to grips with rapid social change remind us that religion is about a lot more than man and God. However, they should not be interpreted as showing that social dislocation can, in any setting, produce a religious response. Despite the horrors and havoc wrought by the First and Second World Wars on the nations involved, they were not followed by religious revivals in Europe.[39] We come back to the centrality of belief and the issue of plausibility. We may well appreciate the secondary social benefits of some idea or practice and yet still not be able to believe. I am ready to believe that a mass turning to Jesus would be of great benefit to my country; anything which reduced alcoholism and drug consumption, made people put their responsibilities before their pleasures, and induced a sense of shared morality would be nice. I am ready to believe that being 'born-again' would make me a better husband, father, and friend. But still I cannot believe. The attraction of the secondary consequences of evangelical religion is not enough to force aside my scepticism about the cosmology and historical claims of Christianity. Indeed, the knowing-ness or reflexivity that allows one to be aware of latent functions is probably corrosive of true belief. If we evaluate a religious belief system on the instrumental grounds of how well it does such other things as produce social harmony, or encourage hard work, our resulting commitment will be weak because it leaves open the possibility that the desired social functions can be better produced by some other ideology or by some non-ideological structures. Of course, people do sometimes think like that. They do find one religion more attractive than another because it has more desirable side-effects, but, and this is the important point, they do so within a culture that assumes that one or more of the religions in the comparison is true and that such secondary consequences as they may value are a gift from God. When the modern missionary tries to persuade you to consider his faith by asking 'Are you happy with your life?', he is expressing the certainty that true happiness is found only through his faith. Within a religious culture, the balance of social benefits may be a reason to find one religion more persuasive than another, but on their own and for people outside that culture, no amount of yearning for a return of community, an end to lawlessness, or the peace of personal contentment will make a religious faith plausible.

The peoples of Latin America who are now converting to Pentecostalism are doing so from an acceptance of the supernatural and from at least a nodding acquaintance with Catholicism. It is no surprise and no challenge to the secularization thesis to find that people in a religious culture can be attracted to a new religion which seems better suited to their changed circumstances than the old one, nor is it a surprise that they are more enthusiastic about the new than the old. What we do not have—and what would be a major problem for the secularization thesis as it is being advanced here—is any example of a major religious revival in a culture which has already become largely secular.

This may seem obvious but it needs stating because it is the main reason for my disagreement with those who assert that secularization must be retarded by universal human needs that can be met only by a supernatural belief system.[40] The mundane usefulness of a religion may make it more appealing but at best it is only one reason to believe and if attended to too directly it undermines faith by having it judged by secular criteria. Only where people still possess a religious world-view are they likely to respond to social dislocation by seeking and being attracted to religious remedies. Cultural defence and cultural transition may keep religion relevant but they will not create a religious society out of a secular one.

## Notes

..................................................................................................

1. Max Weber, *Economy and Society* (Berkeley and Los Angeles: University of California Press, 1978), 391.
2. On the East India Company's attitude to missionary effort, see Stephen Neill, *A History of Christian Missions* (Harmondsworth, Middx.: Penguin, 1975), 232, 274–80.

3. Marcus Tanner, 'Serbia Tries to Rid Itself of a Turbulent Priest', *Independent on Sunday*, 7 Nov. 1993, and 'God Invoked by Rivals in Montenegro', *Independent*, 1 Nov. 1993.

4. Jozef Gula, 'Catholic Poles in the USSR during the Second World War', *Religion, State and Society*, 22 (1994), 10–11.

5. Misha Glenny, *The Rebirth of History* (Harmondsworth, Middx.: Penguin, 1990), 52. On Poland and other ex-Communist countries, see Niels Nielsen, *Revolutions in Eastern Europe: The Religious Roots* (Maryknoll, NY: Orbis, 1991).

6. Miklós Tomka, 'The Changing Social Role of Religion in Eastern and Central Europe: Religion's Revival and its Contradictions', *Social Compass*, 42 (1995), 19.

7. *Religion Watch*, 8 (Nov. 1992), 3.

8. For excellent discussions of the relationship between the Catholic Church, Irish nationalism, and the Irish state, see John H. Whyte, *Church and State in Modern Ireland, 1923–1970* (Dublin: Gill & Macmillan, 1970), and John Fulton, *The Tragedy of Belief: Division, Politics and Religion in Ireland* (Oxford: Oxford University Press, 1991).

9. Seamus Martin, 'Latin Hymns Echo of Old Era', *Herald*, 6 Sept. 1993.

10. The material for this section is drawn from the following sources among others: William A. de Klerk, *The Puritans in Africa: A Story of Afrikanerdom* (Harmondsworth, Middx.: Penguin, 1974); Hermann Gilliomee, 'The Growth of Afrikaner Identity', in Heribert Adam and Hermann Gilliomee (eds.) *Ethnic Power Mobilised: Can South Africa Change?* (New Haven: Yale University Press, 1979), 83–125; and T. D. Moodie, *The Rise of Afrikanerdom* (Berkeley and Los Angeles: University of California Press, 1975).

11. It is significant that, in the few years before the 1994 multi-racial elections in South Africa, the ideological ground of the white right wing shifted markedly. Although some Afrikaners defended their claims to a 'homeland' in religious terms, the need to draw in English-speaking whites led many ultra-conservatives to drop religio-ethnic claims and to promote their campaign on straightforwardly racial grounds.

12. Further details of these data are given in Steve Bruce, *God Save Ulster! The Religion and Politics of Paisleyism* (Oxford: Oxford University Press, 1986).

13. In early 1985 all unionist MPs resigned their seats to fight a co-ordinated by-election as a protest against the Anglo-Irish accord, a policy initiative which for the first time gave the Irish Republic a formal say in how Britain administered Northern Ireland. The DUP and UUP formed a united front to maximize the unionist vote. The evening before the elections, members of Paisley's family and church barracked an ecumenical service in the Church of Ireland St Anne's Cathedral in Belfast. Keeping the faith was more important than keeping Church of Ireland unionist voters sweet.

14. Roger Finke and Rodney Stark, 'Religious Economies and Sacred Canopies: Religious Mobilization in American Cities, 1906', *American Sociological Review*, 53 (1988), 46.

15. Phillip E. Johnson, *The Shopkeepers' Millennium: Society and Revival in Rochester, New York, 1815–37* (New York: Hill & Wang, 1978).

16. In various places I have been highly critical of the Stark–Bainbridge theory of religion, which uses the notion of religion as 'compensator' to argue that, so long as people need compensators, religion will remain popular. They are

inappropriately concluding that, because religions have performed the sorts of social functions described here, only religions can perform such functions and that such functions represent needs that must be met. For further discussion and references, see Rodney Stark and William S. Bainbridge, *A Theory of Religion* (New York: Peter Lang, 1987), and *The Future of Religion: Secularization, Revival and Cult Formation* (Berkeley and Los Angeles: University of California Press, 1985); Roy Wallis and Steve Bruce, 'The Stark–Bainbridge Theory of Religion: A Critical Analysis and Counter-Proposals', *Sociological Analysis*, 45 (1984), 11–27; William S. Bainbridge and Rodney Stark, 'Formal Explanation of Religion: A Progress Report', *Sociological Analysis*, 45 (1984), 145–58; Roy Wallis and Steve Bruce, 'Homage to Ozymandias: Reply to Bainbridge and Stark', *Sociological Analysis*, 46 (1985), 73–6; and Reginald W. Bibby and Harold R. Weaver, 'Cult Consumption in Canada: A Further Critique of Stark and Bainbridge', *Sociological Analysis*, 46 (1985), 445–60.

17. On Sikhs in England, see R. Ballard and C. Ballard, 'The Sikhs: The Development of Southern Asian Settlements in Britain', in J. L. Watson (ed.), *Between Two Cultures* (Oxford: Blackwell); Arthur W. Helweg, *Sikhs in England* (Delhi: Oxford University Press, 1986); and Sewa Singh Kalsi, *The Evolution of a Sikh Community in Britain* (Leeds: University of Leeds Department of Theology and Religious Studies, 1992). On Muslims, see Jorgen Nielsen, *Muslims in Western Europe* (Edinburgh: Edinburgh University Press, 1992). For a general review, see Kim Knott, 'Other Major Religions', in T. Thomas (ed.), *The British: Their Religious Beliefs and Practices 1800–1986* (London: Routledge, 1986), 133–57.

18. Will Herberg, *Protestant–Catholic–Jew: An Essay in American Religious Sociology* (Chicago: University of Chicago Press, 1983).

19. Ibid. 3.

20. Ibid. 19.

21. Peter Brierley, *'Christian' England: What the English Church Census Reveals* (London: MARC Europe, 1991), 97.

22. Ken Pryce, *Endless Pressure: A Study of West Indian Life-Styles in Bristol* (Harmondsworth, Middx.: Penguin, 1979), 221.

23. Ibid. 214.

24. The material in this section is drawn from David Martin, *Tongues of Fire: The Explosion of Protestantism in Latin America* (Oxford: Basil Blackwell, 1990).

25. For good general histories of Methodism, see Robert Currie, *Methodism Divided* (London: Faber & Faber, 1968); Alan D. Gilbert, *Religion and Society in Industrial Society: Church and Chapel and Social Change 1740–1914* (London: Longmans, 1976); and David Hempton, *Methodism and Politics in British Society, 1750–1850* (London: Hutchinson, 1987).

26. Robert Currie, Alan D. Gilbert, and Lee Horsley, *Churches and Churchgoers: Patterns of Church Growth in the British Isles since 1700* (Oxford: Oxford University Press, 1977).

27. Bernard Semmel, *The Methodist Revolution* (London: Heinemann, 1974), 102.

28. Élie Halévy, *A History of the English People in 1815* (London: Penguin, 1937).

29. H. Richard Niebuhr, *The Social Sources of Denominationalism* (New York: Meridian, 1962), 65.

30. Ford K. Brown, *Fathers of the Victorians: The Age of Wilberforce* (London: Cambridge University Press, 1961).

31. Gilbert, *Religion and Society*, 51–121.
32. Vittorio Lanternari, *The Religions of the Oppressed: A Study of Modern Messianic Cults* (New York: Alfred A. Knopf, 1963).
33. Hinduism, of course, offers a way out. Proper performance of the rituals appropriate to one's caste and acceptance of one's social position will ensure a better rebirth next time. But there can be no change in any one life cycle.
34. There is an important theoretical point which I have not pursued here but which may be of value to those interested in arguments over functionalist explanations of religion. My formulation has, I believe, the advantage over the Stark–Bainbridge version in that, by closely relating the attractive secondary benefits of belief to the plausibility of the religion which purportedly produces them, we do not make the mistake of supposing that desire for the secondary consequences can make up for a lack of faith.
35. Penny Lernoux, *Cry of the People* (Harmondsworth, Middx.: Penguin, 1980); Edward Norman, *Christianity in the Southern Hemisphere* (Oxford: Oxford University Press, 1981); Deane W. Fern, *Third World Liberation Theologies* (Maryknoll, NY: Orbis, 1986), and *Profiles in Liberation: 36 Portraits of Third World Theologians* (Mystic, Conn.: Twenty-Third Publications, 1988).
36. Michael P. Hornsby-Smith, *The Changing Parish: A Study of Parishes, Priests and Parishioners after Vatican II* (London: Routledge, 1989), 23.
37. Ibid. 34.
38. A recent study of religion and ethnicity in the USA concludes: 'First, ethnic identification and loyalty to the religion of one's ethnic group have tended to diminish together in the American context. That is assimilation and secularization are correlated. Second, the processes of assimilation and secularization occur at a slower pace in ethnic groups regarded as minorities and thus discriminated against. Finally, decline of ethnic identity appears to precede decline of ethnic religious loyalty . . .' (Phillip E. Hammond and Kee Warner, 'Religion and Ethnicity in Late-Twentieth-Century America', *Annals of the American Academy of Political and Social Science*, 527 (May 1993), 55–66).
39. For a fascinating and sadly neglected analysis of the impact of the First World War on British servicemen, see David S. Cairns, *The Army and Religion: An Enquiry and its Bearing upon the Religious Life of the Nation* (London: Macmillan, 1919).
40. This case is most ably argued by Stark and Bainbridge, *A Theory of Religion*.

# 6

# AMERICA AND GOD

..................................................................................................................................

A T first sight the USA appears the exception to the secularization
model. Here we have an urban industrial modern society, heavily dependent on advanced technology, which apparently shows little or no evidence of long-term decline in church involvement.

According to Gallup survey data, the proportions of Americans
answering 'yes' to the question 'Did you, yourself, happen to attend
church or synagogue in the last seven days?' has remained remarkably stable. Over the period 1939–81 it rose to a peak of 49 per cent
in the mid-1950s and then gently fell back, so that since 1967 it has
fluctuated in the range of 40–43 per cent. According to Gallup polls,
church membership has seen a similar slight fall (from 76 per cent in
1947 to 68 per cent in 1991) but again that is vastly higher than for
European countries.[1] Catholic sociologist Andrew Greeley, in his
summary of surveys since the 1930s, concludes that 'religion does
not in general seem to have been notably weakened . . . in the last
half-century'.[2] Although the proportion of Americans who claim no
religion has risen from just over 3 per cent in the late 1950s to
between 7 and 8 per cent in the 1980s, this remains significantly
lower than the corresponding British figure, which throughout the
1980s has been around 30 per cent.[3]

To confound the secularization thesis still further, the USA in the
1980s saw a vigorous attempt to reimpose religious values in the
public sphere. A number of political pressure groups, known collectively as the 'new Christian right' (NCR) or 'Religious Right', came
to prominence in 1980, when their socio-moral campaigns were
credited with having influenced some senate elections and contributed to the election of the conservative Republican Ronald
Reagan to the presidency. Although he failed to win the nomination,

televangelist Pat Robertson was able to mount a convincing attempt to succeed Reagan as the Republican Party nominee for president in 1988, and the NCR continues to promote candidates and to press its legislative agenda of socio-moral issues.[4]

However, things are not that simple. For some time, social scientists employed by major religious organizations have wondered how they can square the high degree of church involvement claimed by the general public in open surveys with what the churches themselves know of declining members, declining incomes, and shrinking audiences. As Hadaway and his associates put it: 'If Americans are going to church at the rate they report, the churches would be full on Sunday mornings and denominations would be growing. Yet they are not.'[5] Gallup's own data contain an enigma: the proportion of Americans claiming to have attended church in the previous week has remained stable, but when people have been asked how their church-going has changed, the number saying they attend 'less frequently' has always been greater than that of those who now attend 'more frequently'.[6]

The apparent inconsistency between survey claims and church reports is not resolved by noting that the decline in the old mainstream denominations is made up for by growing evangelical denominations (although evangelical churches are indeed growing). First, the evangelical churches are not growing fast enough to explain the discrepancy. Secondly, even those Americans who say they are members of denominations which we know to be contracting claim levels of church involvement that are impossible to reconcile with clergy estimates. Consider the example of the American Episcopal Church. Given the proportion of Americans who claim in surveys to be Episcopalians, the denomination should have grown by more than 13 per cent between 1967 and 1990. Instead, membership declined by 28 per cent: 'Moreover, attendance figures from Episcopal parishes are far below what would be expected if self-defined Episcopalians attended church in the numbers they claim.'[7] In surveys conducted by Gallup and other competent organizations, about 35 per cent of self-defined Episcopalians said that they had been to church in the previous seven days. But the Church's own figures suggest that only 16 per cent actually did so. To confirm their suspicion that survey responses grossly inflated church involvement, Hadaway and his colleagues went to painstaking lengths to estimate accurately attendance at all known Protestant churches in one county of Ohio. They not only took lists of churches from registers and church yearbooks, but they also drove every paved road (and some unpaved) looking for unlisted churches. Where they could not get estimates of attendance from clergymen, they counted cars in the car parks during services and adjusted the figure for the probable number of passengers. They then conducted a standard telephone survey of reported church attendance and discovered that the attendance claimed by their respondents was 83 per cent higher than their best estimate of actual attendance. Although the technique was different, they put similar effort into comparing claimed and actual Catholic attendance and came to a very similar conclusion.

In the conclusion to their report, Hadaway and his associates are careful to be cautious: 'Although the evidence is compelling because it is so uniform, the fact remains that our data pertain to fewer than 20 Catholic dioceses and to Protestants in only one Ohio county.'[8] Though such circumspection is commendable, we are clearly warranted in supposing that they have a general point, because, to return to the observation with which they begin their report, we know that the constantly cited survey data of high church involvement is at odds with what is known to the churches themselves. Furthermore, similar discrepancies are found between survey and church data in England and Australia.[9] Social scientists have often been sniffy about church generated statistics, but the argument for rejecting them has always been that churches *inflate* their membership and attendance, not artificially deflate it.

This chapter will look closely at the changing place and nature of religion in the United States and it begins with the assumption that religion has been and remains more popular in the USA than in most parts of Europe. However, the work of Hadaway and his colleagues is important because it allows us to get the scale of the differences in perspective. The USA is different—in the context of contemporary Western democracies the NCR is unique—but it is not all that different.

## Explaining Resilience

How does one explain the popularity of religion in the United States? Much American thinking starts with the observations of Alexis de Toqueville, a minor French nobleman who toured

America in the 1830s and made a series of insightful comparisons of the old world of Europe and the new world of the United States.[10] He was struck by the voluntary nature of American religion and by its variety. In France, where there was only one church and that church was firmly on the side of the old pre-Revolution order, those social classes who wanted to challenge that order became disillusioned, not just with the Catholic Church, but with religion itself. There was no such compromising connection in the USA. There was no state church promoting the interests of the ruling class. Hence those people who wanted to express social and political dissent could do so without also abandoning religion.

The state church system found in much of Europe contained little incentive for the clergy to recruit a congregation. The nineteenth-century Church of England vicar derived his living from the rental value of lands given to the Church centuries earlier by monarchs and pious lords. Whatever other considerations may have motivated him to take his calling seriously, there was no financial incentive for such a clergyman to increase his congregation or to make himself more popular. The ambitious cleric who sought preferment did so by currying favour with his social superiors who controlled church appointments. In contrast, the clergy of the American churches only ate if they recruited members who were willing to feed them. The key to prosperity was not sucking up to the élites but appealing to the people. In a voluntary system there is a very strong incentive for preachers to build churches, to make their message popular, and to work hard to build a following.

This leads logically to the third observation: the virtue of competition in a free market. Where there is a state monopoly—and, according to such economists as Gary Becker, this is as true of religion as of cars—the product will not be as well adapted to the demands of consumers as when a large number of organizations compete in a free market, all needing to win customers to survive.[11] Instead of there being one state church and a number of small dissenting alternatives, the USA had a vast range of competing religions. Hence there was something to suit everyone.[12]

Although it has attained something of the status of an orthodoxy, de Toqueville's account of American religion has a number of flaws. His claim that a close association of church and state alienates people from religion if they become alienated from the old social order works only for Catholicism (and even then in only some settings). It is certainly the case that the monolithic and authoritarian nature of

Catholicism tends to polarize responses to religion—as de Toqueville saw in his native France. It seems easier for Catholics to abandon Christianity than to retain a version of it that rejects the Vatican's claim to a monopoly of religious truth. In Spain, Italy, and France society divides into two big competing blocks: the Catholic Church and the secularism of the Communist and socialist parties. However, the position in Protestant countries that had state churches was very different. Though the state church might claim a monopoly position, it did so within a theological structure that gave no ideological support to such claims. If one believes that we can all equally well discern the will of God and that there is no need for bishops and priests, then one can form one's own religious organization. And many British people did just that. If they did not like the close ties between squire and vicar, they became Methodists. That the Pilgrim Fathers supposedly sailed to America to avoid religious persecution seems to have caused Americans to exaggerate the extent of religious persecution of British dissenters. In parts of the country, rejecting the state church brought its costs, but none the less Baptists, Presbyterians, Seceders, Free Churchmen, Congregationalists, Quakers, Methodists, and independents of every hue managed it.

We may also note an apparent contradiction in the contrast of the motive structure for state church clergy and their voluntary counterparts. In their explanation of how the 'upstart sects' overtook the better established Congregationalists in early America, Finke and Stark say: 'The uneducated and often unpaid clergy of the Baptist and Methodists made it possible for these denominations to sustain congregations anywhere a few people could gather, for it was the pursuit of souls, not material comfort, that drove their clergy forth.'[13] So here the arduous labours of Baptist and Methodist preachers are explained by the love of souls rather than the love of money. But in other places the economic need to recruit and sustain a congregation is used to explain why the clergy of voluntary associations were supposedly better at adapting their faith to meet the needs of the people, and hence to explain why voluntary religion is more successful than monopolies (state sponsored or otherwise).[14]

It might well be that these apparently contradictory assumptions about what drove clergymen and inspired their ministries could be reconciled by dividing the history into two periods: the early frontier missionary work and the more settled expansion period. But even that leaves us supposing that the clergy of state were not driven to serve their people by a desire to be liked by their congregations, by a desire to serve God faithfully, by a sense of guilt at failing the people, and so on. However, to a large extent this is neither here nor there, because, no matter how well taken is the observation that the officials of state churches did not have the same incentive as their voluntary counterparts to recruit a following, the point does not distinguish religion in the UK and the USA. Although the clergy of the four established churches in the UK (the Episcopalian churches of England, Wales, and Ireland and the Presbyterian Church of Scotland) had little financial need to be popular with their congregations (again, leaving aside whatever other reasons they may have had), there were plenty of ministers in the dissenting denominations who had every good reason to court popularity. That these denominations were not as popular in the UK as in the USA then cannot be explained by the supposed contrast in what motivated their clergy.

A third problem with the free-market explanation of the diverging fates of religion in the old and new worlds is that it rests on claims about the greater cultural diversity of the new world which are not supported by the record. Leeds in 1808 had five Church of England churches but it also had a Scottish Presbyterian church, two English Presbyterian churches, three Independent chapels, a Quaker meeting-house, a Baptist chapel, three Methodist chapels, a Roman Catholic chapel, and an Inghamite meeting-house. By 1851 the number of religious outlets had grown from 17 to 132 and these belonged to eighteen different organizations. Even the Mormons had two churches. By any account this is a decent range of alternatives.[15]

If the UK had far more diversity than de Toqueville and his heirs noticed, the USA was and is far less diverse than is supposed. What is often forgotten is that de Toqueville built his impressions of America while travelling. The USA as a whole had and still has a great range of religious alternatives but any one part—the places that people actually inhabit—shows a high degree of religious concentration. Utah is as Mormon as Spain is Catholic. The southern states are conservative Baptist or Methodist. Catholics are concentrated in pockets. Big chunks of the Mid-West are Lutheran. Religious diversity could only explain the appeal of religion if it were actually the case that the average American was given more choices than the average Britain. In practice they were not. The religious historian Edwin Gaustad defines homogeneity by more than 50 per cent of the population belonging to the same denomination. By that measure, in 1906 twenty-two of forty-eight states of the United States were homogenous. The figures for England were very similar.[16]

Furthermore, there was always a major obstacle to Americans actually benefiting from the supposed pluralism. Many of the churches were and still are ethnic churches. Racial segregation is still such that adding a black Pentecostal church to a town does not in the least increase the choice for white Americans. Adding a German-language Lutheran church makes no difference to the range of options available to a Swedish American. In contrast, with the exception of Catholicism, which was very strongly associated with Irish migrants, almost all the alternatives in late eighteenth- and nineteenth-century Britain were equally available to all British people. Where choice in the USA was constrained by linguistic, ethnic, racial, and class barriers, choice in Britain (with the exception of small parts of Wales and Scotland where language divisions persisted) was constrained only by class. If as wide a range of alternatives was open to the British as was available to Americans, then we cannot explain the popularity of religion in the USA by its diversity.

A more promising contrast between the old and new worlds concerns ethnicity and ethnic conflict. Rather than see people as unattached isolated individuals, the rational choosers of the economists' model, we should note the importance of social identities and, in particular, the constraints of inherited identities. I have already described at length Herberg's 'three-generations' view of the social roles of religion. One reason why Americans are religious is that their churches offer them a way in which they can display their commitment to American values while maintaining their ethnic distinctiveness. To this positive interpretation of ethnic identity, I would add the negative side discussed at length in the previous chapter. For many Americans, religion was important because it served as a means of ethnic exclusion, of social closure: a sign of belonging to a high status group and a source of pleasing justifications for that higher status. And this remains the case today. Although most are not overtly racist, one attraction of independent evangelical Baptist churches (and the independent schools often attached to them) is that they are white.

The settlement of Scots and English people in Ireland in the seventeenth and early eighteenth centuries created one ethnic conflict. The Irish migrating to Britain in the late eighteenth and nineteenth centuries re-created that competition in Liverpool and Glasgow.

And, as we would expect from the argument of the previous chapter, those parts of Britain where the Irish settled were more contentiously religious than the rest of the British Isles. The rest of Britain was relatively free of such ethnic competition until the 1960s, when large numbers of migrants from the former Empire arrived, but, while there was strong anti-immigrant sentiment, it did not produce any accompanying revival of religious interest among the English because the country and the culture were by then thoroughly secular. Ideologies of superiority were drawn upon to defend social exclusion and discrimination but these were very rarely religious.

The problem of explaining some social phenomenon is that why it began and why it continues may be very different things. It is hard to be precise but my impression is that its role in maintaining ethnic identity brought American religion through to the 1950s in robust health. Since then that role has been supplemented or replaced by a more general provision of a sense of belonging. Americans move often and considerable distances. As Herberg noted, one of the ways of making oneself at home in a new place is to find an institution which offers continuity. The Lutheran who moves town or state or even region can expect that the Lutheran church will be familiar to him and provide an opportunity to meet people like himself. As Wuthnow notes, since the 1950s: 'From the traditional one-room meeting-house where a lonely parson offered fiery sermons on Sunday mornings, the modern religious organization had become a holding company for activities and programs for "men and women of all ages" as some advertisements in fact stated.'[17] The fastest growing churches offer what for Europeans would be an astonishing range of facilities. Houston's Second Baptist Church (which calls itself 'Second Exciting' and which journalist Zoe Heller wittily dubs 'The Mall of God') has a membership of 18,000 and a gymnasium, a theatre, a Jacuzzi, a crèche, a school, an indoor running track, a pool hall, an eight-lane bowling alley, a restaurant, an arts and crafts boutique, a bookshop, and somewhere to pray.[18]

To return to de Toqueville, the argument that the cultural and religious pluralism of the USA explains why religion remained popular there when it declined drastically in Europe requires that the USA did display greater religious pluralism than Britain, but that was not the case. Britain in the 1850s had a wide variety of religious organizations and little to stop people creating anything that was missing, but still many people were not interested in any of the variants. A more plausible explanation of the strength of American religion rests on the ethnic and immigrant nature of American churches. Rather than saying that pluralism causes religious resilience, I want to suggest that both are caused by a third factor: the immigrant nature of the United States. The USA has religious diversity because it is a society made up of immigrant groups. It has a strong religious culture because the strains of cultural transition and the need for cultural defence gave each of these groups good reason to remain committed to its religion.

## Changes in American Religion

Comparing societies is always difficult because their histories may be different enough to imply that the appropriate comparison points would be some years apart. The 1851 census reported that more than half the British people lived in cities. The roughly equivalent date for the USA was 1920. The proportion of Britons living in cities stabilized in 1911; that point has not yet been reached in the United States. It would thus be possible, if one took secularization to be a uniform and universal process, to argue that religion in the USA will change in the same way as religion in Europe, but following about seventy years apart.[19] However, as should be obvious from the effort put into describing differences in the evolution of societies, I do not subscribe to the view that social change is predictable in the same way that chemical reactions are predictable. The secularization thesis as outlined in this book is not a summary of invariant causal connections from which predictions can be 'read off'. We cannot know enough about the present to claim such a complete understanding and, even if we could, we would be defeated by the human ability deliberately to defy expectations. None the less, in so far as we can understand why things happened as they did in one setting, we can make guesses about what will happen elsewhere. Thus, while I would not want to endorse the simple claim that religious change in the United States is simply lagging behind that of Europe, I want to suggest that a close look at the evidence shows that the general explanations of change presented in the previous four chapters apply in varying degrees to the American case.

There are signs of weakening commitment within the continued formal church involvement. Americans attend church less often than they used to; the pattern of twice-Sabbath attendance and mid-week prayer or Bible Study meetings has declined except among the smaller and more fundamentalist bodies. A smaller proportion of all reading matter is religious and there can be little doubt that this is so for the churchly as well as for the unchurched. Religious titles were on average 7.4 per cent of books published between 1955 and 1959 but only 5.2 per cent of those published in the early 1970s.[20] In 1992, only 3 per cent of books sold were religious titles.[21] Another useful index is the popularity of religious higher education. Despite the public attention given to the establishment of such evangelical foundations as Oral Roberts University and Jerry Falwell's Liberty University, taking higher education as a whole, the proportion of all degrees that were in theology and divinity has more than halved since the 1950s. It was then 2.5 per cent; by the early 1970s it was just 1.2 per cent.[22]

Considering the very high claimed rates of church attendance, knowledge of elementary facets of Christianity is poor. In 1978 only 42 per cent of Americans could name five of the ten commandments. More than a third failed to get three right. Only 46 per cent could name the four gospels. A slightly smaller proportion knew who delivered the Sermon on the Mount.[23] We lack comparable data from an earlier period to be certain, but it is very likely that such ignorance is recent and growing and is related to the decline in religious reading and to the changes in the purpose of religion which will be discussed below.

While financial contributions to the churches have remained high, they have declined markedly as a proportion of average earnings. Americans give as much to the churches as they did fifty years ago, but what they spend on everything else has more than doubled. In 1963 Catholics gave 2.2 per cent of their income to the Church. By 1983 it was only 1.6 per cent.[24]

There has been a marked decline in commitment to what were once orthodox Christian beliefs. For example, in 1984 Gallup reported that the percentage of those asked who believed that the Bible is 'literally true' had fallen from 65 per cent in 1964 to just 37 per cent.[25] One can see this increasingly selective attitude to traditional beliefs and practices very clearly in changes within US Catholicism. Here too there has been a shift towards liberalism, with Catholics remaining within the Church but becoming much more critical of it and selective about which of its teachings they will accept. Consider the attitude of most American Catholics to contraception. By the late 1970s Catholic birth-rates, family size, and contraceptive practices were indistinguishable from the US norms and that despite the Church's very clear policy.

Gallup polls regularly ask respondents 'How important would you say religion is in your life—very important, fairly important or not very important?' The proportion who think it is very important has fallen from 75 per cent in 1952 to 58 per cent in 1991. Although there are cycles in the proportions of Americans who believe religion is 'increasing in influence', with the 1991 figure of 36 per cent being far higher than the 14 per cent of 1970, no poll since the 1960s has come close to the 69 per cent recorded for 1957.[26]

Throughout this study I have been at pains to stress the importance not just of what people believe but also of how they hold those beliefs. There are signs of important changes in the status that mainstream-church Americans accord to their own beliefs. To use the labels defined in Chapter 4, they are becoming more denominational and less sectarian. For many Americans, there is no longer the certainty that there was, nor are they so dogmatic. In the 1920s Robert and Helen Lynd studied life in a representative small American city (Muncie, Indiana) which they called Middletown. Since then there have been a series of follow-up studies and we can chart important changes. In 1924 the Lynds asked for responses to the statement that 'Christianity is the one true religion and all people should be converted to it.'[27] Ninety-four per cent of those asked—that is, nearly everyone—agreed. When the same question was put in 1977 to a sample of church-going young people, only 41 per cent agreed. The authors of the re-study summarized that section of their book by saying: 'half of Middletown's adolescents who belong to and attend church and who believe in Jesus, the Bible and the here-after do not claim any universal validity for the Christian beliefs they hold and have no zeal for the conversion of non-Christians.'[28]

A series of Gallup studies have made the same point. Americans are shifting from the Church and sect certainty that their organization is the one true faith to the liberal denominational position of supposing that it is right for them but that it might not be right for others and that there is nothing wrong with people who are not Baptists or whatever. With that position of toleration comes a lack of interest in maintaining and spreading the faith. If it is not essential, then why put a great deal of effort into preserving it?

What was also revealing was the support that the Middletown

study gave to Bryan Wilson's argument that American church involvement is in good part explained by non-religious considerations. The Lynds asked why people went to church and the most popular answer they got was because obedience to God required it. In the 1977 re-study, the most popular reason given for church-going was 'pleasure'.[29]

Of considerable long-term significance is the evidence of an increasing polarization around education. Robert Wuthnow trawls through a lot of survey data to show that by the 1980s there was a clear and increasing division between the better educated, who tended to be most liberal in their religion and least attached to churches, and the rest.[30] Whereas in the 1950s a well-educated high-status young person did more religion than his working-class counterpart, he or she now does less. The implication of this change is that religious values and beliefs are no longer given additional legitimacy by being associated with other marks of wealth, status, and prestige to the degree that they were. It is a simplification but we can think of the middle class as being radically divided between those involved in government, public administration, education, and the media (who tend to lean to the left politically) and those who work in private industry (who tend to lean to the right). Instead of there being general élite support for traditional religion and the socio-moral values that are associated with it, the élites are divided and religion (and its place in public life) is a matter of contention.

Finally, we should not forget that our main interest is not so much 'Do people claim to be religious' but 'What difference does being religious make?' Clearly that has to be answered at a variety of levels from that of personal satisfaction and the stability of the psyche up to major social impact. I will return to this but here I will just note that repeated surveys report that 'Little difference is found in the ethical views and behaviour of those who go to church and those who don't when it comes to lying, cheating, pilferage and non-reporting of theft.'[31]

To summarize, I am suggesting that, while our first impression of survey data of church involvement may be of stability, more sensitive approaches to American religious life show a number of important changes, many of which fit well the classic secularization model. It might be argued that we are being misled here by knowing a lot more about the religious life of the present than we did about whatever past we might take as a golden age of religious orthodoxy, but the above observations are based on good longitudinal data and thus can, I believe, bear the weight of the interpretation that I and others put on them.

## Sectarian Sub-Cultures

Imagine a fundamentalist Baptist family in a small city in Virginia. Vern and Tammy were raised as Baptists and as teenagers met at a church 'cook out'. They married and now have three children. They go to church twice on Sunday and usually a couple of other evenings as well. Their children attend the independent Christian school run by the church. Although it is avowedly anti-racist, there are just two black children out of 300. In summer, the children spend three weeks at the church's own adventure camp, which is run by an associate pastor and staffed by young men and women from the church's Christian liberal arts college. Tammy works part-time as a volunteer secretary for the church's television programme, which is aired on thirty-five small local cable networks. On Saturdays, her husband goes with one of the church's associate pastors to visit people in prison. Tammy's mother, who has bought a flat in a church-run condominium for 'retired saints' is active in the church's senior citizens club. The Pioneers, as they are known, have monthly coach outings, coffee mornings, and the like. The more active ones also work as volunteers for the church, helping in the bookstore or in the office.

Vern and Tammy have decided that when the kids finish high school they will go to one of the fundamentalist colleges—Bob Jones University in Greenville, South Carolina, or Jerry Falwell's Liberty University in Lynchburg, or even stay at home and attend the church's own college.

Vern and Tammy's social life revolves almost entirely round the congregation. They like to spend their free time 'fellowshipping' with their friends, who are all church members. They read religious papers and magazines. In the car stereo they have cassettes of Reverend Jim or Reverend Bob expounding a section of the Bible. When they tire of their cassettes, they will tune their radios to a fundamentalist station and listen to Brother Beeny or the Reverend Ike with his 'five steps to heaven salvation plan which can be yours if you mail me ten dollars, just ten dollars at . . .'. Instead of heavy metal music (which Vern and Tammy want banned or at least identified with stickers warning that the records contain dangerous satanic lyrics), the children listen to Christian rock music. The family members watch little secular television but they are keen on the religious broadcasts of Oral Roberts, Jerry Falwell, Jim Bakker (until his sex scandal finished his career), or Jimmy Swaggart (until his sex scandal almost finished his career). Each summer they will spend a week going to the crusade revival tents and hearing new and glamorous out-of-town preachers. They may even have a copy of *The Christian Yellow Pages*, which lists fundamentalist businesses, so they can make sure they stay in a fundamentalist hotel, shop at a fundamentalist grocery store, and buy their cars from a Christian car salesman.

Vern and Tammy are not as cut off from the mainstream world as such communitarian sects as the Amish or the Hutterites but they do their best to recreate at a local level the degree of cultural homogeneity that is needed to sustain the 'church' form of religion. They are not ignorant. They know a lot about the world outside but that knowledge is passed through a very strong ideological prism. They know what is wrong with the rest of America: it has been taken over by homosexuals and secular humanists.

This 'ghetto formation' is a recent phenomenon. It was rejected as a strategy by those conservatives who in the second decade of this century acquired the sobriquet of 'fundamentalists':

They strictly rejected a functional expansion of the church . . . For them the purpose of a congregation was to pursue salvation and to provide a place for the religious community to join together in that pursuit. Functions that went beyond the worship service, Sunday school, and support for evangelists and missions did nothing but distract from these goals.[32]

That there has been such marked functional expansion of conservative Protestant churches is only partly explained by the arrival of such new opportunities for evangelism as mass-media broadcasting; it is largely explained by the increasing barren and even hostile nature of the surrounding culture. That in remaining numerous the saints have circled the wagons is pretty good evidence that the Indians of secularization are a greater threat now than they were in 1910.

## Britain and America Contrasted

The point about the sectarian ghetto of Vern and Tammy is that it could not be created in any European country. The UK, for a variety of reasons but primarily because it is small and relatively homogenous, has a highly centralized structure for government and public and social administration, and most other European countries are closer to the British than to the American models. In Europe it is very difficult to set up an independent school; it is very easy in the USA. American mass media is open to anyone who can afford to buy time on it. Before the advent of satellite TV, the UK had only four television channels, and these remain heavily regulated by the government. Christian broadcasters cannot buy time to air their programmes and they cannot start their own Christian TV networks.[33] American government is federal, with states, counties, and even towns having considerably more autonomy than they have in the UK. When the Conservative government of the 1980s got tired of the policies of the Labour-controlled Greater London Council, it simply reorganized local government and got rid of it.

Its origins as a migrant society led the USA to evolve in such a way as to allow a great deal of freedom to individual ethnic, religious, and regional groups to construct their own worlds. Where many American social scientists see 'pluralism' as something which impinges on ordinary Americans and hence explains the popularity of religion, I see pluralism as the cause of a social and political structure which allows particular groups to recreate culturally homogenous 'ghettos'. The openness of the USA means that, although the country as a whole has far greater cultural variety, many Americans are far better placed than people in the UK to live their lives within worlds that are mono-cultural.

## The Secularization of the Mainstream

I now want to backtrack slightly and consider how the changes in the mainstream of American religion might be described most abstractly before I suggest that slowly but surely similar things are happening in the sectarian worlds of fundamentalism. Although the focus here is on the American case, the same observations could have been drawn from European examples. In describing mainstream American religion, Wilson and others have made the point that it seems to have lost a great deal of its specifically religious *content* and its *distinctiveness*. I will take those two things separately.

The simplest way of describing the changes in content is to say that the supernatural has been diminished and that it has been psychologized or subjectivized. Religion used to be about the divine and our relationship to it. God was held to be a real force external to us. The Bible was his revealed word. Miracles actually occurred. Christ was the son of God and died for our sins. Heaven and hell were real places. Gradually over the last hundred years a quite different interpretation of these things has affected much of mainstream Christianity. God is no longer seen as an actual person but as some sort of vague power or our own consciences. The Bible is no longer the word of God but a historical book with some useful ethical and moral guidelines for living. Miracles are explained away; either they did not really happen or they were natural phenomena misunderstand by ignorant peasants. Christ is no longer the Son of God but an exemplary prophet and teacher. Heaven and hell cease to be real places and become psychological states.

These changes have two obvious values in adjusting Christianity to the modern world. First, they save most of the specific content from refutation by increasingly popular secular knowledge. Secondly, they remove the necessity for arguing with other religions. If hell is a psychological state, there is less necessity to argue about its nature and how to avoid it.

Harry Fosdick Emerson, a leading liberal Protestant clergyman of the 1930s, said that the starting-point of Christianity was not an objective faith but faith in human personality. The problem of increasing irreligion was not that people were going to go to hell but that 'multitudes of people are living not bad but frittered lives—split, scattered, uncoordinated'. The solution was a religion which would 'furnish an inward spiritual dynamic for radiant and triumphant living'.[34] Religion as relationship to the supernatural was replaced by religion as personal therapy. It was no longer about glorifying God by obeying his commands but about personal growth. To put the point in traditional sociological language, shared religion has always had 'latent functions' or 'secondary consequences' in addition to the primary purpose of linking this world with the divine. Previously, those latent functions have been primarily *social* and have been directed to the lives of societies and communities, to the preservation of shared moral values and social mores, to an identity beyond the individual.[35] Now the secondary benefits of religion are individualized and they have largely displaced the primary purpose. Previously, one intended to worship God and accidentally maintained the cohesion of society. Now one pursues personal satisfaction and accidentally worships God.[36]

This fundamental shift in American Protestantism began in the 1930s and reached its zenith in the popularity of Norman Vincent Peale. Peale was a liberal Presbyterian minister, pastor of one of the biggest churches in New York (which he built from just forty souls to over 900) and the originator of what he called 'the power of positive thinking'.[37] In the first two years after its publication, the book of the same name sold over 2 million copies.[38] For Peale the Christian message was reduced to a battle between good and evil, but these were no longer objective and external forces. They were within us and 'evil' was that which held back our development; it was a lack of self-confidence. Good becomes 'positive thinking'. Those people who think positively (while conforming in behaviour to the norms of suburban middle-class 1950s America) will be successful; this is salvation. Those who do not will be damned. That is, they will be unhappy. The contrast between this psychologized and internalized gospel and the traditional American Protestantism can be neatly seen in a contrast between the radio sermons of Peale and those of one of the leading conservative evangelicals of the 1950s, Charles Fuller. There are other ways of trying to quantify and compare elements of the content of a sermon or speech, but researchers used an interesting technique of counting the number of things that were mentioned as bad or undesirable and the things that were mentioned as good or desirable. Table 6.1 shows the breakdown and gives the words in order of frequency of use.

The contrast is stark. For Peale the forces of evil are internalized as character defects, frustrations, and personal failures. God is a benign force which can help you overcome those defects and live a full and happy life. Fuller wants his audience to realize that they are in imminent danger of death and damnation and need to get saved to avoid that fate. Fuller was popular with conservative evangelicals but Peale was popular with Americans. As Schneider and Dornbusch note of the general trend in religious literature of the 1950s:

while concern with the next world fades increasingly, salvation comes quite conclusively to mean salvation in this world; release from poverty or handicapping inhibitions in personal relations or from ill health or

**Table 6.1.** Peale's and Fuller's sermons contrasted

|  | Peale | Fuller |
|---|---|---|
| Undesirable | defects | death |
|  | unhappiness | darkness |
|  | wrong | alienated |
|  | problems | Satan |
|  | troubles | world |
|  | worries | blind |
| Desirable | happy (-iness) | God |
|  | prayer | Christ |
|  | Jesus Christ | Bible |
|  | peace of mind | gift of grace |
|  | wonderful | believer |
|  | simplicity | spiritual |
|  | God | body of Christ |

Source: Everett C. Parker, David W. Barry, and Dallas W. Smythe, *The Television–Radio Audience and Religion* (New York: Harper and Brothers, 1955), 138–49.

emotional disequilibrium . . . suffering has lost its 'meaningfulness' and more and more is described as senseless misery, best gotten rid of. No longer divinely or transcendentally significant, suffering figures as a pathological experience calling for a psychiatrist or a minister trained in counselling.[39]

Peale's rewriting of Christianity to make it a self-help growth therapy was immensely popular. Forty years after its first publication, his *Power of Positive Thinking* is still regularly reprinted.

Of course, this major change in the interpretation of Christianity did not occur in a vacuum. It was part and parcel of a new optimistic spirit that swept the country as industrialization made people richer than they had ever imagined and as the USA rose to be the major world power. Its economic strength and political might were living proof of the power of positive thinking.

At the same time as the faith was being stripped of its traditional supernaturalism, it was also losing its behavioural distinctiveness. Asceticism was out. Church-goers no longer gave up smoking, drinking, dancing, or going to the theatre. They wore the same clothes as other people, lived in the same kinds of houses, and had the same increasingly liberal moral and ethical standards. They got divorced.

It is a commonplace of recent criticisms of the secularization thesis to ridicule Wilson's observation that American churches have secularized from the inside. Wilson is chided for wanting to have it both ways in suggesting that, while formal religion in Europe has lost adherents, religious institutions in the United States have retained support but at the price of reducing the distinctiveness of their message. But ridicule is not refutation. It seems abundantly clear that contemporary American mainstream Christianity is quite different from that of the nineteenth or eighteenth century. Religion is no longer a set of rules which must be obeyed because God says so. It is a personal therapy which can be adopted, if you like, because it will make you feel better. Its key terms no longer have any referents beyond the psyche. As this basic change involves replacing the other-worldly with the mundane, there seems no obvious reason not to regard it as secularization.

## The Secularization of Conservative Protestantism

Conservative Protestants (especially the fundamentalists and Pentecostalists) stayed out of this round of change. They were able to resist new ideas and attitudes for a long time because they were not so immediately affected by the social changes that encouraged them. Prosperity was slow to come to the deep South and to the rural areas of the West and Mid-West. Oral Roberts, who by the late 1950s was the best-known and most popular Pentecostal preacher in the United States, grew up in considerable poverty in rural Oklahoma. As a child his entire wardrobe was a single set of overalls. When he graduated from elementary school, he was elected 'King of the Class'. He had saved money from selling newspapers to buy a new set of overalls so that he could be fittingly attired to escort the 'Queen of the Class'. She turned up for the party wearing a white satin evening gown. His teacher told Oral he still had time to go home and change into his good clothes.[40]

One of the things that religion does is to make sense of people's lives and reconcile them to what cannot be changed. Conservative Protestantism, in its fundamentalist and Pentecostal forms, involved a rejection of material things and of the loose moral and ethical standards that seemed to come with them. Liquor, tobacco, exciting music, and sexual promiscuity were forbidden. Strict dress codes were enforced: women could not wear short sleeves or jewellery. Going to baseball games, the movies, circuses, dance halls, or state and county fairs was prohibited. But eventually the prosperity of industrial America began to seep down to the communities in which fundamentalism and Pentecostalism were strong. The conservatives refused televisions because they transmitted Satanic messages but they also rejected them because they could not afford televisions. It is not surprising then that, when they could afford televisions, the injunction against watching TV gradually weakened. Fancy clothes were the work of the devil until poor whites could afford fancy clothes, and then the lines gradually shifted. So long as Pentecostalists were so poor that the break-up of the family would have pushed them over the edge into destitution, divorce was entirely unacceptable. As they became better-off, so too that line was moved.

The extent of the changes is ably documented by James Hunter, who in 1982 surveyed a large number of young evangelical students in a variety of colleges with a series of questions that had been used in full in 1951 and in part in 1961 and 1963 (the results of which he combines). For each of the items described in Table 6.2, the respondents were asked if it was 'morally wrong all the time', and the per-

**Table 6.2.** Mores of young evangelicals, 1951, 1963–3, and 1982 (%)

| The following are 'morally wrong all the time' | 1951 | 1961–3 | 1982 |
|---|---|---|---|
| Studying on Sunday | 13 | 2 | 0 |
| Playing pool | 26 | 4 | 0 |
| Playing cards | 77 | 33 | 0 |
| Social dancing (tango, waltz, etc.) | 91 | 61 | 0 |
| Folk dancing | 59 | 31 | 0 |
| Attending 'Hollywood-type' moves | 46 | 14 | 0 |
| Attending 'R'-rated movies | — | — | 7 |
| Smoking cigarettes | 93 | 70 | 51 |
| Drinking alcohol | 98 | 78 | 17 |
| Smoking marijuana | 99 | — | 70 |
| Casual petting | — | 48 | 23 |
| Heavy petting | — | 81 | 45 |
| Premarital sexual intercourse | — | 94 | 89 |
| Extramarital sexual intercourse | — | 98 | 97 |

*Source*: James D. Hunter, *Evangelicalism: The Coming Generation* (Chicago: University of Chicago Press, 1987), 59.

centages given are those who agreed that the activity was, indeed, entirely unacceptable.

Individual items are fascinating. For anyone acquainted with British evangelical circles, it is remarkable that more than half Hunter's 1982 sample thought 'heavy petting' could ever be acceptable. The general import of the table can be readily gauged from the empty slots at the bottom left of the table and the zeros at the top right. The final four items were so awful to evangelicals of the 1950s that the issues were not even raised. The first six items are now fully accepted though they were rejected by large numbers in the 1950s. That alcohol is now acceptable but smoking is not suggests that general public health concerns weigh heavier with young evangelicals than do the behavioural restrictions of their parents.

Beyond this sort of survey data there is a vast body of impressionistic data that could be drawn upon. By and large the same consumer goods and cultural products are now found in evangelical and fundamentalist homes as in the homes of other Americans. Plainness in appearance, once the outward mark of asceticism, is now entirely absent. The young men and women who make up the gospel choirs and audiences on televangelism shows are as glamorously coiffured and dressed as their secular counterparts.

To observe that, as they have prospered, the evangelicals have abandoned a lot of their social distinctiveness may sound like a crassly reductionist treatment of beliefs and values; beliefs are secondary or epiphenomenal and people readily change their beliefs to fit their circumstances. I am not suggesting that wealth will always corrupt and that the religions of the oppressed will always be compromised to accommodate newly available patterns of consumption, but asceticism is easier when one is poor. Increased prosperity means that the required sacrifice gets relatively bigger and bigger, and, not surprisingly, some people begin to reinterpret the social teachings of their gospel to discover that, actually, wearing make-up and nice clothes and going to dances do not make you a bad person. The two realms—the material world and the world of culture—move with each other.

To summarize so far, much of the behavioural distinctiveness has gone from conservative Protestantism since the 1960s. Has there been a corresponding change in religious beliefs? There are certainly signs. Hunter's study of young evangelicals showed that, while their views on what they had to do and believe in order to attain salvation remained orthodox, they had softened considerably their views of other people's chances of being saved. There was no longer the certainty that there was only one way to heaven. An element of choice has entered our relationship with the divine.

There is also evidence of a clear shift in one of the most abstract elements of Christian religion. In comparing Peale and Fuller, I noted that Fuller was maintaining a traditional view of the nature of religion. If one examines the message of the major televangelists of the 1980s and 1990s, it appears that something like Pealism has arrived there too. One of the classic divisions in human thinking concerns the essential nature of the human self. Are we essentially good and made bad only by our circumstances and experiences or are we essentially bad and made good only by our circumstances and experiences? Until recently the dominant position in Christianity was that, since the Fall and the expulsion from the Garden of Eden, we have been bad and that only the dramatic intervention of God can make us good again. Liberal Protestantism rejected that and proposed—as in Peale's *Power of Positive Thinking*— that the self is improvable and even perfectible. Although fundamentalists, evangelicals, and Pentecostalists rejected that shift in the 1950s and 1960s, even they are now influenced by it. Hunter makes the point economically by listing the titles of best-selling evangelical books of the 1980s: *The Undivided Self: Bringing Your Whole Life in Line with God's Will, You Can Become the Person You Want to Be, The Healthy Personality and the Christian Life, How to Become Your Own Best Self,* and *Self-Esteem: The New Reformation*.[41] God is still there, but he is no longer the strict father whose job it is to smash the human self and bring us to see our own worthlessness. He is the psychotherapist who can help us to be more fulfilled and to achieve more in this life. Arguments between this new evangelicalism and the more traditional version are rife in conservative Protestant circles, but at least one professor in an evangelical seminary thinks the modernizers are winning:

It seems that God has become a rather awkward appendage to the practice of evangelical faith. . . . The centre, in fact, is typically the self. God and his world are made to spin round this surrogate centre. . . . Without serious engagement with God's truth and serious reflection upon this world and the Christian's place in it, the Church is left empty of meaning and an idol has been erected in its place.[42]

Another evangelical innovation that can fairly reasonably be interpreted as evidence of secularization is 'prosperity theology', known to its detractors as the 'health and wealth' gospel, or 'Name it and Claim it!'[43] Conservative Protestants have always supposed that getting right with God would have benefits in this world, but the preaching of a major Pentecostalist such as Oral Roberts suggests that the behavioural part of the equation—the obedience to God—has all but disappeared. Roberts takes the biblical references to casting your bread on the water and it returning tenfold and 'Ask and it shall be given unto you' as promises of material prosperity. Televangelist Pat Robertson offers as one of his 'Kingdom Principles' the law of God's reciprocity:

If we want to release the superabundance of the kingdom of heaven, we first give. . . . I am as certain of this as of anything in my life. If you are in financial trouble, the smartest thing you can do is to start giving money away. . . . Your return, poured into your lap, will be great, pressed down and running over.[44]

The crucial biblical text is Mark 10: 28–30:

Then Peter began to say unto him, Lo, we have left all, and have followed thee.

And Jesus answered and said, Verily I say unto you, There is no man that hath left house, or brethren, or sisters, or father, or mother, or wife, or children, or lands, for my sake and the gospels,

But he shall receive an hundredfold now in this time, houses, and brethren, and sisters, and mothers, and children . . .

Leading televangelist Kenneth Copeland interprets this text as a financial promise: 'Do you want a hundredfold return on your money? Give and let God multiply it back to you.'[45] As the base communities of American Pentecostalism have become more affluent and a large number of Pentecostal preachers and televangelists have become rich celebrities, not only has wealth become acceptable (even desirable) but there has been a discernible shift in thinking about how one might achieve it. Where the Puritan might hope to see the fruits of his diligent labours as a sign of his status as a member of the Elect (but be prepared, Job-like, to accept whatever God's divine and inscrutable providence might send), some modern Pentecostalists believe that the faith to ask for God's blessing (coupled providentially for the televangelists with a sacrificial donation to television ministries) is sufficient to produce the reward. So much for the Protestant ethic.

To summarize again, people can organize their world so as to protect their distinctive beliefs and life-style, but it takes a great deal of sacrifice and hard work. As we saw with Vern and Tammy, American fundamentalists do a great deal to immunize themselves against liberal and secularizing influences, but they are not as cut off as such communitarian sects as the Amish and the Hutterites, and they have changed. They have lost much of their asceticism. They have become more 'denominational' and less 'sectarian'. And they have gone some way down the road of psychologizing and internalizing religion.

So that all the arguments can be considered at their strongest, it is only proper to add a rejoinder to the above. It might be argued that, while there have been real changes in the nature of the conservative Protestant rejection of the dominant mores, the degree of deviance has remained much the same. While the line that marks the acceptable from the sinful has moved, conservatives have held the same position relative to liberal cosmopolitan America. The puritans of the 1920s enjoyed sentimental ballads but rejected the blues and lascivious show music; 1980s evangelicals enjoy the Beach Boys and pop music but reject heavy metal, grunge, and funk. To caricature, one could suppose that, over the century, conservative Protestants have consistently rejected cultural innovations until they were a decade old and then enthusiastically embraced them. Rather than describe this process as accommodation to the mainstream, one could depict it as constantly maintaining a culture that is just distinctive enough to allow those who support it to feel different.

There is something in such a line of reasoning. Though there is not scope to pursue the point here, it is important that we are careful in weighing the implications of changes and do not carelessly judge any shift from what a previous generation held to be important as 'secularization'. None the less, recent changes in conservative Protestantism—personal growth in place of obedience, the exaltation of the self, the demise of asceticism—do seem to be of such a nature as to be regarded as a fundamental alteration and not merely a shift in degrees.

## Religion in Public Life

At first sight, the rise of the new Christian right (NCR) in the 1980s might seem to have been a strong refutation of the basic secularization approach to religious change. Hadden makes exactly this case by coupling the NCR with Iranian fundamentalism as proof that religion still affects politics.[46] In this section I will examine closely the nature and career of the NCR and suggest that, while the recent political entanglements of American fundamentalism would indeed discomfort anyone who thought that the secularization approach amounted to the claim that no members of modern industrial democracies will ever try to reintroduce religious values to the public domain, a realistic approach to the NCR confirms the arguments advanced in the second chapter of this book.

Although the federal and diffuse nature of American public life allows the creation and maintenance of distinctive subcultures and thus offers one solution to the problem of accommodating cultural diversity within a single nation-state, there remain the problem of defining the centre and the possibility of disputes about the boundaries. There have been frequent religiously inspired movements to define what Neuhaus has called the 'public square'.[47] In the best-known example, 1920s conservative Protestants succeeded in making illegal the manufacture and retail of alcoholic beverages.

In explaining the rise and nature of the NCR, there are two important points. First, the culture of the core constituency of the NCR—sunbelt fundamentalists—has been increasingly encroached upon since the end of the Second World War. On many matters of social and moral policy, geographical and cultural peripheries have become increasingly subject to the core of cosmopolitan America. The reach of government has massively increased: in 1976 there were seventy-seven federal regulatory bodies, fifty of which had been created since 1960.[48] The sheer size, the diversity of ethnic groupings, and the federal system of American government has long permitted regions considerable autonomy, but the recent trend is for polity and culture to become more centralized (mass media, for example, are becoming more centralized and homogeneous in output), and for the centre to become more liberal. So fundamentalists have found themselves harder pressed by a more permissive culture. Where once two-thirds of the states were willing to vote for the prohibition of alcohol, there was open campaigning for the legalization of marijuana. Conservative sexual mores were openly questioned and sometimes publicly flouted. Abortion was made legal. A more aggressively secularist interpretation of the constitutional doctrine of separation of church and state meant that school prayer was now threatened.

A more subtle threat was posed by the increasing frequency of claims to rights from members of some previously disadvantaged group (a notion which was anathema to fundamentalists with their individualist Arminianism). First blacks, then women, and then homosexuals claimed that social arrangements should be changed to improve their position. And the state seemed willing not only to accept such claims but to impose new social patterns on subcultures which had previously been permitted to go their own way. Since the 1960s the southern states have been under constant political, judicial, and legislative pressure to promote racial integration and equality. All of these changes appeared as threats to the life-style and socio-moral values of conservative Protestants and hence also as threats to the religious beliefs which fundamentalists held to legitimate such socio-moral positions. The more prescient knew that electing conservative and fundamentalist councilmen in Greenville, South Carolina, had little influence where the important decisions were increasingly being made: the federal and Supreme courts, the Presidency, and Congress. They were willing to listen to people who argued that fundamentalists had to become involved politically if they were to maintain (or restore) the Christian culture which had made America great.

At the same time as some fundamentalists were becoming more politically concerned, a number of professional conservative political activists were coming to see fundamentalists as an important bloc in a new populist conservative grouping which would differ from the old Eastern establishment conservatism in mobilizing people around social and moral issues as well as more traditional concerns with foreign policy, the welfare state, the economy, and the regulation of business. They persuaded a number of leading fundamentalists to become politically active.

The key figures in the mobilization of the NCR were televangelists. James Robison of Dallas and Pat Robertson of the 700 Club and the Christian Broadcasting Network played a part, but the most influential and consistently involved figure was Jerry Falwell of Lynchburg, Virginia. Interest was mobilized at two levels. Nationally, the audience for Falwell's televised church service, his computer mailing lists of supporters, and other lists of known socio-moral conservatives were used to create a base from which to raise funds and produce the appearance of a large united movement. At the same time, Falwell and other fundamentalist leaders used their ministerial networks to influence other independent fundamentalist Baptist pastors, who in turn mobilized their con-gregations.

Falwell's Moral Majority and similar organizations such as Religious Roundtable, Christian Voice, and American Coalition for Traditional Values raised money to campaign as pressure groups on a range of public policy issues (such as abortion, homosexuality, the teaching of evolution in schools, the threat of 'secular humanism', minority-rights legislation, and prayer in public school). The cam-paigns had two related purposes. The first was to mobilize conserva-tive opinion so that legislators, judges, journalists, and educators would temper their liberalism (either from genuine respect for the opinions of conservatives or from fear of retribution). The second was to turn that opinion into electoral clout. Legislators at state and congressional level who had a record of voting the 'wrong way' found themselves the targets of well-funded negative campaigns. Funds were also spent on behalf of acceptable conservative candidates.

The precarious position of the Protestants of Ulster has given them a long history of sustained political involvement (the ethnic religion described in Chapter 5). American fundamentalists have alternated short bursts of activism with long periods of 'quietist' retreat from the impure world.[49] A major NCR tactic was voter reg-istration, and this seems to have succeeded in 1980 and 1984. However, this would have been significant only if liberals had failed to register a similar number of new voters, if the new conservative voters had all voted the same way, and if their involvement was sus-tained.

For a variety of reasons (not least the value of incumbency) there is a long history of third parties failing. Even if fundamentalists had been sufficiently numerous seriously to consider forming a party, the activists knew it was doomed. So the attempt to displace liberal politicians and mobilize conservative voters was accompanied by infiltration of the Republican Party at local level.

To put it bluntly, none of this had any very great lasting effect.[50] Few NCR supporters were elected to national office, some of the few whose success was claimed by the NCR repudiated that sup-port, and a number of the 1980 successes failed to get re-elected. Not surprisingly given that only four or five senators were ever 'move-ment' conservatives and that the Democrats controlled the House of Representatives, the NCR had no legislative success at the con-gressional level. Although he made supporting noises, President Reagan conspicuously refused to use his influence to mobilize congressional votes for NCR-promoted bills on school prayer and abortion. The NCR had some legislative success at state level in those states which had always had sizeable fundamentalist populations, but even these victories were often hollow. As in the case discussed below of the Arkansas creation science bill, many NCR issues touched on basic constitutional rights and thus could be challenged through the federal courts. The centripetal tendency of the court system then allowed the more liberal and universalistic values of the cosmopolitan middle classes to over-rule the particularisms of the NCR.

If electoral and legislative politics failed to produce any major changes, were there more subtle effects? Even the much vaunted shift to the right in the political agenda which the NCR was supposed to have effected turned out to be candy floss. Measured studies of attitude surveys during the Reagan era showed that the turn to the right on defence and economic policy was not accompanied by any significant shift to the right on socio-moral issues. It might also be supposed that there will be a long-term NCR effect through the training of large numbers of evangelicals and fundamentalists for conventional party politics. There is no doubt that many young conservative Protestants acquired an interest and some expertise in politics through NCR involvement, but, as with voter registration, this advantage was blunted by a similar and counter-balancing revival of interests among liberals.

Furthermore, the relative absence of religious or socio-moral concerns from the central interests of the Republican party was not an accident, a condition to be rectified simply by the presence of fundamentalists. The party's relative neutrality on socio-moral issues and its unwillingness to become identified with a particular religious position were a sensible response to the problems of maximizing voter support in a culturally plural society. This is very much the view of mainstream Republicans who believe that the party's adoption of an anti-abortion platform in 1992 helped it to lose the presidency.

Those NCR activists who remained most aggressively fundamentalist failed to get anywhere. Those who got anywhere did so by compromising and becoming largely indistinguishable from secular conservatives. Instead of following the eight years of vacuous rhetoric of Reagan with the real support of televangelist Pat Robertson, the NCR got as president George Bush, an old-fashioned eastern moneyed conservative and in 1992 saw Bush displaced by the Democrat Bill Clinton.

A minor but significant NCR tactic was the initiation of lawsuits. Although 'unelected' judges were frequently a focus for conservative ire, having been largely responsible for many of the changes they most resented, the NCR was willing to use the same avenues for change. When a number of courts made it clear that the price to be paid for religious freedom was that the public arena had to be free of religion, fundamentalists responded by trying to have 'secular humanism' (a catch-all notion to cover anything which did not overtly recognize the supremacy of Christianity) judged to be a religion so that it too could be banned from schools.

The presentation of Christianity and secular humanism as two 'matching' religions had some initial success, but it was exposed as sleight of hand when it came to detailed discussion of the issues. In a major case in Alabama, Judge Brevard Hand found for Christian plaintiffs who wanted a range of textbooks banned for unconstitutionally promoting secular humanism, but the judgment was overturned by the 11th Circuit Court of Appeals, which ordered Hand to dismiss the case. The finality of the ruling was accepted by the National Legal Foundation, a right-wing pressure group, when it decided not to appeal the case to the Supreme Court. Reagan and Bush were able to appoint a number of conservatives to the Court, but, though they were prepared to see a slight weakening of the judicial support for the right to abortion, they did not shift the line on public religion and gave no encouragement to those who wished to see 'creation science' taught as an alternative to evolutionary theories in school.

The problem for the NCR is that politicized fundamentalists are only a small minority of the American people. To have any national effect and to be able to claim national legitimacy, they have to work in alliance with conservative Catholics, Jews, black Protestants, Mormons, and secular conservatives. They have also to accept the rhetoric of the separation of church and state so that their crusades are promoted not on the superiority of fundamentalist religious beliefs and values but with a number of secular motifs. The limitation on this tactic is that their claims are then judged on secular criteria.

The Arkansas 'equal time' bill is a good example. In the early 1970s fundamentalists shifted the defence of the Genesis account of Creation from saying 'we believe it because the Bible says so' to exploiting differences between evolutionary models to argue that creation science (as it was now called) fitted the facts every bit as well as evolution. The Arkansas state legislature passed a bill to force schools which taught evolution to give 'equal time' to the biblical creation account. The American Civil Liberties Union took the case to the courts, arguing that creationism was a religious belief, not a science, and that the bill meant that schools were promoting a particular religion. The creationists had to give good reason why anyone who did not accept the Bible should believe in 'special creation'; their presentation of such a case was dire. The judge decided for the ACLU.[51]

It is ironic, given the fundamentalist dislike for the notion of group rights, that the NCR was most successful when it appealed to 'fairness' and presented itself as a discriminated-against minority. Such very limited progress as was made was the result of appealing to the secular value of fairness rather than to theological rectitude. Attempts to go beyond a demand for a little more social space for their own culture to claiming some sort of hegemony were firmly opposed.[52]

The problem was not only one of external opposition to fundamentalist aspirations. There was also an internal problem of motivation. The alliance with non-fundamentalist conservatives was precarious. The NCR asked fundamentalists to get involved in politics to defend their religiously inspired culture and then asked that, in order to do politics well, they should leave behind their religion. On Sunday they believed Catholics were not 'saved'; on Monday they had to work with Catholics in defence of our 'shared Judaeo-Christian' heritage. But placing religion and politics in separate compartments governed by different criteria is exactly the feature of modern religion which they reject. My extensive interviewing in South Carolina and Virginia in the early 1980s made it clear to me that fundamentalists cannot be pragmatic without conceding that which defines them. They are themselves aware of the problem and are troubled by it. And even if they could abandon their anti-Semitism, racism, and anti-Catholicism, Catholics, blacks, and Jews have long enough memories to be suspicious. Additionally, there has usually been an organizational block on Catholic participation in pressure-group politics: the Catholic Church prefers its campaigning to be directed through its own agencies. Although organizations such as Moral Majority Inc. and American Coalition for Traditional Values could always find a few black, Catholic, or Jewish figures to appear on their letterheads and platforms, such alliances were not successfully built at local levels, where NCR organizations remained primarily fundamentalist.

Furthermore, what the NCR campaigns have demonstrated is that most Americans are happy with the status quo. Well-funded and organized NCR campaigns have backfired in that they have created an equally aggressive response from liberals and have allowed Americans to make the choice. We can see what choice they make in the presidential election campaign of Pat Robertson. Against those who saw Jerry Falwell's announced retirement from politics in November 1987 as the end of the NCR, some activists and some commentators construed Pat Robertson's presidential campaign as a major step forward for the NCR. It certainly represented an important increase in aspirations and inadvertently provided a mass of opinion-poll data from which a number of general conclusions about the strength of the NCR can be drawn. These can only be sketched here but are discussed in detail elsewhere.[53]

The more people considered the issues raised by such a candidacy, the more anti-Robertson feeling outstripped pro-Robertson sentiment. Even those people who should have been most sympathetic were not mobilized. In one poll, even self-identified conservative Protestants said that Robertson's status as a former clergyman made them less rather than more likely to support him (by a margin of 42 to 25 per cent). Many preferred a secular politician who had some of the right positions to a born-again televangelist who had them all; in a poll which was confirmed by the voting patterns in the Southern states primaries, Southern fundamentalists and evangelicals divided 44 per cent for George Bush, 30 per cent for Bob Dole, and only 14 per cent for Robertson.

General public sympathy for some NCR values did not translate into widespread support for NCR policies or politicians. Much of the mistake of the likely impact of the NCR came from misunderstanding survey data and the relationships between attitudes and actions. An oft-cited indicator of likely NCR support is a study of 1977 survey data which showed that almost a third of Americans accepted the Moral Majority platform in its entirety and a further 42 per cent were ideological fellow-travellers.[54] Read one way, the survey did show a remarkable amount of support for conservative mores, but other readings were as plausible. Many of the issues for which a view was sought from survey respondents were extremely general, and it is not obvious which of the range of responses should be taken as the Moral Majority position. For example, one question offered the proposition 'It is much better for everyone involved if the man is the achiever outside the home and the woman takes care of the home and family' and asked if respondents strongly agreed, agreed, disagreed, strongly disagreed, or did not know. Which of those should be taken as the thinking of the NCR? If we take only 'strongly agree', we get 18 per cent of respondents, but if we take both assenting positions, we get the massive 64 per cent. Multiply the consequences of such technical choices over a range of questions and one can see how the same body of statistical survey evidence can create quite different impressions.[55]

Furthermore, even when we agree that there is a general sympathy for conservative socio-moral positions, we cannot assume that such sentiments translate into shared commitment to the particular policies of the NCR. It is one thing to be 'against abortion'; it is quite another actively to support this or that measure to outlaw or severely limit abortion.

Nor can one assume that even shared policy commitments translate into a powerful socio-political movement; fundamentalists have other interests which divide them. Not all socio-moral conservatives place those interests at the top of their agendas. Anyway, they are unlikely to be mobilized around those concerns unless the political circumstances focus attention on those issues. American domestic politics seems much more concerned with such secular and mundane matters as the economy, crime rates, the welfare system, and public health-care provision than with school prayer, creation science, and abortion.

Finally, we need to remember that the NCR has not had the field to itself. A large part of its very limited success was the result of surprise. Liberals took their political and cultural domination for granted and had forgotten that their values required active promotion. Once well-known natural scientists such as Stephen Jay Gould realized that they had to defend their evolutionist thinking, they did so convincingly. I will give just two very different examples of successful liberal counter-attack. Fundamentalists had exerted considerable influence over textbook content because of the legal structure of the Texas school book review procedure. Only books that had been approved by a committee could be bought from state funds. The review procedure permitted members of the public to criticize books and for many years fundamentalists had dominated these hearings. It did not permit lay people to defend books against their critics. Rather than face the possibility of criticism and rejection, many publishers had taken to censoring their textbook offerings. People for the American Way successfully campaigned to have the procedure changed so that liberal lay groups could defend those works attacked for 'secular humanism'. As a result, fundamentalist influence was drastically reduced.

People for the American Way was also successful in countering Pat Robertson's attempts to shed his evangelist past. Like all good politicians, Robertson presented different faces to different audiences. To his religious following he continued to offer a born-again Baptist view of political events; to the general public he presented himself as a conservative businessman whose business interests just happened to include running a Christian broadcasting network. People for the American Way prepared a video compilation of Robertson's utterances as an evangelist and circulated these free to hundreds of television stations so that Robertson's own publicity material was balanced by presentations of a self which he preferred to downplay.

A similar observation can be made about the emotive issue of abortion. Many liberals feared that any weakening of the Supreme Court's support for the right to abortion would mean that right would be lost. Instead, the whole question has returned to the place where many think it should be decided: the political arena. What was significant about the elections of 1992 was that those politicians who supported the right to abortion did well and those who supported the NCR platform did badly.

The pressure-group politics of the Christian right have been discussed at length for two reasons. First, the NCR is often glibly cited as refutation of the secularization thesis. Secondly, a close look at how those pressure groups have operated and at their results tells us a great deal about the place of religion in modern pluralistic democracies. That such a movement as the NCR could be mobilized in the USA tells us that many Americans are fundamentalists, that many fundamentalists are socio-moral conservatives, and that the diffuse and open nature of American politics gives such people a far better chance of bringing their concerns to public attention through the political process than they would have in any European country.[56] An understanding of why such a movement failed to make any significant advance on its political agenda illustrates some of the key themes of the secularization approach. To have any realistic chance of making headway, the fundamentalists had to accept the principles that lie at the heart of all culturally pluralistic modern industrial democracies. Religious preferences are desirable only when confined to the private home and leisure world. Goals which stem from religious preferences have to be defended on the secular grounds of fairness and social usefulness. While religious minorities can claim some room for their cultures, they cannot hope to impose their values on the society at large.

## Conclusion

To return to the place where this chapter began, the USA is often (increasingly so in the last decade) presented as the case which refutes the secularization approach. The argument can be made from the enduring popularity of church involvement and from the persistence and revival of religiously inspired attempts to reshape public consciousness. In the first part of this chapter I argued that a detailed look at changes first in the mainstream denominations and then in the evangelical world offers considerable evidence of secularization. In the second part I argued that, once we get beyond surprise that a movement such as the NCR should exist at all and look closely at its nature and significance, we again find little reason to abandon the secularization paradigm. I now want to put American religion (which primarily means Christianity) in a bigger historical and theoretical context.

It is clear that the bulk of such a decline in church membership and attendance as there has been in the USA has largely occurred in the mainstream liberal denominations. Although the fundamentalists and Pentecostalists show little sign of growing as a proportion of the American people, they are becoming more influential because they are a proportionately larger part of American Christianity. There are a number of ways of explaining this trend. Stark and Bainbridge offer an elaborate version of an idea that has a long and honourable sociological pedigree: people have needs which can only be well met by religion.[57] This would explain why the mainstream denominations which compromised with modernity by abandoning those parts of their belief systems apparently most at odds with secular culture have declined. The conservatives grew because they were offering the supernatural product that people wanted.

There is a problem with this. If the difference between mainstream and conservative Protestantism is to be explained by the greater success of the latter in meeting needs, a major part of the growth of conservative Protestant churches should be accounted for by defections from liberal churches. There has, in fact, been very little of that. By and large they are separate worlds. Conservative Protestantism survives—as I have suggested with my archetypal couple Vern and Tammy—by keeping its own children within the faith. Liberalism declines because its children become indifferent to it. But—and this is the major point overlooked by Stark and his associates—as the conservatives have grown relative to the rest and become more affluent, they have also lost a great deal of what made them distinctive. As we have seen, the psychologized gospel of 'positive thinking' that was anathema to conservatives in the 1950s and 1960s is now well established in fundamentalist and Pentecostalist circles, and much of the behavioural distinctiveness that marked those groups off has also gone. This in turn has produced a series of new schisms with congregations hiving off from what were once conservative organizations.

This suggests a very general pattern. Conservative sects grow and gradually become more liberal and more mainstream. Some conservatives resist this direction and break away to form new purified conservative sects. The new mainstream becomes more liberal and declines further. The new sects grow until they too become increasingly denominational and mainstream, and so on.

The difference between my point of view and that of Stark and his colleagues is that they see these cycles as operating in a religious economy which is essentially stable. The total amount of religion in a society should remain the same because the needs it meets are universal. There is an alternative route that can be taken at this point. One could argue that the universal needs can be met by some other institution which is the 'functional equivalent' of religion; sport, nationalism, and socialist politics have all been offered as candidates. However, to suggest that is to endorse the sense, if not the language, of the secularization thesis. If we are going to insist that religion and only religion can properly satisfy human needs (because only it can offer rewards big enough to compensate for our failures in this life and explanations of our sufferings that are sufficiently convincing) then it has to be the case that the decline in the popularity of previously powerful religious organizations and the internal secularization of those that remain popular must be creating a market for new religions. The next chapter will consider that proposition.

It is all too easy in trying to capture the essence of major social changes to end up presenting a story which invites caricature. I have tried to present the secularization thesis in a way that is properly sensitive to the vast differences in the religious histories of different societies and cultures. The purpose of this examination of American religion is not to suggest that those who are struck by the American fondness for religion have been entirely misled by surface appearances (though they may well have been misled about the extent of American divergence from the European norm). There are great differences between old- and new-world religion. However, I think they are often misunderstood. If we have to choose just one major social variable to explain American religion, it would not be pluralism or voluntarism but *ethnicity*. American religion drew its strength from its role as the guardian of ethnic interests and the emblem of ethnic identity. That role has diminished, but, as we can see from the radical division between black and white churches, it is far from written out of the script. Furthermore, along with such other considerations as the size of the USA and the colonial history of conflict with the UK (the classic centralized nation-state), ethnicity was a major cause of the diffuse structure of American public life. That open texture permits religious interest groups, even after their religion has become loosened from ethnic identity, to maintain the distinctive sub-societies which in turn allow the maintenance of strong religious cultures.

However, though Americans differ from Europeans in their fondness for their churches, those churches have changed. Radical sects have become denominations. The mainstream denominations have become tolerant and ecumenical. The gospel itself has been rewritten to remove much of the specifically supernatural. Conservatives were largely unaffected by the moderating currents that dragged through the mainstream churches in the first half of the century, but even in their hard-wrought sub-societies they are now shifting in a direction which, for want of a better term, can be called secular.

## Notes

1. Robert Bezilla (ed.), *Religion in America 1992–93* (Princeton: Princeton Religion Research Centre, 1993).
2. Andrew M. Greeley, *Religious Change in America* (Cambridge, Mass: Harvard University Press, 1989), 128.
3. John G. Condran and Joseph B. Tamney, 'Religious "Nones", 1957 to 1982',

*Sociological Analysis*, 46 (1982), 415–23. Most recent figures provided by Professor Tamney.

4. For general accounts of the NCR, see Clyde Wilcox, *God's Warriors: The Christian Right in Twentieth Century America* (Baltimore: Johns Hopkins University Press, 1992); Michael Cromartie (ed.), *No Longer Exiles: The Religious New Right in American Politics* (Washington: Ethics and Public Policy Centre, 1993); Ted G. Jelen, *The Political Mobilization of Religious Beliefs* (New York: Praeger, 1991); and Matthew C. Moen, *The Transformation of the Christian Right* (Tuscaloosa, Ala.: University of Alabama Press, 1992).

5. C. Kirk Hadaway, Penny L. Marler, and M. Chaves, 'What the Polls Don't Show: A Closer Look at US Church Attendance', *American Sociological Review*, 58 (1993), 742.

6. Bezilla, *Religion in America*, 44.

7. Hadaway, Marler, and Chaves, 'What the Polls Don't Show', 742.

8. Ibid. 750.

9. David Barker, Loek Halman, and Astrid Vloet (*The European Values Study 1981–1990 Summary Report* (London: European Values Study Group/Cook Foundation, 1992) ), give a monthly church-attendance figure for Britain of 23%, which Peter Brierley, drawing on a series of MARC Europe studies of actual church attendance, thinks is about twice the correct figure. Monthly figures from survey data are awkward to assess. If the world divided into weekly attenders and non-attenders, survey data could be readily compared with clergy estimates. If a significant proportion attended, say, every third week, that would go some way to explaining why there are fewer people in church on any Sunday than say that they attend 'once a month'. According to the 1991 British Social Attitudes survey, the proportions of weekly, fortnightly, and monthly attenders were 100 : 21 : 56. This would give a figure of around 12% claiming to attend for the average Sunday, which is about 2% higher than the figure generated from clergy estimates. Peter Kaldor (*Who Goes Where? Who Doesn't Care* (Homebush, NSW: Lancer, 1987) ), summarizes 1984 Australian Values Study survey data and compares it with two clergy-based figures for church attendance. In one case the church-generated figure was 75% of that produced by the survey; in the other it was only 42%.

10. For example, de Toqueville is favourably cited by Theodore Caplow, 'Contrasting Trends in European and American Religion', *Sociological Analysis*, 46 (1985), 101–8, and Roger Finke, 'Religious Deregulation: Origins and Consequences', *Journal of Church and State*, 32 (1990), 609–26.

11. Gary Becker, 'The Economic Approach to Human Behavior', in Jon Elster (ed.), *Rational Choice* (Oxford: Blackwell, 1986), 108–22.

12. For a detailed critique of the extension of economistic models of behaviour to religion, see Steve Bruce, 'Religion and Rational Choice', *Sociology of Religion*, 54 (1993), 193–205.

13. Roger Finke and Rodney Stark, *The Churching of America 1576–1990: Winners and Losers in our Religious Economy* (New Brunswick, NJ: Rutgers University Press, 1992), 83.

14. Finke, 'Religious Deregulation'. 617.

15. C. Cayley, *The Leeds Guide: Giving a Concise History of that Rich and Populous Town* (Leeds, 1808), and British Parliamentary Papers, *1851 Census, Great Britain, Report and Tables on Religious Worship, England and Wales, 1852–53*

(Cork: Irish University Press reprint, 1970). Efforts to test the accuracy of the 1851 Census data by checking local registers show that the Census under-reports small dissenting denominations and independents. For example, see G. Patterson, 'The Religious Census: A Test of its Accuracy in South Shields', *Durham County Local History Society Bulletin* (Apr. 1978), 14–17, or Ian Beckwith, 'Religion in a Working Men's Parish', *Lincolnshire History and Archaeology*, 4 (1969), 29–38.

16. Edwin S. Gaustad, *Historical Atlas of Religion in America* (New York: Harper & Row, 1962). See also Steve Bruce, 'Pluralism and Religious Vitality', in Steve Bruce (ed.) *Religion and Modernization: Sociologists and Historians Debate the Secularization Thesis* (Oxford: Oxford University Press, 1992), 170–94.

17. Robert Wuthnow, *The Restructuring of American Religion* (Princeton: Princeton University Press, 1988), 64.

18. Zoe Heller, 'The Mall of God', *Independent on Sunday Review*, 2 June 1991, pp. 2–7.

19. Callum Brown suggests this: 'A Revisionist Approach to Religious Change', in Bruce (ed.) *Religion and Modernization*, 50.

20. Robert Wuthnow, 'Recent Patterns of Secularization: A Problem of Generations', *American Sociological Review*, 41 (1976), 856–67.

21. *USA Today*, 25 June 1992, p. 1.

22. Wuthnow, 'Recent Patterns of Secularization'.

23. George H. Gallup, Jr., and Sarah Jones, *100 Questions and Answers: Religion in America* (Princeton: Princeton Religion Research Centre, 1989), 42.

24. Greeley, *Religious Change*, 68.

25. Wuthnow, *Restructuring*, 165. So that I am not accused of opportunism in cit-ing survey data where it suits my argument and arguing against the reliability of surveys on other occasions, let me state my general principle. I do not sup-pose that survey data are randomly misleading. Rather I assume that surveys consistently over-report beliefs and actions which are widely regarded as decent and honourable (hence more people claim to have voted than actually did so) and consistently over-report what people used to think and used to do. Hence they tend to be biased in the direction of the past and the consensually decent. As a very loose rule of thumb, we can suppose that surveys which show evidence of declining orthodoxy and interest in Christian religion in the USA can be used to make that point because the true picture is likely to be an even greater shift in the same direction.

26. Bezilla, *Religion in America*, 54–7.

27. Robert S. Lynd and Helen M. Lynd, *Middletown: A Study in Contemporary American Culture* (New York: Harcourt, Brace, & Co., 1929), 316.

28. Theodore Caplow, Howard M. Bahr, and B. A. Chadwick, *All Faithful People: Change and Continuity in Middletown's Religion* (Minneapolis: University of Minnesota Press, 1983), 98.

29. Ibid. 100.

30. Wuthnow, *Restructuring*, 162.

31. Undated Gallup advertising leaflet for the Religion in America series of reports.

32. Martin Riesbrodt, *Pious Passion: The Emergence of Modern Fundamentalism in the United States and Iran* (Berkeley and Los Angeles: University of California Press, 1993), 91.

33. For a detailed comparison of broadcasting structures and their opportunities for different sorts of religious broadcasting, see Steve Bruce, *Pray TV:*

*Televangelism in America* (London: Routledge, 1990).
34. Ibid. 84.
35. This, of course, is Durkheim's point about the social consequences of religion. I would add that it is quite possible to accept the accuracy of Durkheim's observation of such consequences without endorsing his claim that such functions *explain* religion or the allied claim that the need for such functions to be met from somewhere means that secularization is impossible.
36. The change in secondary consequences and the shifting relationship between manifest and latent functions are very ably discussed by Bryan R. Wilson, *Religion in Sociological Perspective* (Oxford: Oxford University Press, 1982).
37. Peale was born in 1898 and died on Christmas Eve 1993. He was described by the Sales Executive Club of America as the 'Most Sales-Minded Clergyman' and once played himself in a thirty-minute inspirational film entitled *How to Raise Your Batting Average in Selling*. See his obituary in the *Guardian* (20 July 1988), which was published five years before he died! See also Carol V. R. George, *God's Salesman: Norman Vincent Peale and the Power of Positive Thinking* (New York: Oxford University Press, 1994). Although this section concentrates on Protestantism, there are clear and obvious parallels with American Catholicism, where the figure corresponding to Peale would be Bishop Fulton Sheen, whose television broadcasts in the 1950s were extremely popular; see Bruce, *Pray TV*, 32.
38. Louis Schneider and Sanford M. Dornbusch, 'Inspirational Religious Literature: From Latent to Manifest Functions of Religion', *American Journal of Sociology*, 62 (1957), 476–81.
39. Ibid. 478.
40. David E. Harrell, Jr., *Oral Roberts: An American Life* (Bloomington, Ind.: Indiana University Press, 1985), 28–9.
41. James Davidson Hunter, *Evangelicalism: The Coming Generation* (Chicago: University of Chicago, 1987) 69–70.
42. Jackson W. Carroll and Penny Long Marler, 'Culture Wars? Insights from Ethnographies of Two Protestant Seminaries', *Sociology of Religion*, 56 (1995), 1–20.
43. Dennis Hollinger, 'Enjoying God Forever: An Historical/Sociological Profile of the Health and Wealth Gospel in the USA', in John Fulton and Peter Gee (eds.), *Religion and Power: Decline and Growth* (London: British Sociological Association Study Group of Religion, 1991), 53–66.; David E. Harrell, *All Things Are Possible: The Healing and Charismatic Revivals in Modern America* (Bloomington, Ind.: Indiana University Press, 1975); and D. L. McConell, *A Different Gospel: A Historical and Biblical Analysis of the Modern Faith Movement* (Peabody, Mass.: Hendrickson, 1988).
44. Quoted in Jeffrey K. Hadden and Anson D. Shupe, *Televangelism: Power and Politics on God's Frontier* (New York: Henry Holt, 1988), 131.
45. Hollinger, 'Enjoying God', 56.
46. Jeffrey K. Hadden, 'Toward Desacralizing Secularization Theory', *Social Forces*, 65 (1987), 587–611; repr. in slightly abridged form as Reading 48 in Anthony Giddens (ed.), *Human Societies: A Reader* (Cambridge: Polity Press, 1992), 230–7. See also Jeffrey K. Hadden and Anson D. Shupe, 'Introduction', in Hadden and Shupe (eds.), *Prophetic Religions and Politics: Religion and the Political Order* (New York: Paragon House, 1986).

47. Richard Neuhaus, *The Naked Public Square: Religion and Democracy in America* (Grand Rapids, Mich.: Eerdmans, 1984).

48. Morris Janovitz, *The Last Half-Century: Societal Change and Politics in America* (Chicago: University of Chicago Press, 1978), 368.

49. The US fundamentalist luxury of quietism is partly explained by the lesser threat from hostile political forces and the greater degree of freedom in the more open US structure, but theology is also implicated. The Calvinism of Ulster and Scottish Presbyterianism lends itself much more readily than Arminian fundamentalism to the notion that the state or 'civil magistrate' should legislate for righteousness.

50. For a recent review of the effects of the NCR, see Steve Bruce, Peter Kivisto, and William H. Swatos (eds.), *The Rapture of Politics: The Christian Right as the United States Approaches the Year 2000.* (New Brunswick, NJ: Transaction, 1994).

51. For an account of the case from a protagonist on the liberal side, see Langdon Gilkey, *Creationism on Trial: Evolution and God at Little Rock* (Minneapolis: Winston Press, 1985).

52. An excellent lawyer's account of the NCR's progress with its agenda is given in John H. Garvey, 'Fundamentalism and American Law', in Martin Marty and R. Scott Appleby (eds.), *Fundamentalisms and the State: Remaking Politics, Economics and Militance* (Chicago: University of Chicago Press, 1993), 28–49.

53. Bruce, *Pray TV*, 162–97.

54. John H. Simpson, 'Moral Issues and Status Politics', in Robert C. Liebman and Robert Wuthnow (eds.), *The New Christian Right: Mobilization and Legitimation* (New York: Aldine, 1983), 188–207.

55. L. Sigelmann and S. Presser, 'Measuring Public Support for the New Christian Right: The Perils of Point Estimation', *Public Opinion Quarterly*, 52 (1988), 325–37.

56. Compare, for example, the tactics and relative successes of the NCR and the British Nationwide Festival of Light: Roy Wallis, *Salvation and Protest: Studies of Social and Religious Movements* (London: Frances Pinter, 1979), 130–71.

57. As suggested a number of times, we can produce two versions of this simple idea. The Durkheimian tradition stresses the *social* needs or the needs of the social system; the Stark and Bainbridge version owes more to George Homans'a exchange theory and rests the theory on universal *individual* needs.

# 7

# THE NEW RELIGIONS OF THE 1970s

O NE of the least expected features of the last thirty years has been the creation and growth in the USA and Western Europe of a large number of new religious movements.[1] At the same time as the mainstream churches were losing members and authority, young people in large numbers began to experiment with a wide range of new cults and sects. Some of these were Hindu and Buddhist imports from the Orient, a not entirely novel borrowing. The nineteenth-century new religious movement Theosophy drew on Eastern traditions and there were representatives of the major Hindu and Buddhist schools at the World Parliament of Religions in Chicago in 1893.[2] Zen Buddhism was briefly fashionable in the late 1950s. However, it was really only in the counter-culture of the late 1960s that large numbers of Westerners started to look to the spirituality of the East for sources of the transcendence apparently no longer available in the urban and industrial West. In the early 1970s, 3 per cent of San Franciscans surveyed claimed to have tried Zen Buddhist meditation and 5 per cent claimed to have tried Transcendental Meditation (TM). This is perhaps to be expected from America's west coast, but a national survey showed that 4 per cent of a sample of Americans also claimed to have tried TM. There was also the Meher Baba Movement, the Divine Light Mission, Krishna Consciousness, and the Healthy-Happy-Holy movement of Yogi Bhajan (a variant of Sikhism).[3]

The counter-culture also saw a flowering of psychotherapies that bordered on the religious. Some became very popular. Werner Erhard's Erhard Seminar Training or est (always with lower-case letters) claims to have trained over 20,000 people in the first three years of its life.[4] There were also Arica, Bioenergetics, Silva Mind Control, Insight, Scientology, The Farm, Kerista, Primal Therapy, Co-Counselling, Rebirthing, and many many more.[5] All were in the business of improving the self, but they differed from conventional psychotherapy because 'of an additional ingredient, namely the obsession with perfection. Perfecting the self leads almost inevitably into the religious.'[6] It does so, of course, because the claims made are so extravagant that one has to believe in some sort of supernatural to find them plausible, even if it is merely the supernatural nature of the human self. After all, Primal Therapy claims to produce 'complete consciousness'.

In this chapter I will describe a variety of new religions, explain their appeal, and consider what implication the phenomenon has for our understanding of the place of the supernatural in the modern world.

The variety of new religious movements is such that they seem often to have little in common other than being 'new' and being 'religious', and even those terms require stretching to accommodate some examples. None the less, we can make sense of them by grouping them into two types according to their relationship with the wider society and their response to the world (which, as I have suggested above, are the key questions for conceptualizing older religions as churches, sects, denominations, and cults).[7] Some of the new religions *reject* the world while some positively *affirm* it.

## World-Rejecting Movements

One of the best known (or most notorious) of the new religions is the Unification Church, which was founded in Korea in 1954 by the Revd Sun Myung Moon, the son of a Korean convert to evangelical Presbyterianism, as the Holy Spirit Association for the Unification of the World. The movement appeared in California in the early 1960s, where it had the good fortune to be studied by John Lofland, who called it the 'Divine Precepts' in his book *Doomsday Cult*.[8] The Moonies, as they were popularly known, had a very slow start in America and did not experience significant growth until the early 1970s, when Moon himself moved to the United States.

Moon's religion was a development of evangelical Christianity which believed that the Kingdom of God could be established on this earth with the overthrow of godless communism. Moon believed that Christianity needed to be superseded because it had failed to unite all the peoples of the world under the heavenly father. Disunity had paved the way for a decline in moral virtue among young people and the decline of the Christian Churches. Moon saw his role as one of completing the work that Christ had started but not finished: establishing the Kingdom of Heaven on earth. Hence its name: the *Unification* Church.

The Moonies view the mundane secular world as an evil place to be avoided as much as possible until one dies and leaves it for good. In the Moonie world-view, man's greed and pursuit of material gain have ruined the world and perverted all social relationships.

The typical world-rejecting movement is ascetic. The self-denial may take place in a communal setting, as was the case with the members of the International Society for Krishna Consciousness (ISKCON), who lived in considerable poverty in an 'ashram'. They rose at 3.00 a.m. to worship the Hindu deities in the Temple, spent two hours chanting sixteen rounds of the Hare Krishna mantra on their string of 108 beads, and then worked on domestic tasks in the ashram, or spent time fund-raising or proselytizing on the streets.[9] The Moonies did not require communal living but they did expect single adherents to devote most of their energies to promoting the movement and that usually meant working full time for it for very small rewards. A former Moonie offered this description of his typical day 'witnessing':

I have been flower selling for a week now. At the end of each afternoon, we return to the van, exhausted. For dinner—if lucky, we would receive a generous donation of unused burgers someone had begged from the McDonald's franchise down the road by telling the manager we were poor missionaries. If we weren't so lucky, we might dine on donated stale doughnuts and cold pizza.

Our group was collecting over a thousand tax-free dollars a day.

Each morning we picked up our order of roses from the San Francisco flower district. We slept in vans at night, eight in a row, brothers at one end, sisters at another. When family members were on the road for several days, we couldn't change clothes or shower. To even change a shirt in this crowded smelly vehicle could tempt the sisters to fall again, might stir and excite the sexual drives now buried deep within our unconscious.

Night after night we worked until two in the morning, doing bar runs . . . coaxing drunks to buy wilted roses for the angry wives awaiting them at home. At 2.30 we would drive to a local park, praying in unison in the darkness . . . After the gruelling ritual ended, we settled down for a night's sleep, a full hour and a half, for we must soon be up for pledge service Sunday morning.[10]

As we see in that description, world-rejecting movements were also puritanical. Ironically the new religions were often collectively condemned by middle America for encouraging promiscuous sex and drug-taking. The accusation of sexual impropriety is commonly levelled against any sort of religious experimentation and, given the heightened emotions involved in ecstatic religion, it is not always false, but more often than not it is deployed irrespective of a movement's actual teachings and practice. It is certainly a long way from the mark with the Moonies. Although they developed the slightly unusual practice of having mass weddings of members presided over by Revd and Mrs Moon, the Moonies had very old-fashioned views of the purpose of sex and rather an exalted view of the nuclear family, in which relations are meant to mirror those between the Heavenly Father and his earthly children. Moonies took vows of premarital celibacy and believed that sexual intercourse should be permitted only within monogamous heterosexual marriage. They not only avoided drugs but they were also opposed to smoking and drinking alcohol.

The world-rejecting new religious movements were demanding. Self-denial is a high price to pay and followers are expected to pay it, with a change in their lives drastic enough to be described as 'conversion'. There was often also a high price in the more immediate sense. For many recruits the breaking of ties to the old world and old identity was accompanied by handing over savings to the movement. Moses David's Children of God was largely funded by new recruits donating their wealth.[11]

Finances for People's Temple members were fairly simple: everything went to Jim Jones. Families signed over homes, property and pay checks to the temple. To raise additional money for the cult, some members occasionally begged on street corners.

Members who did not live in the Church had to tithe a minimum of 25 per cent of their earnings. Those living on church property gave everything to Jones, who returned to them a two dollar weekly allowance.[12]

The practice of donating all one's worldly goods to the movement caused considerable offence. Given the widespread hypocrisy about sexuality in Western cultures, where a rhetorical commitment to monogamy coexists with a very high rate of extramarital affairs, the hostility to the alleged promiscuity of new religious movements could be interpreted as middle America's anger at having its lack of integrity exposed. But the rejection of wealth was a straightforward attack on a dominant social value. Many middle-class Americans could simply not believe that their sons and daughters would willingly hand over their cash to some guru or swami unless they were under malign influence.[13]

The world-rejecting movement typically accords a very low value to the human self. Just as in traditional Christianity, the self is essentially sinful and perfection is reached by taming it and subordinating it to some higher authority. The self is to be developed only in so far as that development glorifies God (usually through glorifying the leader of the movement). As Beckford says of the Moonies:

it is important to cultivate and refine one's spirituality to the point of . . . perfection. But this is no part of a programme of self-discovery for its own sake. Human potential is deliberately realized for the sake of 'Father' (that is, Moon). Nearly everything is dedicated to him or done in his name. . . . Consequently the self is conceived as an inferior, subordinate entity that can only achieve perfection in and through the recognition of its necessary dependence on Father.[14]

Finally, the typical world-rejecting group is hierarchical, with the founder being seen as being especially close to God, if not actually being God incarnate.

## World-Affirming Movements

While exotic and sectarian world-rejecting religions attracted most attention, the most popular and influential new religious movements were very different. The world-affirming movements generally lacked most of the features associated with 'religion': they had no church, no collective ritual of worship, no fully developed theology, and no ethical system (in the sense of general principles which tell us what to want and how to behave). They were happy with much of the secular world and had a generally positive attitude to humankind and to the 'self'. Embodying that incurable 'can-do' optimism that produced Norman Vincent Peale and his *Power of Positive Thinking*, the world-affirming groups argued that people are not so much evil as *restricted*. We all contain enormous potential power which we need to be taught to utilize. Particularly, we need to be taught to free ourselves from the internal constraints that are the legacy of the way our parents raised us.

An early example of this sort of movement is Silva Mind Control, invented by Mexican American José Silva in the early 1950s. It is a training involving techniques of self-hypnosis and visualization which takes about forty-eight hours and which

can train anyone to remember what appears to be forgotten, to control pain, to speed healing, to abandon unwanted habits, to spark intuition so that the sixth sense becomes a creative problem-solving part of daily life. With all this comes a cheerful inner peace, a quiet optimism based on first hand evidence that we are more in control of our lives than we ever imagined.[15]

Similar in its belief that we all possess vast untapped potential is Insight.[16] Insight trainers believe that all of us have a 'centre' which already knows everything we want to know. We can be liberated from fear, guilt, and anxiety; from the residues of the past which dominate our present responses and produce inappropriate reactions; from self-limiting images that make us feel inferior; from the sense of ourselves as victims. The purported point of the training is to make people accept responsibility for their lives. To do that we must abandon our rationalistic and cerebral culture and appreciate that the heart is as powerful a centre of energy as the mind.

The techniques for achieving this 'empowering liberation' varied from movement to movement but most involved role-playing designed to force people to abandon their inhibitions, to discuss their problems openly, and to mix freely with others. That is, they were modelled on the now quite common form of the encounter group.

## Scientology

Chapter 3 described the ways in which the church and sect forms of religious expression evolved into the denomination as they accommodated to the realities of a culturally diverse world. Though that is the major trend, not all organizational evolution is in the direction of toleration and accommodation. The creation of the Church of Scientology is an example of a shift in the other direction. L. Ron Hubbard first presented his thoughts on what he called 'Dianetics' in an article in *Astounding Science Fiction*.[17] Hubbard believed that the human mind was a marvellous computer. Operating perfectly, it would have total recall of all sense impressions and vastly improved mental agility. This state Hubbard called 'clear'. His contrast with clear was that of a mechanical calculating machine that had one or two keys stuck down so that all its calculations went wrong (in the 1950s that was an arrestingly modern metaphor!). Hubbard believed that the source of these stuck keys was the mind's natural desire to avoid pain. Painful experiences in our past were stored in our subconscious as 'engrams' and prevented our functioning fully. The various techniques of Dianetics were designed to discover the origins of these engrams and, by forcing the patient to confront them, clear them away until the mind was free to function at full capacity, as a 'clear'. To add scientific credibility to what sounded like an easy-listening version of Freud's theory of the subconscious, Hubbard brought in a machine. The E (for engram) Meter was a primitive lie detector. Holding a tin can wired to a dial which could be seen only by the Dianetics counsellor, the subject would be questioned until a swing of the needle suggested that a sensitive topic had been discovered. Then that area was probed for evidence of engrams.

Initially Dianetics was taken up as just one therapy among many by people who dabbled in a whole range of similar popularized derivatives of Freudian psychoanalysis. They did not join anything or commit a great deal of their time, money, or identity to the enterprise. Nor did they regard it as being superior to a variety of other kinds of psychotherapy technique they used. It is typical of the cultic world that cult members see themselves as seekers who have a right to select ideas and practices and to synthesize them into their own package. Hubbard quickly became unhappy about his lack of control over Dianetics. In particular, he resented the way in which Dianetics practitioners added their own tuppence-worth to his teachings and thus asserted equal insight into the human condition. Hubbard was also disappointed with the small numbers who stayed loyal to his therapy. People took up Dianetics in the search for a cure for a particular psychological problem. Perhaps it worked. Perhaps, as with most of our psychological problems, the bad bit just passed. Either way, a lot of people dabbled and then moved on.

Hubbard's response was to claim new revelations and insights that he used to change Dianetics into the sectarian religion of Scientology. The doctrines and the practices were codified and presented as a series of stages in a clear and lengthy career structure for consumers. Part of Hubbard's new revelation was a belief in rebirth. When you completed the first round of courses and eliminated all the engrams from this life, there were still those from previous lives to be removed before you became an 'operating thetan'! An additional advantage of the staged career was that it could be used to reinforce consumer commitment. The courses were expensive. The more of them you did, the more you had invested in Scientology, literally as well as figuratively, and the greater the pressure to continue to believe. Furthermore, members were given large discounts on course costs if they recruited and trained others. The consumer started out as an autonomous client buying the psychotherapeutic services of Scientology, but the product was marketed so as to draw clients into becoming followers.

Scientology, Bioenergetics, and Silva Mind Control were popularized lay psychotherapies with their roots in humanistic psychology. Transcendental Meditation (TM) and Rajneeshism offered a similar outcome but from a very different tradition.[18]

## Transcendental Meditation

TM is a meditational technique taught to those who are initiated in a brief ceremony in which the initiator conveys to the new mediator a personal mantra. The person then meditates on that mantra for twenty minutes morning and evening every day. It was brought to the West by the Hindu Mahareshi Mahesh Yogi in the early 1950s, but Western interest was stimulated in 1968 when, prompted by George Harrison (whose involvement lasted more than a weekend), the Beatles travelled to India to visit the Mahareshi.

Although meditation in its original Hindu context is usually associated with a rigorous programme of discipleship and with renouncing the world, TM is now promoted as a technique for becoming more efficient and effective in the here and now. As we can see from the following text of a 1995 newspaper advertisement, the primary appeal is to instrumentalism, and the ease of acquiring the technique is stressed.

A technique for the New Year which relaxes, revitalises and recharges your energy to get more out of life. It leaves you feeling positive, alert and clear with the calmness and inner contentment to tackle life with enthusiasm. It helps to protects you from stress and future ill-health.

Transcendental Meditation has been thoroughly verified by over 500 independent scientific research studies. Hundreds of UK doctors have learnt TM and many recommended it to patients. A simple technique to develop your true potential. It requires no belief or change in lifestyle. It takes just a few minutes everyday, but will work for you for a lifetime.[19]

Claims to supernatural powers have not been dropped entirely, but they have been shifted to the background. Meditators can, if they wish, 'upgrade' by enrolling in the Siddhis programme, which is supposed to equip one with such special powers as the ability to levitate.

Although it is thoroughly individualistic, TM claims that the supernatural powers it channels have beneficial social consequences. There is the obvious cumulative effect: if enough individuals get saved, then the world will change. But TM also claims that, if a critical mass of people meditate regularly, the level of cosmic consciousness will rise sufficiently to have a beneficial effect far beyond that created by the sum of the individuals. Thus the movement sometimes sends 'Governors of the Age of Enlightenment' to crisis spots, where they sit in their hotel rooms and meditate. As a TM magazine puts it, they 'enliven the ground state of natural law deep within themselves and produce the gentle impulses of coherence which neutralise turbulence and disorder in collective consciousness . . . Violence naturally calms down.'[20]

Such claims were elaborated and widely advertised in 1992 when the Natural Law Party (NLP) fielded some 300 candidates in a British general election. The party's manifesto offered the improvement in cosmic consciousness which will result from meditation as a solution to unemployment, crime, and all the other ills for which the conventional parties were suggesting more mundane solutions. A paragraph from the NLP manifesto is well worth quoting, as it shows the extent to which TM (like many world-affirming movements) attempts to position itself, not as rejection of conventional Western scientific thought, but as its full and final development. Instead of presenting itself as a Hindu religion which is true because the Vedic books and Hindu tradition say it is true, TM now offers natural science as proof of its correctness. The manifesto of the NLP says:

In response to the call of the nation we offer something new from the field of science; we offer our discovery of the Constitution of the Universe. The Constitution of the Universe, ever lively in its eternal wakefulness within every grain of creation, governs the universe with perfect orderliness and without a problem. The Unified Field of Natural Law, the field of pure consciousness or pure intelligence, is at the unmanifest basis of creation and governs all levels of life through Natural Law. The Unified Field Theories of Quantum Physics ($N = 8$ Supergravity and Heterotic Superstring etc.) from the standpoint of modern science have identified this ultimate reality of life, the Unified Field of Natural Law.[21]

## Rajneeshism

The Bhagwan Shree Rajneesh was a professor of philosophy at an Indian university before he founded an ashram at Poona.[22] Thousands of young affluent middle-class Westerners flocked there to hear his message. Unlike the rigorous discipleship of traditional Hinduism, the Bhagwan's neo-sannyasin or 'new-disciple' movement was fun. All that was necessary was to wear something of an orange colour, to take on a new name given by the Bhagwan, to wear his picture, and to practice the Bhagwan's meditation technique. Most meditation involves relaxing the body and clearing the mind by focusing on some simple thought or phrase. In Rajneesh Dynamic Meditation, the meditator deliberately increases his or her stress to an acute level before letting go and relaxing. This is done by rapid, chaotic breathing, through which repressed tension and emotion is contacted and brought to the surface. The repressed feelings are then released through catharsis—screaming, shouting, crying, laughing, or whatever form it takes. This is followed by a third stage in which the meditator jumps up and down, arms in the air, shouting 'Hoo! Hoo! Hoo!' Only after these three active steps, each lasting ten minutes, does the meditator relax into silence and stillness.

The movement became notorious for its sessions in which small groups of people were locked in a bare padded room and encouraged to 'let it all hang out'. One unusual feature of these events was that they often ended in group sex.

Unlike Hubbard, the Bhagwan was happy to endorse eclecticism. As one would expect from someone with his roots in Hinduism with its central proposition that diversity is an illusion that distracts us from the fundamental one-ness of all things, Rajneesh was content to allow his followers to bring with them any and all of the previous therapies in which they had been involved. Thus the Rajneeshies offered sessions of aromatherapy, Alexander technique, est, and so on. Michael Barnett, a leading figure in a variety of human potential movements in Britain, became a prominent neo-sannyasin and many participants had a background in a range of secular self-oriented disciplines. According to a University of Oregon survey, 11 per cent of the sannyasins had higher degrees in psychology or psychiatry and the same proportion had first degrees in those subjects.[23]

Perhaps because most of his followers were from the United States or perhaps, as some critics have suggested, because he was facing a very large tax bill in Poona, Rajneesh decided to move to the USA, and in 1980 the Rajneesh Foundation bought a 64,000-acre ranch near the small town of Antelope, Oregon. The neo-sannyasins took over the town and named it Rajneesh and on the ranch built the much bigger community they called Rajneeshpuram. Relations with the locals degenerated. There was arson, burning, threats of violence, and much recourse to law before the community broke up under the strain of its own internal divisions. In 1985 the Bhagwan was expelled from the USA and a number of his senior lieutenants were jailed for serious offences.

Rajneesh returned to Poona in 1987 and died three years later. Liberated from the erratic behaviour of the living Rajneesh but able to present him on large video screens, his followers have made Poona into a major New Age tourist resort, and, under the name 'Osho' (which he took in his last years), Rajneesh's books still sell well.[24]

From the examples of Scientology, TM, and Rajneeshism we can describe the typical world-affirming new religion in summary as follows. It does not require renunciation of the world; in principle the world is good. The great evil is that more people are not able to enjoy the good things of life because their abilities remain hidden or constrained. The movement offers techniques that will free the inner self and its potential. Not much is required by way of commitment. In order to give the movement some continuity and stability, there is usually a higher level of knowledge which is revealed only to a select group of extra-committed devotees. Thus Scientology, TM, and Rajneeshism developed a strong inner circle of practitioners who worked for the movement and who might sensibly be described as followers, but most people who participated in the movements did so as consumers. They learnt the basic meditation techniques; or, in the case of est and Insight, they spent a couple of weekends at a conference centre and then returned to their conventional lives. The organizations operate more like corporate commercial enterprises than churches. They advertise and employ marketing techniques to promote services which are offered on a commercial basis, with a set fee structure and discounts for bulk purchasing or payment in advance.

And they do not require much by way of change of belief. Although they tend to be informed by quite complex ideologies and the inner core of adepts will be well versed in the justifications for the therapies and empowering techniques, it is not necessary for ordinary clients or consumers to understand these or be committed to them. As it says in the TM advert, no belief is required.

World-affirming movements differ in the extent to which there is some power other than the self, something which, if it is not sufficiently personal to be worshipped, one can at least merge with in an ecstatic experience. Whether or not Rajneeshism and TM are 'theistic' is rather a matter of which layer of the onion one happens to be peeling off at the time. In the Hinduism from which they grew, the supernatural power can present itself or be seen as a God or Gods (Vishnu or Shiva, for example), but even these entities are 'really' only the embodiment of a force which, while it has moral purpose, is none the less impersonal. Such a force is clearly a long way from the personal God of Christianity or Islam, but it still has sufficient presence to give Rajneeshism and TM a more theistic feel than such explicitly self-oriented movements as est and Exegesis. In those, the experience of God that is offered is of the God within.[25] This difference reflects their origins: the former an industrialized version of Eastern mysticism; the latter a mysticized version of industrial therapy. They meet in drawing on some notion of a cosmic consciousness to explain how the individual self may have powers and potentials beyond its obvious material constraints but it is the self, the I, the me, which is the main focus of attention.

While conventional Christianity does offer benefits in this life, its major claims are located in the next world and are thus relatively immune to refutation. I can discover that getting right with Jesus does not save my marriage but I cannot know that it does not 'save us from the grave'. Likewise the claims of world-rejecting movements. We might imagine that world-affirming movements would have a major problem with their claims to empower people: the real world would refute them at every turn. Meditating does not save my marriage nor win me that promotion. It is very obvious that much of what happens to us is not within our control; our ability to alter the circumstances in which we work and live is slight. Although personal qualities may raise or lower our chances of getting a job, they can do so only within the constraints of the labour market, and it seems that even national governments have only a small influence on the macro-economic forces that shape unemployment rates. We might suppose, then, that those who turn to world-affirming movements to make themselves more effective and powerful would quickly become disillusioned, but those movements that have endured have been able to put an interestingly ambiguous gloss on what counts as evidence that the therapy or technique is working. There is a paradox in that what many promote both as the road to success and as the proof of success itself, is acceptance of the way things are. As Werner Erhard put it in an est seminar: 'Life is always perfect just the way it is. When you realise that, then no matter how strongly it may appear to be otherwise, you know that whatever is happening right now will turn out to be all right. Knowing this you are in a position to begin mastering life.'[26] Or is that passively accepting life?

One finds the same breadth of interpretation in the accounts of the effectiveness of their 'chanting' given by members of Soka Gakkai. They chant for real changes in the world—a new job, a better car—but when they are asked if the chanting worked, they may say the change initially desired did not occur but none the less it worked because they realized that they were meant to be in the job they were in, that that was really the place for them.[27]

## The Social Origins of the New Religions

Many world-affirming religions are opposed to ratiocination and rationality. Werner Erhard, founder of est, described understanding as the booby prize.[28] What is sought is feeling and experience, not cerebration. Doing is more important than thinking and being is more important than doing. None the less, the world-affirming religions, as much as the world-rejecting ones, owe their popularity to the rationalization of the modern world. Rationalization is the process whereby life has become organized in terms of instrumental considerations: the concern with technical efficiency, the maximization of calculability and predictability, and the subordination of nature to human purposes. Rationalization carries in its wake what Weber, in quoting Schiller, liked to call 'the disenchantment of the world': a loss of a sense of magic, mystery, prophecy, and the sacred.[29]

Rationalization greatly affects our private as well as our public lives. The family is separated from production, children from adults (in schools and leisure pursuits), where we live from where we work, and so on. Modern life is for many people so fragmented that they find it increasingly difficult to draw on their public roles for a satisfying and fulfilling sense of identity. Many jobs are routine and mechanized; they lack intrinsic interest or opportunities for job satisfaction. Moreover, achievement—what one can do rather than who one is—has become a major preoccupation for people whose image of how they should live, derived from the mass media, leads them to believe that comfort, happiness, and satisfactory relationships are achievable by everyone. Old community structures have broken down and mobility, social and geographical, makes it increasingly difficult to recreate them in the anonymous world of the city.

Rationalization in these various forms provides the backdrop to the emergence of the new religions. It affects particularly those experiencing the transition from home to the wider social world of work and college, thus most sharply striking those in late adolescence and early adulthood. It was precisely such people who, in the counter-culture of the 1960s and early 1970s, reacted against the dehumanization of the public world. Through political protest, the hippie movement, and the commune movement, young people sought to transform or re-create the world in which they lived. But political protest faced severe repression, and hippie culture and the commune movement largely disintegrated under the impact of drugs and exploitation.[30] Young people committed to a sense that the world could be radically created anew came to see that the transformation they sought could not be achieved solely by human effort. Some had been led towards a more spiritual and mystical view of the world as a result of their drug experiences. By the early 1970s, many young people in North America and Europe were available for a movement which claimed that some divine agency or power was poised to intervene in the world, that the millennium would be brought about by supernatural means if people would commit themselves zealously to the endeavour. The failure of the counter-culture was thus the principal source of recruits to the world-rejecting new religions.

The world-affirming new religions had their origins in more enduring and pervasive features of advanced capitalist societies. Such societies create widespread aspirations for the values of power, status, personal attractiveness, happiness, and the like but distribute these resources (or the legitimate means to gain them) unequally among the population. For those people who find the idea of the supernatural at all plausible but whose interests are focused on the here and now rather than on the next life, the world-affirming new religions offer a promise to enhance the individual's capacity for rational action by religious means that transcend whatever educational or socialization facilities characterize the wider society, and . . . to teach the individual the potency of extra-rational agencies and facilities that will allow him to transcend the merely rational with a superior and arcane wisdom.[31]

The new movements provided the recipe, technique, or knowledge required to reduce the gap between aspiration and actuality. Either, in such movements as TM or Scientology, people would learn to increase their abilities so as to be able to achieve their goals or, in such movements as est or Rajneeshism, they would learn that the present was the only moment there is and that happiness lay in wanting, experiencing, and celebrating what they already had, rather than in trying to get what they thought they wanted.

Those who participated in these movements were typically from the more comfortable sectors of Western societies, from social groups which had benefited from above-average education and incomes; the working-classes were absent from the new religions. Cost no doubt had something to do with it. An Exegesis weekend cost £200 at 1984 prices; an est weekend $400. But there was also an ironic resonance of class interest. Consider Sir Henry Newbolt's famous lines:

> And it's not for the sake of a ribboned coat
> Or the selfish hope of a season's fame
> But his Captain's hand on his shoulder smote
> 'Play up! Play up! and play the game!'

They were written about cricket in an English public (that is fee-paying and élite) school and addressed to the upper classes of the foremost world power (and those who would emulate them). Just as the injunction that how one plays the game is more important than winning makes most sense to those who are assured of victory, so an invitation to abandon all striving, all desire for power or achievement, and all ambition is least offensive to those who are doing rather well. Such apparent self-abnegation has little attraction for those who have yet to sample the good things that success and affluence may bring. Hence the notable absence of the working-class and of racial and ethnic minorities.

In an achievement-oriented society there develops a market for securing success but success may have a high price in repression and the postponement of gratification. A high level of self-control and repression of instinctual desires is normally the price paid for achievement by the middle classes. A participant in an Actualizations training seminar said:

All my life, I've been an achiever. I've always won all of the 'Best of Everything' awards. I've been rising fast in the corporation I work for, looking forward—somewhat uneasily—to the day when they make me president of the company. It's a goal I have absolutely no doubt that I'll achieve. There's just one drawback. I feel the closer I get, the less human I am. It's robbing me of my humanity.[32]

While they have become comfortable in material terms, some people may feel that they have done so at the price of repressing their 'real' selves, creating a strait-jacket around their expressive desires, and placing barriers between themselves and their loved ones. Thus there arises a demand—met by some of the world-affirming new religions—for a context and method for liberating spontaneity, for contacting the real self behind the masks and the performances, and for feeling and sharing intimacy and love, if only for a weekend, before the return to the impersonal realities of urban industrial life.

However, it is not just the human problems which world-affirming new religions aim to solve which point to a middle-class market. There are also entry qualifications. I will return to this when discussing New Age religion, but it seems clear that to feel at home among the neo-sannyasins or the students of est you need a degree of self-regard and self-confidence in order to believe that you deserve and can benefit from that sort of attention. It is a lot easier to imagine that, appropriately adjusted, the self is a powerful autonomous agent if you work in a job which offers some autonomy and some opportunity for creativity than if one is part of a large semi-skilled manual labour force and pressingly aware of how little one can affect anything. It also helps to be literate and articulate. There are books to be read and there are workshops in which you must talk about your problems.

There is a further sense in which the world-affirming new religions are a product of the rationalization of the modern world and that is in their view of the self as an appropriate site for remedial action. In Chapter 1 I introduced Berger, Berger, and Kellner's work on the implications of technology.[33] Although the styles of thought and assumptions that inevitably come with the use of technology have their origins and their most immediate impact in the world of work and the economy (for example, in leading managements to model relations between personnel on the form of a production-line process), they spread into other areas of life and they affect even those spheres which were thought to be not only relatively immune to rationalization but to provide 'rest and recreation' for a soul dehumanized by the world of work. We see the rational industrial commitment to improving productivity and efficiency in our remedial approach to our bodies and our personalities. We are no longer expected to be 'ourselves'. Indeed, we have a duty to discover our 'real' selves by working at it. This is one of the paradoxes of naturalism. We are supposed 'just to be ourselves' but we attain that authentic state by working hard to change into the sort of person the instructor or therapist or 'resource person' thinks we ought to be. Relationships have to be 'worked at'. A room of middle-class people talking about their childhoods is a 'workshop'. The publishers of those monthly magazines—'Buy Part 1 and get Part 2 free!'— that build into a comprehensive library of instruction for gardening, home decorating, or car repair now offer manuals for improving fitness, beauty, and personal development.

But notice the point of such work and attention. Unlike the disciplines of the medieval monk or the 'Method' of the Methodists, these modern techniques are not designed to help us conform to an external ethical code or better to glorify God. They are designed to make us happy: to allow us to fulfil our human potential. As Philip Rieff puts it: 'a sense of well-being has become the end, rather than a by-product of striving after some superior communal end.'[34]

## Human Potential and the Organization Man

One of the features of human behaviour that makes its study so rewarding is our ability to go beyond simply accommodating ourselves to the world around us and to attempt to reverse major social change. In being able to see which way the wind is blowing we can bend with it but we can also fight against it. One of the interesting developments of the human-potential movement has been its co-option by people who are determined to reverse the division of the modern world into two spheres: the public and the private, the world of work and the home. A large number of individuals and organizations now offer 'human-potential' training for corporate management. Cunard Ellerman has sent half its British staff on courses influenced by est. In the USA, Pacific Bell has sent thousands of its employees on a course based on the teachings of Gurdjieff.[35] There are even capitalist companies staffed entirely by 'self-religionists'. Heelas has written at length about Programmes Ltd., which was Europe's largest direct telephone selling company in the mid-1980s and the staff of which were all Exegesis graduates.

This paradoxical inversion of the expected relationship between self-religion and the bureaucratic rationality which most self-religions regard as the root of many personal evils could be viewed cynically as just another example of youthful rebellion compromised, the old hippie's sell-out, but this would be a little unfair to those involved and would miss the most interesting feature of the *modus vivendi*. Rather what we see is a complex accommodation between the goal of self-realization and the massive solidity of bureaucratic capitalism. The self-religions elevate the self to such potency that they deny the normal laws of causation. An est staff member working in telephone sales told Tipton: 'Here I sat, dialling the phone, hour after hour—nobody home. Finally I realized that it was me who wasn't "home"!'[36] The liberated self has power. If you fail, it is because you are at fault. The key to success is to stop trying. Success comes from cultivated detachment rather than from striving. I am reminded of two traditional Zen Buddhist stories. A master calligrapher was chiding his disciple, who was trying to write the symbol for enlightenment on a large banner. Every version was criticized. The harder the disciple tried, the more hostile the master's response. Frustrated the disciple, shouted 'Look! Out the window!' and while the master's back was turned he hurriedly scribbled another version. On turning back, the master judged that work to be perfect. The second story concerns the Zen archers. Rather than practise their archery, they practised their meditation, so that, once they had attained enlightenment, they could fire blindfold and hit the target. The assumption is that there is a order to the cosmos. Properly attune yourself to its rhythms and you will succeed effortlessly and do so in circumstances where no amount of conscious striving could produce the result. The self-religionist can offer his skills to a corporation because, like the Zen archer, he is not aiming for material success. The rewards no longer matter to him. Furthermore, success will not taint him because he knows its shallowness. A third Zen story will make the point. An elderly monk and his disciple, riding in a pony cart, come to a pretty maiden standing by the side of a muddy road. The monk stops the cart, descends, carries the girl across the track, sets her down on the far side, reas-

cends and drives off. The disciple fumes for miles. Eventually the
monk asks him what is wrong and the disciple chides his master for
carrying the young woman. The master replies: 'I left the girl
behind on the roadside. Are you still carrying her?' The enlightened
person loses this-worldly desires. Having lost them, he no longer
needs to be pious or self-denying in actions because his soul has
become Teflon-coated. The harmful residues of the material world
no longer stick to the true inner self. The rewards of successful striving no longer matter to the enlightened soul. To reject them is to
show they still matter. So one might as well accept them. So carry
on being a yuppie banker.

The thinking of the corporation that buys such training will be
quite different. On the one hand, there is the belief that the rationality of modern bureaucracies discourages initiative and thus fails
to make the best use of staff. On the other hand, there is the reasoning that anything is worth trying that might improve productivity and competitiveness, no matter how unlikely it looks.

## Secularization and New Religious Movements

What does the rise of new religious movements in the 1970s tells us
about the place of religion in the modern world?

Even with the increased life span and affluence of the industrial
West there are still sufficient occasions for us to feel dissatisfied with
the mundane world and hence to remain interested in the possibility of the supernatural. Unlike most other animal species, human
beings have no natural limits on their desires. There is nothing in
our biological make-up that sets limits to our wants and so ensures
that we can be satisfied.[37] Indeed, there is a certain perversity that
means that improvement in our standards of living and an increase
in consumption seem to fuel rather than satisfy desires. Emile
Durkheim argued that case well in his explanation for suicide rates
increasing, not just in times of economic depression, but also in
times of unexpected prosperity.[38] But even without the difficulty of
our desires in this world constantly outstripping our capacity to satisfy them, we would have the problem of an intellect that is capable
of imagining beyond our lives; the very fact that we must all die is a
potent and persistent source of unhappiness.

Stark and Bainbridge have offered an extremely complex and

scholarly version of these points to argue that religion is inevitable or, to put it the other way round, that secularization is impossible.[39] We all have desires which cannot be met and so we are in the market for 'compensators', which can be either substitutes for those things we really want or promises that we will get them in the next life. Stark and Bainbridge believe that only religions can provide sufficiently powerful compensators because only they can invoke the supernatural. Hence, so long as life is nasty, brutish, and short—and because our expectations rise with our circumstances we will always see it as that, no matter how sweet and long it is—we will be in the market for religion. If this is the case, then the religious 'economy' should always be in steady state because demand is created by universal needs. In a mistaken belief that modern people cannot accept what seemed reasonable to the peasants of the Middle Ages, the mainstream Christian churches move away from supernaturalism and become more secular and decline (as they have done in the last thirty years) and new religions will arise to fill the gap. Stark and Bainbridge are wise enough not to predict which new religion will be the one to fill the gap, but they insist that one will.[40]

Do new religious movements fill the gap left by the decline of the major churches? The increasing unpopularity of the major religious traditions certainly leaves a lot of people free and available for recruitment to some alternative. Without accepting Stark and Bainbridge's major claim that enduring human needs can only be met by a religion, we can expect some connection between the decline of the majors and the proliferation of the alternatives. But, while the collapse of the mainstream churches in Britain and Europe has made a large number of people available to join new religious movements, relatively few have taken up the offer. At the start of the century around 25 per cent of the adult British population was in membership of the mainstream Christian churches. Now it is around 10 per cent. That leaves somewhere around 36 million adults outside the churches. In the 1980s alone more than five million people were lost to the mainstream churches but the total membership of new religious movements in Britain was less than five or six thousand. If it was six thousand, then only one in every six thousand available British adults joined a new religious movement. Though the major churches in the United States have not declined to the same extent, the same point obtains, and recent figures from Canada have been used to argue the same case.[41]

There is also a problem of distribution. According to the Stark and Bainbridge theory, new religious movements come in two types. When the religious tradition is strong, then various social tensions produce schisms from the main traditions and these are sects. When the society is not very religious, then new religions of a distinctly different and innovative kind appear. These, according to Stark and Bainbridge, are cults. Or, as they put it: 'sects reflect efforts by the churched to remain churched . . . cults reflect efforts by the unchurched to become churched.'[42] It follows then that the more innovative, 'cultic' (in their term) new religious movements should be stronger in Europe, a very secular place, than in the USA. Although Stark and Bainbridge claim that to be the case, the evidence is by no means unambiguous.[43] Reliable membership figures are almost impossible to find. Many active seekers after new religious forms of enlightenment travel from country to country and the total numbers involved are so small that the presence of a few hundred young Americans enjoying the permissiveness of Stockholm or Amsterdam can distort any international comparison. It is possible to count the number of cult offices or headquarters per country, but, given that any movement with a universal mission will want a presence in most capital cities, this will make smaller countries look relatively more receptive to religious innovation than large ones, even if the number of Moonies and Rajneeshies in Norway is minuscule.

A more firmly established problem with the Stark–Bainbridge thesis is that the wrong new religions have been the most successful and enduring ones. The notion that new religious movements act as a counter-balance to the internal secularization or decline of the mainstream churches would be more persuasive if it were the more obviously 'religious' movements—that is, the sectarian and world-rejecting ones—which were most popular and most persistent. But it is the world-affirming ones—those that promote individual instrumentalism, the psychologizing of religion, and offer mundane this-worldly gratifications—that have done best. In so far as people who chant in Soka Gakkai or meditate in TM or attend est seminars or Insight weekends feel that these things have worked for them, the benefit has been in terms of reconciling them to the world as it is and allowing them to continue to perform the mundane social roles they were performing anyway. Either involvement has no lasting effect or it makes the people involved more effective in their mundane roles. Far from providing any sort of challenge to the dominant political structure, economic structure, or culture, the world-affirming new religion confirms people in either their acquiescence in or their active commitment to the status quo. That is, joining Soka Gakkai UK makes very little difference to the world of the Soka Gakkai 'chanter' and none at all to the rest of the world. The 'expressive' capitalists of the self-religions who are working on their 'selves' while carrying out a mundane job may see themselves as being driven by quite different motives from their unenlightened colleagues who just do the job. The difference in motivation might matter a great deal to the est and Exegesis graduates, but it makes little or no difference to the job. The business is the same and, with the exception of an increase in 'psycho babble', the world is still the same. There are no consequences for the operation of the social system.

This is in considerable contrast to the new religions of the eighteenth and nineteenth centuries. Though Methodism, for example, was thoroughly individualistic and promoted personal philanthropy as an alternative to radical political and social change, it made a difference. First it dramatically and visibly changed the lives of its adherents and secondly it changed the world around them. The dissenters were to the fore of the anti-Slavery movement; they founded savings banks and mutual insurance societies; they created temperance organizations; and they promoted widespread literacy. It is hard to see any comparable impact of the present wave of new religious movements.

The years since the 1960s have been particularly hard on the world-rejecting new religions. The disappearance of the counter-culture and the onset of recession meant that fewer young people were available, rebellious, and rejecting materialism to provide continuing cohorts of recruits. Members aged and produced children. Some movements adapted to these changes in the time-honoured fashion (as outlined in Chapter 4) of becoming less hostile to the world around them, more conventional in structure and appearance, more denominational in character, and drifting towards a more world-accommodating position. This approach can be seen in the Unification Church, which has established a more conventional parochial ministry to service a constituency that may attend its services but which is disinclined to commit everything to the movement. Similarly, the Hare Krishna devotees have begun to find a new clientele and basis for support among the Indian communities of Europe and North America, willing to donate funds, attend temple ceremonies, and otherwise use the services and facilities of the movement, but without a total commitment.

In some cases the movement so intensely rejected the surrounding society that it produced a reaction that destroyed it (Charles
Manson's Family[44] in California), or that led it to destroy itself in
anticipation of external attacks (the mass suicide in 1978 of the
members of Jim Jones's Peoples Temple in Jonestown, Guyana).[45] In
other cases reactive hostility and the fear of severe control have led
the movement virtually to go underground, as is the case with the
Children of God (also known as the Family of Love or the Family).[46]
In short, such movements have largely disappeared as a consequence of social-control measures evoked by their disregard for, and
hostility towards, conventional society.

The world-affirming movements have not generally evoked such
severe opposition, largely because they endorse many conventional
social norms and values. Moreover, the clientele for their services
has not disappeared; indeed it seems likely to persist as long as there
is unequal distribution of valued attributes and a widespread sense
of everyone's right to possess them. However, these movements
exist in a market for the services and commodities they offer. They
must compete with new brand names entering the market more
effectively packaged or more closely geared to the latest market
needs. The demand for means of self-expression and overcoming
repression may be high when the economy is buoyant and everyone
wants to relax and enjoy life. When recession appears, movements
too heavily committed to an earlier market trend may go to the
wall, while other forms which provide recipes for success in the corporate jungle when unemployment threatens may flourish.

But in coming to a measured judgement of the impact of the new
religious movements of the 1960s and 1970s we should note that,
though exotic, they were always very small and most people's
involvement was very short-lived. What Wuthnow says about the
USA can readily be extended to Europe: 'the new religions scarcely
constituted a major reshaping of American religion. Many age categories and many segments of the population were scarcely affected
by these movements at all.'[47]

## Notes

1. This chapter was drafted in collaboration with the late Roy Wallis and its
virtues owe a considerable amount to his extensive writings on new religious
movements. Its vices are all my own.

2. J. Stillson Judah, *The History and Philosophy of the Metaphysical Movements in America* (Philadelphia: Westminster Press, 1968), and Peter Washington, *Madame Blavatsky's Baboon: Theosophy and the Emergence of the Western Guru* (London: Secker, 1993).
3. Robert Wuthnow, *The Restructuring of American Religion* (Princeton: Princeton University Press, 1988), p. 151.
4. Ibid. 151.
5. For extensive descriptive listings, see J. Gordon Melton, *Encyclopedic Handbook of Cults in America* (New York: Garland Publishing, 1986), and *The Encyclopedia of American Religions* (Detroit: Gale, 1989).
6. Paul Heelas, 'Western Europe: Self-Religions', in Stewart Sutherland and Peter Clarke (eds.), *The World's Religions* (London: Routledge, 1988), 925.
7. Roy Wallis, in the original formulation given in his inaugural lecture *The Rebirth of the Gods?* (Belfast: Queen's University, 1978), had just these two types. In later developments, for example, in *The Elementary Forms of the New Religious Life* (London: Routledge, 1984), he added the third category of 'world-accommodating'. By noting that some NRMs radically divided the world so that they affirmed some spheres but not others, this addition allowed some interesting observations to be made; however, for the sake of keeping this discussion within manageable limits, I have reverted to the framework of his original presentation.
8. John Lofland, *Doomsday Cult: A Study of Conversion, Proselytization and Maintenance of Faith* (Englewood Cliffs, NJ: Prentice-Hall, 1966).
9. E. Burke Rochford, *Hare Krishna in America* (New Brunswick, NJ: Rutgers University Press, 1985); Larry D. Shinn, 'Conflicting Networks: Guru and Friend in ISKCON', in Rodney Stark (ed.), *Religious Movements: Genesis, Exodus and Numbers* (New York: Paragon House, 1985), 95–114; and J. Stillson Judah, *Hare Krishna and the Counter Culture* (New York: Wiley, 1974).
10. Christopher Edwards, *Crazy for God: The Nightmare of Cult Life* (Englewood Cliffs, NJ: Prentice-Hall, 1979), 161–2.
11. Roy Wallis, *Elementary Forms*, and 'Charisma, Commitment and Control in a New Religious Movement', in Roy Wallis (ed.), *Millennialism and Charisma* (Belfast: Queen's University, 1982), 73–140. For a good participant observer's account of COG, see David E. Van Zandt, *Living in the Children of God* (Princeton: Princeton University Press, 1991). For an ex-insider's exposé, see Deborah Davis with Bill Davis, *The Children of God: The Inside Story by the Daughter of the Founder Moses David Berg* (Grand Rapids, Mich.: Zondervan, 1984).
12. Phil Kerns (with Doug Weed), *People's Temple, People's Tomb* (Plainfield, NJ: Logos International, 1979), 159.
13. Such sacrifice was an important element in the general impression that recruits were not acting out of free will and that conversion should be explained by some form of social or psychological coercion. For a general discussion of conversion to NRMs and an extensive bibliography of relevant literature, see Thomas Robbins, *Cults, Converts and Charisma: The Sociology of New Religious Movements*, special issue of *Current Sociology*, 36 (1988).
14. Cited in Wallis, *Elementary Forms*, 52.
15. José Silva and Phillip Miele, *The Silva Mind Control Method* (New York, Pocket Books, 1977), 12–13.

16. Roy Wallis, 'Inside Insight', *New Humanist*, 95 (Autumn 1979), 94.
17. Roy Wallis, *The Road to Total Freedom: A Sociological Analysis of Scientology* (London: Heinemann, 1976).
18. H. Johnston, 'The Marketed Social Movement: A Case Study of the Rapid Growth of TM', *Pacific Sociological Review*, 23 (1980), 333–54.
19. *Herald*, 17 Feb. 1995, p. 30.
20. *World Government News*,2 (Nov.–Dec. 1978), 6.
21. Natural Law Party, *Election Manifesto* (May 1992).
22. Lewis F. Carter, 'The "New Renunciates" of the Bhagwan Shree Rajneesh: Observations and Identification of Problems of Interpreting New Religious Movements', *Journal for the Scientific Study of Religion*, 26 (1987), 148–72, and *Charisma and Control in Rajneeshpuram: The Role of Shared Values in the Creation of a Community* (Cambridge: Cambridge University Press, 1990).
23. Frances Fitzgerald, 'A Reporter at Large: Rajneeshpuram', *New Yorker*, pt. I (11 Sept. 1986), 46–96 and pt. II (29 Sept., 1986), 83–125.
24. Danny Ben-Tal, 'Welcome to Club Meditation', *Independent Weekend*, 28 Aug. 1993.
25. Paul Heelas, 'Western Europe: Self-Religions', in Stewart Sutherland and Peter Clarke (eds.), *The Study of Religion: Traditional and New Religion* (London: Routledge, 1991), 167.
26. Wallis, *Elementary Forms*, 28.
27. Bryan R. Wilson and Karel Dobbelaere, *A Time to Chant: The Soka Gakkai Buddhists in Britain* (Oxford: Oxford University Press, 1994).
28. Roy Wallis, 'Being with Werner', *New Humanist*, 96 (Spring 1981), 23.
29. Hans H. Gerth and C. Wright Mills, *From Max Weber: Essays in Sociology* (London: Routledge, 1970), 51.
30. This argument is elaborated in Steven M. Tipton, *Getting Saved from the Sixties: Moral Meaning in Conversion and Cultural Change* (Berkeley and Los Angeles: University of California Press, 1982).
31. Bryan Wilson, 'The Functions of Religion: A Reappraisal', *Religion*, 18 (1988), 207.
32. James M. Martin, *Actualizations: Beyond est* (San Francisco: San Francisco Book Co., 1977), 55.
33. Peter L. Berger, Brigitte Berger, and Hansfried Kellner, *The Homeless Mind* (Harmondsworth: Middx.: Penguin, 1974). As a matter of bibliographical commentary and because it points to a topic that deserves further research, it is worth highlighting what is implicit in my use of this source: there are two different but related themes in *The Homeless Mind*. In private conversations, Paul Heelas has described the main point for him as the book's specification of the socio-psychological problems of modernity and the value of those as causes of new religious movements—a Durkheimian anthropologist's reading which stresses 'needs' created by rationalization. Influenced more by the Weberian tradition, my reading of *The Homeless Mind* stresses the general change in consciousness (especially the application of a 'problem-solving' perspective to spheres previously shielded from rationalization) rather than in specific needs.
34. Philip Rieff, *The Triumph of the Therapeutic* (Harmondsworth, Middx.: Penguin, 1973), 224.
35. Paul Heelas, 'The Sacralization of the Self and New Age Capitalism', in Nicholas Abercrombie and Alan Warde (eds.) *Social Change in Contemporary Britain*

(Cambridge: Polity Press, 1992), 153. See also his 'Cults for Capitalism? Self-Religions, Magic and the Empowerment of Business', in John Fulton and Peter Gee (eds.), *Religion and Power, Decline and Growth: Sociological Analyses of Religion in Britain, Poland and the Americas* (London: British Sociological Association Sociology of Religion Study Group, 1991), 27–41, and 'Exegesis: Methods and Aims', in Peter Clarke (ed.), *The New Evangelists: Recruitment, Methods and Aims of New Religious Movements* (London: Ethnographica, 1988), 17–41.

36. Tipton, *Getting Saved from the Sixties*, 214.

37. This observation, articulated by the German philosophical anthropologist Arnold Gehlen, leads to Peter Berger's potent description of the human condition as being one of unusual 'world-openness'. It is in order to deal with the potential problems that result that we create limits on our desires through culture. See the first chapter of Peter L. Berger, *The Social Reality of Religion* (London: Faber & Faber, 1969), or the fuller discussion in Peter L. Berger and Thomas Luckmann, *The Social Construction of Reality* (Harmondsworth, Middx.: Penguin, 1973).

38. Emile Durkheim, *Suicide* (London: Routledge Kegan Paul, 1970).

39. Rodney Stark and William S. Bainbridge, *The Future of Religion: Secularization, Revival and Cult Formation* (Berkeley and Los Angeles: University of California Press, 1985), and *A Theory of Religion* (New York: Peter Lang, 1987). For one detailed critique, see Roy Wallis and Steve Bruce, 'The Stark–Bainbridge Theory of Religion: A Critical analysis and Counter-Proposals', *Sociological Analysis*, 45 (1984), 11–27.

40. Stark seems to be putting his money on the Mormons: 'It would be rash to suggest that . . . I expect the immediate replacement of secularized religious organizations by new, more otherworldly and vigorous bodies. What I propose is that in the long run this is what happens . . . it is irrelevant to cite the small absolute numbers attracted by the British branches of groups such as the Children of God or the Moonies . . . in order to show that new religions are insignificant responses to the march towards secularity. Religious revolutions are not the work of hundreds of new religious movements. It only takes one. And that is why this paper has concentrated on the Mormons' ('Modernization, Secularization and Mormon Success', in Thomas Robbins and Dick Anthony (eds.), *In Gods We Trust: New Patterns of Religious Pluralism in America* (2nd edn.; New Brunswick, NJ: Transaction, 1991), 201–18).

41. Reginald Bibby and Harold R. Weaver, 'Cult Consumption in Canada: A Further Critique of Stark and Bainbridge', *Sociological Analysis*, 46 (1985), 445–60.

42. Stark and Bainbridge, *Future of Religion*, 491.

43. The issue is argued in Roy Wallis, 'Figuring Out Cult Receptivity', *Journal for the Scientific Study of Religion*, 25 (1986), 494–503, and Rodney Stark, 'Europe's Receptivity to New Religious Movements', *Journal for the Scientific Study of Religion*, 32 (1993), 389–97.

44. Vincent Bugliosi (with Curt Gentry), *Helter Skelter: The Manson Murders* (Harmondsworth, Middx.: Penguin, 1977).

45. John H. Hall, *Gone from the Promised Land: Jonestown in American Cultural History* (New Brunswick, NJ: Transaction, 1987).

46. Roy Wallis, 'Hostages to Fortune: Thoughts on the Future of Scientology and the Children of God', in David G. Bromley and Phillip E. Hammond (eds.), *The*

*Future of New Religious Movements* (Macon, Ga.: Mercier University Press, 1987), 80–90. In the 1990s COG members in Australia and France were arrested for alleged child abuse but released and no one was charged; see Will Bennett, 'Cult Denies Child Sex Abuse', *Independent*, 2 July 1993.

47. Wuthnow, *Restructuring*, 152.

# 8

# THE NEW AGE

We are passing out of 2,000 years of Piscean astrological influence into the influence of Aquarius, which will affect all aspects of our culture, as we move from Piscean structures of hierarchical devotion to more fluid and spontaneous relationships that dance to an Aquarian rhythm.[1]

A STROLOGERS have a notion of a 'Great Year' made up of twelve 'months', each 2,160 years in duration and each represented by a star sign in the Sidereal Zodiac. It is supposed that Stonehenge was built at the start of the Age of Aries, that the start of the Age of Pisces was marked by the birth of Christ, and that we now stand at the beginning of the Age of Aquarius, a period, as Bloom puts it, of 'more fluid and spontaneous relationships', a time of new powers.

'New Age' is a term used loosely to describe a very wide range of beliefs and practices which became popular in the late 1980s.[2] Many have their roots in the esoteric culture of the late nineteenth century; others are extensions of the new religions and human-potential movements discussed in the previous chapter. Despite those roots, there are sufficient differences of belief and of structure to justify treating New Age religion as a subject in its own right and not merely as a continuation of older movements.

While many of the best-known 1970s new religions were sectarian, most elements of the New Age are cultic and are organized as 'client cults' and 'audience cults'.[3] The client cult is structured around the individual relationship between a consumer and a purveyor. Typical is the alternative therapist who advertises his or her services in an appropriate magazine or the bulletin board of a health-food shop and provides individual consultations for a fixed fee. Thus a classified advertisement in *Fortean Times* invites one to 'Make the pilgrimage to Middle Earth—Tarot, crystals, oils, lava lamps, jewellery, incense, cards, tarot readings by appointment', and then gives the address and phone number to call to arrange such a reading.[4]

Audience cults are generally structured around the mass distribution of the word, spoken and printed. The circulatory system of the New Age body is made up of books, magazines, audio cassettes, and public lectures. The *Fortean Times* notice board section lists periodicals for witches: '*Wicca-Brief*—newsletter for Wiccans and pagans in German'. For those interested in a range of esoteric information, there is '*New Dimensions* . . . The best for occult articles, Qabalah, metaphysics, psychology, book and music reviews. Dynamic in origin. The best all-rounder. Magic at its best.' Those who wish to investigate 'contact with non-human intelligences' can read '*The Wild Place* Issue 6 out now!' Such personal contact as there is usually takes place in a lecture and workshop circuit. Promoters of particular revelations or techniques use New Age magazines to advertise their meeting in the Central Halls, Westminster, or their weekend retreat in a converted mill in peaceful Cumbria. They present their insights and therapies and move on. New Life Promotions, which organizes the annual Mind, Body, and Spirit conventions in London, also arranges national tours for prominent New Age teachers. The work of such itinerants complements the routine and regular meetings organized by such bodies as the Society for Psychical Research ('Exploring Dowsing', 'Clairvoyance—How Far Can We See?', and 'Alien Contact, the Inner Dimension of the UFO Mystery') and the London Earth Mysteries Circle ('Reclaiming Our Heritage', 'Earth Mysteries and Magnetism', and 'UFOs and Psychic Phenomena').

That the New Age is organized around client and audience cults means that its popularity cannot be measured by estimating the membership of particular organizations. Furthermore, as we shall see, many of its key ideas are widely diffused throughout the culture; we have to ask to what extent people are influenced by the New Age rather than how many New Agers there are. There have been a few attempts to use surveys to do this, but these suffer from all the obvious problems. A 1992 survey asked almost 2,000 teenagers (divided into a 'school' or non-church-going group and a 'church' group) 'Have you ever been involved in any of the following?' and listed eight occult practices. The results are given in Table 8.1. The author of the study reports the findings as a matter of urgent concern, but one has to wonder what the respondents thought was meant by 'involved'. It is also worth noting that those

**Table 8.1.** Teenagers involved in occult practices, England, 1992 (%)

| 'Have you ever been involved in any of the following?' | School | Church |
| --- | --- | --- |
| Ouija | 26 | 8 |
| Astrology | 18 | 10 |
| Tarot | 13 | 6 |
| Hypnosis | 5 | 3 |
| Crystals | 3 | 2 |
| Reflexology | 3 | 2 |
| Channelling | 3 | 1 |
| I Ching | 2 | 1 |

Source: Peter Brierley, *Reaching and Keeping Teenagers* (London: Christian Research Association, 1993), 80.

elements of occultism which had been most sampled—if that is what the question tested—were those which date from the turn-of-the-century interest in the occult and which are well established as part of our cultural wallpaper. Those that are novel to the contemporary New Age—channelling and the use of crystals—are almost unknown.

However, there are less ambiguous markers of new activity in the New Age milieu.[5] The annual Mind, Body, and Spirit convention, held in London, began in 1977 as a one-day event with only a small number of exhibitors. In the late 1980s it was extended to five days. In 1993 over a hundred individuals and organizations presented their products or ideas from stalls in the main hall, and there was sufficient interest in the lectures and workshops for the convention to run over ten days.

The New Age's reliance on the printed word gives us a more convincing way of illustrating the increase in popularity of New Age beliefs and practices. The number of bookshops in the United States known to specialize in New Age materials doubled between 1980 and 1988.[6] It is obvious to any browser in British bookshops that far more space is devoted to 'Mind, Body, and Spirit' than to Christianity. Waterstone's shop in Aberdeen (not obviously the most fertile field for New Age phenomena) has some 70 metres of shelves of New Age books, but fits its more traditional Christian titles into 5 metres. We can also make some inferences from data on book publishing. In the twenty years between 1970 and 1990, the total number of new titles published in Britain just about doubled. The number of published books that were 'religious' (including the occult) increased by close to that proportion: 90 per cent. But the occult section grew by 150 per cent. Table 8.2 shows the relative proportions. What is clear is that the occult has been growing steadily as part of the total market but enjoyed a significant leap forward in the 1960s when compared with conventional religion titles. Furthermore, if we consider the weaknesses in the data, we can conclude that the trend is stronger than it here appears. Many New Age titles will be classified as medicine, psychology, or ecology, and many titles are not published in the UK but are imported from the USA, where the market and output are considerably larger. The largest of the specialist New Age publishers, Element Books, was founded in 1978 and in 1993 had a list of over 300 titles in print. As good a sign as any that the market is large and thought to be stable is the entry into it in the late 1980s of all the major publishing houses, with specialist labels for their New Age offerings. Thus Penguin has its Arkana imprint. HarperCollins has Aquarius, Mandala, and Thorsons imprints, and Random Century has Rider/Shambala.

As will become clear, one of the dominant characteristics of New Age thought is its eclecticism. One of Element's most successful lines is its series of titles called 'Elements of . . .'. The nouns that follow demonstrate both the diversity of the New Age and the lack of any attempt to define a canon of acceptable revelations. The following is a list of the current topics in the series:

**Table 8.2.** Books published, United Kingdom, 1928–1990

| Year | Religious titles (inc. occult) as % of all titles | Occult titles as % of all titles | Occult titles as % of religious titles |
|------|------|------|------|
| 1928 | 6.8 | 0.22 | 3.3 |
| 1940 | 4.7 | 0.36 | 7.7 |
| 1950 | 5.7 | 0.31 | 5.6 |
| 1960 | 5.2 | 0.29 | 5.6 |
| 1970 | 3.7 | 0.49 | 13.4 |
| 1980 | 3.6 | 0.54 | 15.0 |
| 1990 | 3.7 | 0.64 | 17.3 |

*Source*: Peter Brierley, *A Century of British Christianity: Historical Statistics 1900–1985 with Projections to 2000* (Research Monograph 14; London: MARC Europe, 1989).

Alchemy, Astrology, Buddhism, Christian Symbolism, Creation Myth, Dreamwork, Earth Mysteries, Feng Sui, Herbalism, Human Potential, Meditation, Mysticism, Natural Magic, Pendulum Dowsing, Prophecy, Psychosynthesis, Shamanism, Sufism, Taoism, Aborigine Tradition, Chakras, The Goddess, The Grail Tradition, Greek Tradition, Qabalah, Visualisation, Zen.[7]

With eclecticism comes a diffuseness that means that there are few clear divisions and boundaries, few organizations, but rather a milieu in which people acquire, absorb, and learn a variety of beliefs and practices that they combine into their own pockets of culture.

## Involvement and Commitment

As might be expected from the description of the New Age as cultic rather than sectarian, there are enormously differing sorts and degrees of involvement. For some people, it is no more than reading a book and entertaining an idea; for others it is a change of world-view and direction comparable to conversion in more traditional religions. Consider the ways in which people show an interest in astrology. A very small number of people make their livings as astrologers. A larger number strongly believe that the solar system is the symbol of a living energy pattern and that its arrangement tells us something useful about human personality and the course of events. They will use birth maps and birth signs as a guide to interpreting the behaviour of themselves and others, and will con-sider the lie of the planets before making major decisions. This may be done with more or less seriousness and consistency. Beyond them, we have those whose involvement is restricted to reading horoscopes with no conviction that they are useful but with the gen-eral supposition that it cannot do any harm. In this circle there are a very large number of people. The fourth best-selling book of 1993, behind three novels, was *1994 Horoscopes*, which sold 480,000 copies in the UK, which is about one for every 100 adults.[8]

Then there are those who glance at their horoscopes in popular magazines and newspapers; many of them have acquired enough information to be able to describe people in terms of the supposed characteristics typical of their birth sign: 'She's a typical Arian!' A survey of implicit religion in Leeds conducted in 1982 showed 75 per cent of people saying that they looked at their horoscopes but only 19 per cent saying that they 'believed in it'.[9]

There are also varying degrees of general cultural acceptance. Astrology, once a noble science, then a damnable heresy, has become so thoroughly accepted that there can be few Western Europeans who do not know their zodiac signs. Most popular periodicals carry a horoscope. I even found a hobbyist's home-improvements magazine with a horoscope: for every birth sign, the astrologer gamely insisted, this month was a particularly auspicious time for some home-improving! Celebrity astrologers grace breakfast television programmes. Yet the nature of the acceptance is important. It seems to be the case that we are happy with astrology as a 'bit of fun', a 'laugh', but regard as deviant those who take it too seriously. Thus the same tabloid newspapers which carry horoscopes roundly condemned the wife of President Reagan when a biographer claimed that Nancy's advice to her husband was influenced by the professional astrologer she regularly consulted.

## The Themes of the New Age

To give some flavour of the New Age, I will first quote from the publicity material for a number of New Age teachers and then summarize the key themes. The advertising material for Nicki Scully's seminar 'The Path of the Warrior as Healer' says:

Nicki spent her formative years in the late 1960s in southern California. It was during this time that she met Rock Scully, then manager of the famous music group the Grateful Dead. The relationship immersed her in the world of music and events within which energetic alchemy was a way of life. Out of that psychedelic cauldron, she emerged with a new understanding of the sacred, and the motivation to explore her life's work in the fields of healing and metaphysics. In 1969 she was introduced to shamanic healing in the Native American tradition and has continued to study and honour native American religious and traditional ways. A deep interest in Egypt led Nicki to make several trips to that country and her explorations created a physical link to the culture whose relevant ancient truths are brought forth in her current work. . . .In 1981 Nicki moved to Eugene, Or., and was initiated to the first 2 degrees of Reiki by the late master, Bethel Phaigh. Direct access to energy for healing served to redirect her life to one in which the alleviation of pain and suffering is of fundamental importance. . . . She combines energetic healing techniques with shamanistic principles to provide integrated and balanced healing and growth techniques.

The leaflet then describes the seminar.

This workshop is a journey and the journey is about being fully in your power, strong and clear in everything you are doing. It's about taking a stance in life; stalking and reclaiming your power. It's about honoring yourself and owning who you are, now. You will learn appropriate means of protecting yourself, building your own internal shield, and how to move without doubt or question. Sekhmet is the lion goddess in the Egyptian Pantheon. It is she who protects the truth of Maat, the rule of Law (cosmic law, not people's laws). Sekhmet's teaching results in powerful internal transformation and healing and she shares shamanistic healing techniques that are extremely potent.[10]

Jill Purce offers pioneering 'Inner Sound and Voice' workshops.

Interested in the magical properties of the voice she learned Mongolian and Tibetan overtone chanting. The latter she studied in the Himalayas with the chantmaster of the Gyütö Tibetan Monastery and Tantric College. She has been following the philosophy and practice of Dzogchen since 1978 when she first met the Tibetan Lama, Namkai Norbu Rinpoche. She has worked with American Indians and Shamans from different traditions.

Her literature offers the following description for a lecture with 'demonstration and audience participation' which takes the metaphor of getting 'in tune' with the universe at face value:

Traditional knowledge describes the creation of the world through sound. It defines the laws of cosmology in the subtlest harmonies of heavenly music. Both physiology and psychology it sees as our microcosmic resonance with these cosmic tones. In music itself, it finds the mediator between the two. This lecture examines the sonorous universe from antiquity and sees how it relates to the findings of modern science, as well as to our own healing and transformation individually and collectively. We will experiment with the psycho-physical effects of breathing, chanting, mantric and sonic meditations and look at the wider implications, which include the use of mantra and musical medicine, as well as 'objective music', apparently miraculous workings by means of sound.[11]

As can be seen from these brief descriptions, the eclecticism of the New Age is not just a consequence of the sampling attitude of the audience as it moves from one workshop to another, from one technique to another. Even the purveyors of quite specific products call on a range of traditions, cultures, and disciplines to legitimate their work. The enormous range of New Age interests can be even more clearly seen in the output of the 'broad-band' producers who offer general guidance rather than specific therapies, many of whom receive their ideas through 'channelling'. In the 1960s Eileen Caddy, one of the three founders of the Findhorn community, received daily messages from an inner voice.

I could sit and meditate for a long time and nothing would come, but as soon as my pen touched the paper it was like switching on an electric current. The words flowed. I was told: 'I work through each of you in different ways. You know when you need guidance from Me, you can receive it instantaneously. Like a flashing of lightening it is there. You can find the answer immediately; therefore you hold great responsibilities in your hands.'[12]

Eileen Caddy initially regarded her revelations as coming from God, rather traditionally conceived. Later she came to see the source as being her higher self: 'There is no separation between ourselves and God, there is only "I am". I am the guidance. It took me so many years to realise this.'[13] In the 1970s and 1980s it became more common for channellers to conceptualize their source in highly abstract terms as 'an energy vortex' or some such, but also to give the source a personal name and even imbue it with quasi-personal characteristics. One example would by 'Bartholomew', who is channelled by Mary-Margaret Moore. During a hypnosis session designed to relieve back pain, Moore began to hear Bartholomew's voice.

During the first year of her association with Bartholomew, Moore struggled with the fear that her channelling experiences were, in reality, grandiose self-delusions. She attempted to assess the validity of the information received from Bartholomew by monitoring Bartholomew's suggestions and predictions to verify their beneficial effects and their accuracy. In addition, she consulted the I Ching. . . . Of the 64 possible hexagrams . . . Moore's question 'How should I view the phenomenon called Bartholomew and our workings together?' yielded designs representing the first hexagram, 'The Creative', which refers to the creative action of the Deity; the fourteenth, which recommends modesty at the height of power; and the fiftieth, which refers to a 'hollow' ruler who wisely makes himself/herself receptive to the power of the sage. Moore interpreted herself to be the ruler and believed Bartholomew to be the sage, and thus accepted her channeling experiences as genuine.[14]

Bartholomew's advice, which Moore published in two books, ranges over such diverse topics as sex, AIDS, group souls, emotional detachment, ego surrender, and prayer. In Melton, Clark, and Kelly's *New Age Almanac* entry for Moore, there is an interesting coda which hints at the social composition of her audience (a question I will pursue shortly): 'Today Moore channels Bartholomew in a variety of locations around the globe that Bartholomew considers to have transformative power. Fans of Bartholomew travel to these points as a group, under the auspices of Inward Bound Tours.'[15] Scully's teachings can also be acquired with a sun tan: she leads tours to Egypt.

An even wider range of concerns are addressed by 'Lazaris', who is ' a nonphysical entity. He is a consciousness without form—a Spark of Light, a Spark of Love—an energy that has never choosen to take human form.'[16] In over 500 audio cassettes, Lazaris offers guidance on the nature of health and the purpose of illness, the use of crystals in healing, 'the Negative Ego and how it grows', 'methods to set up programmes for specific realities we want to create', 'the Crisis of Martyrhood that we must encounter as we move from the Human Potential into our Spiritual Potential', 'Unseen Friends who want to help us', 'power points and standing stones as well as other qualities of the Earth', 'The Mysterious Power of the Chakras', 'the components that make up Self-Confidence and how to work with them', and 'the economics and the national and world political situations of 1991'.

The above examples, selected rather randomly from a variety of New Age magazines and the advertising literature mailed with them, would suggest that improving the self is the primary concern of most New Agers, but it is by no means the only one. In the introduction to a beginner's New Age reader William Bloom summarizes New Age thought under four main headings. *New Science/New Paradigm* includes 'all the new theories which are reworking our intellectual understanding of the structures of life'. What informs such theories is the belief that the Newtonian view of matter (the basis for conventional scientific thinking) is wrong. The world is not made up of 'tangible bits and pieces following certain reliable laws of interaction' but is instead composed of matter and energy 'connected and formed in invisible ways that we are only just beginning to understand'.[17] The inter-connectedness of everything informs New Age attitudes to health and healing. In place of the medical-science treatment of symptoms and organs, there is claimed attention to the whole person. Then there is *New Ecology*, which is concerned with our responsibilities to the earth, which should be recognized as a complete living organism. This interest is evident in the work of such 'intentional communities'[18] as Findhorn in Scotland, Auroville in south India, and the Bear Tribe in Washington State, USA. Thirdly, and this is where we come back to the self, there is *New Psychology*, which regards as limited conventional psychotherapy's goal to identify and remedy problems with our unconscious minds so that we can return to 'normal' functioning. Like Dianetics, New Age psychology claims to be able to liberate our real and vast potential so that we become 'integrated, fulfilled and completely loving human beings'.[19] Underlying these three themes is *New Spirituality*. Bloom, himself a practising magician, says: 'for me the hallmark of the New Age is the power of *Spiritual Dynamics*.'[20]

## New Science

For outsiders, one of the most startling features of the New Age is its apparent deviation from the rational scientific world-view which dominates Western culture. The first clash concerns how we discover knowledge. This summary simplifies, of course, but what allowed conventional science and medicine to break out of such premodern dead ends as alchemy, astrology, and the theory of the four humours was their insistence on experimentation, observation, and testing.[21] And the field for observation is restricted to the material world. New Agers tend to have little interest in conventional notions of testing. That one or two people assert that a therapy worked for them is enough to establish its efficacy. New paradigms are not discovered by painstakingly trying to explain observations that do not fit with existing well established theories, but by revelation, metaphor, and textual synthesis from a variety of archaic traditions.

New Agers will happily believe that a book apparently written by Jane Roberts is actually a message from Seth, 'an energy personality essence no longer focused in physical reality'.[22] They will happily believe that the ability to channel the thoughts of spirit guides, 'ascended masters', long-dead historical figures, and even animal and vegetable spirits is now widely distributed. Incidentally, this represents a democratization of mediumship, which in the nineteenth century was thought to be available only to a small number of 'adepts'. New Agers will believe that in the early 1980s 'Alper' (the founder of the Arizona Metaphysical Society) received three volumes of channelled instruction about the lost ancient civilization of

Atlantis. According to Alper's source, the Atlanteans had a crystal technology that allowed them to power their cities and mass transportation systems from a very large central power crystal.[23] Alper's detailed channellings about their use for psychic healing and personal growth were extremely influential in promoting the New Age interest in crystals.

Tradition is also a major legitimator of New Age ideas and therapies. By reasoning backward from the observation that modern societies have many defects, New Agers conclude that pre-modern cultures must be morally and ethically superior. Tibetans, Eskimos, Native Americans, and Aborigines are then invested not only with superior social mores but also with great insight into the workings of the material world.

There are people in the New Age milieu (the proponents of parapsychology, for example) who are keen to prove their case to sceptical scientists, but the dominant attitude is best described as having it both ways. Most often the new idea is supposed to be plausible because it is traditional, but one also finds the language of science being invoked wherever possible. Hodgkinson's *Spiritual Healing*, a sweeping review and endorsement of the field, has a chapter called 'The Scientific Rationale'.[24] In so far as the New Age is hostile to any facet of science, it is the supposed close-mindedness and authoritarianism of the professional scientific and medical communities which is criticized.

Especially in promoting their alternative models of the body and the psyche, many New Agers stay fairly close to the modern consensus by confining their interests and their claims to areas which might plausibly be accommodated within conventional theories of causation, even if they are not tested in conventional ways or to the extent which conventional science and medicine would demand. For example, though there is no evidence that the body's healing processes are assisted by magnetism, we have enough experience of radiography and electric-shock therapy at least to imagine magnotherapy being assimilated to conventional models of the body.

As we saw in the advertising material for TM described in the previous chapter, proponents of what are essentially spiritual exercises are happy to give them added legitimacy by borrowing the language of science. A therapy the name of which suggests Buddhist roots none the less describes itself as a technology: 'Bodhisoul © Breathwork is a technology which utilises natural, connected breathing to clear negative energy from your life in a rapid and safe way.'[25]

Although the supposed mechanics remain the same, New Age channelling is considerably more sedate than the Victorian seance, and its products—new knowledge, improved psychological states, or changes in the material world—are presented in ways which minimize the challenge to conventional notions of causation. Eileen Caddy heard a voice within. A learned enquirer offered the following description of a nineteenth-century seance:

Bells ringing over the heads of the circle, floating in the air, and dropping upon the table; a spirit hand seen to extinguish the light; spirit hands touching the hands or garments of all present; pocket books taken out of pockets, the money abstracted and then returned; watches removed in the same manner. . . . the bosoms of ladies partially unbuttoned . . . a basket containing artificial oranges and lemons emptied and its contents distributed around the circle, and the basket successfully placed upon the head of every one around the circle.[26]

Such showmanship has been replaced with much more mundane proofs of efficacy: a friend's cancer goes into remission, the marriage of a member of the circle does improve.

Different elements of the 'new science' sit variously well with the logic of conventional science. Velikovsky's cosmology (earth was colonized by spacemen who were responsible for our ancient civilizations) could be judged to be scientific, but it also clear that it is rather poor science, based on weakly specified theories which do not fit well with well established principles, which have a poor observational track record, and which seem too readily to elude testing. Much New Age medicine has the same character of superficially meeting some criteria and failing abysmally on others. For example, double-blind testing has rarely been carried out on alternative medical claims.[27]

In so far as the proponents of alternative therapies offer to explain them, the specification of the effective causal mechanisms rarely gets beyond metaphor and highly contestable notions of temperament that have hardly developed since the Middle Ages' four humours of blood, phlegm, choler, and black choler (or melancholy). For example, Edward Bach's flower remedies, which were first formulated in the 1930s and are now popular again, were informed by the principle that illness is caused by unbalanced mental states and that there are twelve basic moods which can be manipulated with the appropriate flower essences.[28] Dinshah Pestanji Ghadiali's Chromotherapy was also first developed in the 1930s and revived in the late 1970s when health journalist Linda

Clark related it to a number of other New Age themes (such as the therapeutic use of crystals) in two books—*The Ancient Art of Color Therapy* and *Health, Youth and Beauty through Color Breathing*.[29] Ghadiali believed that coloured light stimulates the glands, with a different colour for each gland: red for the liver, orange for the thyroid, lemon for the pancreas, violet for the spleen, and so on. The association of particular colours and glands is part physical (livers are usually red) and part cultural (the spleen is traditionally associated with anger and angry people get purple in the face).

This point of metaphor can be pursued. One way in which New Age thought does appear to differ significantly from conventional science is in the logic of its synthesizing activity. Conventional scientists tend to work in discrete specialisms. In so far as they connect the ideas of one discipline to those of another, it is usually only when the links can be supported by a body of experimental observations arrived at over a range of experiments and a considerable period of time and when rigorous logic allows the connections. Thus Einstein's work allowed the connection of mechanics to theoretical physics and astronomy. What we often find among New Agers is an *ad hoc* connecting of ideas taken from radically different fields. The Hindu yogic tradition has a notion of *chakra* points: the human body supposedly has seven such centres for absorbing energy from the cosmos. From the entirely different culture of Chinese geomancy (Feng Sui) comes the idea of 'dragon lines' (lines of earth magnetism): certain places on the earth's surface and certain routes across it are auspicious. The same model is metaphorically applied to the human body in the therapy of acupuncture. Some New Agers synthesize these two superficially similar models with the idea of 'ley lines'. In 1921 a 65-year-old brewer and magistrate Alfred Watkins was struck by the insight that a series of ancient sites of spiritual significance—churches, standing stones, and ancient burial mounds—were arranged in straight lines.[30] His book *The Old Straight Track* became popular, and the essential ideas have since been developed along Velikovskian lines as a story about ancient spacemen and taken as confirmation of Chinese Feng Sui.

In many New Age lectures and workshops, there is a conspicuous attempt to appeal to as large a number of adherents of different forms of esoteric knowledge as possible by showing that their ideas really are all interlocking, and that what is evidence for one set is evidence for the others. In a talk on angels in 1993, June Marsh Lazar frequently used the rhetorical device of the encompassing aside. So

she explained the heightened spiritual awareness of Australian aborigines by saying 'Well, you know about *chakra* points. Well, the
earth has its *chakra* points too and one of the most important is in
the Australian outback.' Here is a body of ideas built up by a style of
research which does not challenge the correctness of any particular
established theory (by matching its strong explanations and resolv-
ing some of its weaknesses) but merely looks for resonances or coin-
cidences that allows each to be added to the other. Of course, if the
issue is pressed there is a sound reason for such all-embracing and
uncritical synthesis. In the end everything is cosmic consciousness.
All is one.

New Age research is not experimental but text based. Ethno-
logical sources are plundered for theories and therapies which are
then only tested to the extent that the proponents try them out. If it
works for them, then it works. That each of us may have different
experiences stops such experiential testing leading to the accumulation of sound knowledge, but it also prevents argument. That it does
not work for you is no evidence for it not working.

Despite our clear sense that what such New Agers are doing is
very different from what people in university science departments
do, many New Agers combine criticism of the scientific and medical
establishments with the belief that they are doing what will some-
day be recognized as science. Scientific explanations are not yet
available because prejudice and professional interest prevent scientists from asking the right questions. One important point of disagreement between conventional science and the New Age can be
seen if we compare the attitudes towards 'accidents' in pre-modern
(what anthropologists used to call 'primitive') and modern thought.
Evans-Pritchard makes the point perfectly.

In Zandeland sometimes an old granary collapses. There is nothing
remarkable in this. Every Zande knows that termites eat the supports in
course of time and that even the hardest woods decay after years of service.
Now a granary is the summerhouse of a Zande household. People sit
beneath it in the heat of day . . . . Consequently it may happen that there
are people sitting beneath the granary when it collapses and they are
injured, for it is a heavy structure. . . . Now why should these particular
people have been sitting under this particular granary at the particular
moment when it collapsed? . . .We say that the granary collapsed because
its supports were eaten away by termites. That is the cause that explains
the collapse of the granary. We also say that people were sitting under it at
the time because it was the heat of the day and they thought it would be a

comfortable place to talk and work. This is the cause of people being under the granary at the time it collapsed. To our minds the only relationship between these two independently caused facts is their coincidence in time and space. We have no explanation of why the two chains of causation intersected at a certain time and in a certain place, for there is no interdependence between them.[31]

The Zande does not accept that the process of explanation should be cut short there. The Zande knows about termites and he knows why the people were sitting under the granary, but 'he knows besides why these two events occurred at a precisely similar moment in time and space. It was due to the action of witchcraft.'[32] The pre-modern world looked for *meaning* in the universe, for ways of connecting what are for us unconnected patterns of causation, because outcomes could not be accidental or unintended. Modern science takes the view that there are regularities in the world that follow from the laws of natural science. Pure water at a certain atmospheric pressure boils at a fixed temperature and always do so. The sun rises and the sun sets. Acid corrodes metal. But there is no moral purpose to any of this, or at least, if there is, science offers no techniques for discovering that purpose, which leaves a large gap for New Age thought.

To summarize, while New Age interest in esoteric knowledge and the occult would seem at first sight a major counter-trend to increased rationality, it is important to appreciate the extent to which much New Age thought is shaped by the presuppositions of conventional science; or, to be more precise, is seen by its proponents to be compatible with conventional science and is marketed by them in those terms. However, such *rapprochement* is only skin-deep. If one takes the view that science is not a body of conclusions about the nature of the world but a series of principles of discovery and testing, then it is clear that New Age science has more in common with religion than with science.

## New Ecology

New Agers are 'Green'. The Findhorn community first came to public notice because of the founders' success in vegetable growing, which they achieved, not with fertilizers, but with guidance from Eileen Caddy's inner voice and Dorothy Mclean's conversations with plant spirits she called 'Devas'. Alongside human-potential work, environmental concerns remain central to life at Findhorn. As funds have allowed, the old caravans which were the first residences have been replaced by high-insulation buildings made using wood from sustainable forestry projects. Firms developing and marketing insulation and wind generators have been assisted by the Findhorn Foundation.

However, New Age environmentalism differs from its mundane counterpart in two important respects. First, environmental problems (and their solutions) are closely linked to personal problems:

The root cause is a gross distortion of the human relationship with the earth we live on, caused by the increasing stimulation of material desire. Thus the real solution requires a major personal and collective re-evaluation of the meaning of human life on earth, and of the source of happiness. More sensitive, inwardly directed people make less demands on natural resources and have a much greater appreciation of the wonder of human interaction with the planet.[33]

Secondly, the planet is seen as an organism. We know that elements of our physical environment interact to form something like a self-regulating system. For example, the ozone layer plays an important part in maintaining the temperature of the earth; the massive increase in carbon emissions with industrialization appears to cause holes in the layer, and this threatens our survival. New Agers have taken the system model one step further to suppose that earth is really an animate object—a 'super organism' that James Lovelock named Gaia, after the Greek Goddess of Earth, which has the rights of a person.[34] The secular Green protects the environment out of self-interest; the New Age Green does so out of respect for a superior being.

This involvement with environmentalism raises an interesting tension within the New Age milieu. On the one hand, it is critical of aspects of the modern world, especially those such as pollution that can be seen as the side-effects of greed and over-consumption. New Agers tend to be fans of Schumacher's *Small is Beautiful* and other such critiques of late capitalism. In that sense they are part of the alternative subculture. But they are not pessimists. There is little of the blanket condemnation of the present world one finds in out-and-out world-rejecting new religions. After all, we are now in the Age of Aquarius. Although there are social and economic problems, still the human self is perfectible and improving. Individuals are being 'empowered'.

## New Psychology and New Spirituality

In describing a number of psycho-therapies as self-*religions*, Heelas correctly observed the tendency of once-secular human-potential movements to become increasing spiritual.[35] One facet of the claim that the self is potentially or actually perfect is belief in its indestructibility. The New Age takes for granted reincarnation. It can vary in explicitness from those people who remember the experiences of previous lives to those who simply think that death is not real. Interestingly, reincarnation has even become popular among traditional Christians. One survey in Belgium showed that 20 per cent of the Catholics who regularly attended Mass believed in it.[36] The explanation for this probably lies in the effects of secularization on our ability to imagine. Traditional Christian cosmology, a heaven and a hell to which the soul or self goes on death, has been made awkward by our knowledge of astronomy. Christians could have spent the last 200 years shifting the supposed location of heaven further and further away as we learnt more about the heavens, but most simply gave up and turned the physical reality of the promised place into a psychological state. Reincarnation has the value that, provided one does not question too much the actual state of the soul in between its various corporeal embodiments, it does not require an actual place. Though one has to swallow a rather large theological gnat in accepting the process of reincarnation, the actual effects of it are easy to accept because they are simply the facts of human history. People die and people are born. There may be logical difficulties in believing in a cosmic consciousness but because it is abstract and ephemeral it solves the evidential problems of the traditional Christian idea of heaven and hell.

## Toleration and Eclecticism

I have already noted that the typical attitude of most New Agers towards their own beliefs and practices is that of the cult rather than the sect. Even those purveyors of a particular piece of esoteric knowledge who may wish to recruit a committed and enduring following have little choice but to recognize the operating principle of the New Age milieu, which is one of almost complete acceptance of alternative views. Thus, even when someone as dominant in a field as Tisserand is in aromatherapy (his books sell very well and he is the founder and leading light of two international organizations for 'training' and accrediting aromatherapists) wishes to assert the superiority of his brand of practice over alternatives, he does so by suggesting a hierarchy of knowledge and competence in which what others do is fine for their 'level'.[37]

The reasons for this inclusivism are not hard to find and most have already been touched upon. In the first place, a key element of New Age thought is the power or divinity of the self. If knowledge comes from learning to listen to an inner voice, the light within, then each person's revelation is as good as any other. The individualism and democracy inherent in the Protestant notion that we can all equally well read the Scriptures and discern God's will are amplified in the New Age. Protestantism is given a degree of cohesion by having an external source of authority—the Bible—and the long history of the Christian Church. The failure of the Holy Spirit and of tradition to prevent Protestants from developing competing interpretations of the Bible has ensured constant argument; but generally the argument has remained within a relatively narrow range of options, and until this century it did not give rise to overt relativism. Though Protestantism developed a small 'universalist' wing, most Protestants continued to believe that there was only one God with one will, however many competing claims there might be as to what that will was.

As an aside, it is worth noting that the democratic epistemology of New Age thought does not prevent recognition of a hierarchy of expertise. After all, the Eastern tradition gives an honoured place to sitting at the feet of a guru. Nor is it an obstacle to commercialism. The counter-cultural stream that fed the world-rejecting new religious movements often had great difficulty with 'bread heads', to use the Californian term. Those people who made a living by selling drugs, drug-use paraphernalia, and other counter-cultural accessories were often bitterly criticized by the idealists who wanted a consistent rejection of capitalism. The world-affirming human-potential wing of the new religious movements always had fewer problems with the notion of paying for a worthwhile product. The democratic impulse demonstrates itself, not in the insistence that everyone's present state is as good as anyone else's but in the right to select which claims to expertise will be recognized. The fact that the revelation is paid for actually strengthens the hand of the consumer. Instead of the enduring obligation to follow a leader that is found in charismatic religious movements, there is the limited contractual relationship of the purchaser. Having paid to attend the workshop or buy the book, the purchaser can decide the extent and nature of his or her commitment.

There is, of course, a major clash between the *laissez-faire* attitude of New Agers to ideas and techniques and the stress on professionalism and validation of knowledge which dominates modern societies. In so far as practices are presented as 'religious' they avoid the pressure to be tested and certified, but the closer they come to medicine, the greater the societal demand for regulation.

Some of that demand comes from conventional secular professions which wish to maintain the superior effectiveness of their techniques. Although the attitude of the medical profession to therapies that present themselves as complementary rather than alternative medicine is softening (some general practitioners now recommend meditation), there remains understandable annoyance that, while conventional medical innovations are subjected to all manner of bureaucratic constraints, anyone can set up as an alternative therapist.

Some of the demand for regulation comes from lay people who feel that they have suffered at the hands of unconventional therapists, either directly because the therapies have done them no good or some harm, or indirectly through the effect of such therapies on others.[38] A particularly contentious area is the claim of some psychotherapists to assist victims of sexual abuse to discover and externalize repressed memories. Some parents who have been accused by their adult children of rape in childhood have formed organizations to campaign for the regulation of therapists; some have started legal actions for damages against such therapists.[39]

Interestingly, some New Age practitioners are in favour of the codification and regulation of their expertise. For all that New Agers are generally critical of the hierarchical and authoritarian model of knowledge implied in the social institution of the profession, some see in that model a way of preserving their knowledge, improving the training of others, and increasing the status and public acceptance of their skills. The astrologers who formed the Faculty of Astrologers have so far failed to convince fellow practitioners of the value of professional organization, but the very attempt, and the existence of such bodies as the American Aroma Therapy Association, the National Council and Register of Iridologists, and the Confederation of Radionics and Radiesthetic Organizations, shows the influence of the professional model.

None of this detracts from the main point I wish to make in describing the New Age as a 'cultic milieu'. The sociological important observation about the themes of the New Age is that they are not limited or censored by having to accord with any master principles which shape a coherent ideology. Anyone who attends a large number of New Age seminars, listens to a large number of cassettes, or reads sufficient issues of *One Earth or Kindred Spirit*, quickly appreciates that certain revelations would be unacceptable. It is hard to imagine (though doubtless such things are there on the fringes) a channelling which supported racism, sexism, hierarchy, authoritarianism, cruelty to animals, or the overt promotion of increased consumption, but pretty well anything else must be accepted as being someone's inner guidance. The limited value consensus of the New Age reflects the value consensus of the culture from which its adherents are drawn, but it gives little guidance as to which new revelations of esoteric knowledge one should accept, or how one should conduct oneself in any particular setting.

A dispute in the Findhorn community neatly illustrates the point and is worth recounting.

A small group of people began visiting the community, and some became members, who felt that only with certain kinds of decoration and design, and particularly through the use of crystals, could the appropriate energy be properly channelled here. Indeed, it was not so much divine energy, but the energy of the fabled past civilisation of Atlantis which was to be incorporated into our almost completed Universal Hall through a special configuration of crystals and wires. The whole conception was not properly communicated to the membership, and Peter's [Caddy] authority was such that there was considerable acceptance of the new idea.

A specially cut quartz crystal, about the size of a grapefruit, was prepared and suspended on gold wires in the centre of the Hall. The gold wires led to the supporting pillars, from which silver wires led down into the foundations. In the basement, a smaller crystal was embedded in the floor, and a piece of meteoritic iron sat above it. A third crystal was fixed to a light in the centre of the ceiling. The Hall was closed for some time before this occult arrangement was finished and then, around Christmas 1978, a special ceremony of invocation was held to inaugurate the energy transfer. Craig Gibsone, the present focaliser of the Foundation, remembers walking out of the ceremony and leaving the community, so great was his disgust.

A year and a half later, during a presentation by a visitor from the Edgar

Cayce Foundation,[40] the wires snapped and the crystal fell, smashing a two-inch-thick glass panel in the floor and narrowly missing the speaker, who had 'providentially' not chosen to stand in the centre of the Hall. The crystal shattered into many pieces, to almost everyone's great relief. Eileen [Caddy] was not present at the talk, but her comment when informed of the event was: 'Thank God'. She collected the crystal fragments and, following her guidance, they were returned to the earth from which they came. This curious incident ended a period which taught the community some hard lessons.[41]

That one of the founders and many members of the community could allow an occult practice to which they were opposed to be given a central place in the symbolism and ritual of the community for over a year and do nothing until an accident gave them their opportunity shows the problem. The individualism of the cultic milieu means an attitude to revelations so tolerant and inclusive that there are very few widely acceptable grounds for disagreeing with any idea.

Findhorn also offers examples of the difficulty of conducting a personal life on the basis of New Age beliefs. The founders may have been guided by the divine within, but their personal lives were a shambles. Eileen left her husband and five children to run off with Peter, only to be periodically abandoned by him to the malign influence of his first wife, Sheena, who abused and dominated Eileen and even abducted Eileen's first child by Peter. Peter, a handsome, glamorous, and powerful figure, was attractive to many of the young idealistic women who visited the community. He fell in love with some, and in 1979 he left Eileen for a Californian. In all he married five times. One obituarist tries to find a silver lining in what others might reasonably view as a history of failure by noting that each change of partner 'coincided with a major change of direction'.[42] Talk of loving everyone masks the more commonplace reality that New Age personal and sexual relationships are as or more messy than the entanglements of those of us who are not in tune with our divine selves or the cosmic consciousness. With no comprehensive and binding ethical code, in the New Age there is always the danger that pursuing self-growth actually means pursuing self-interest.

Judith Boice's fascinating and frank account of her sojourns at various Gaian communities (including Findhorn) describes many difficult personal encounters.[43] Even in the mundane business of managing the work of the communities, the avoidance of hierarchical structures and specialization meant that disputes simmered unaddressed until they flared up in often extremely childish fracas. Rather than reducing the potential for conflict, the insistence that people be 'authentic' increased what was at stake in any interaction and provided no means other than cathartic outburst for handling the trouble that resulted.

## The Social Origins of the New Age

With some idea of the core beliefs of the New Age, we can consider what sort of people are attracted to it. In the absence of a well-developed research literature, some of this has to be guesswork. It is possible to identify and study the membership of a movement organization. It is very difficult to identify the inhabitants of a cultic milieu. It will also be obvious that different elements of the New Age will attract different sorts of people. That very small group of 'New Age travellers' which lives a nomadic life, moving caravans and old buses from one free music festival to another, will have little in common with those who lead outwardly conventional lives but who receive channelled wisdom from their spirit guides or meditate better to get in touch with their inner light. At present little is known about New Agers beyond the following fairly obvious points. First, there is an inverse relationship with the strength of traditional religions. The New Age is strongest in those parts of Britain, Europe, and America where Christianity is weakest. Hence there is a lot of New Age activity in the south-east of England, in Amsterdam, and in San Francisco. The popularity of places like the north of Scotland, the English lake district, and Wales for New Age centres is accounted for by what demographers call 'counter-stream migration'. New Agers from the liberal, cosmopolitan, and densely populated centres of societies move to the sparsely populated edges in order to get back to nature and to acquire cheap property which can be used to generate income through hosting workshops and residential conferences. The Findhorn Foundation in Moray, on the north-east coast of Scotland, attracts people from the south of England and the metropolitan centres of Europe; it has very few recruits from Moray. A similar point could be made about the lack of receptivity to New Age ideas in traditional communities that are based on shared working lives rather than shared religion, though there are fairly few of these left. Those people who have been socialized into the life and values of a Yorkshire mining village or a Banff fishing village, for example, are not likely to be in the market for something so centred on the 'self' and so at odds with a world informed by traditional communal values. Like the hippie communes of the 1960s, the communities of the New Age appeal most to those for whom community is an ideal rather than a reality.

Secondly, and this is related to the first observation, there is a clear class element in New Age religion. There are very few working-class New Agers. As with the new religious movements of the 1970s, spiritual growth appeals mainly to those people whose more pressing material needs have been satisfied. Unmarried mothers raising children on welfare benefits in poor housing tend to be too concerned with finding food, heat, and light to be overly troubled by their inner lights; when they do look for temporary release from their troubles, they tend to prefer the bright outer lights of bars and discothèques to the quiet introversion of the encounter group. That many of the virtuosi New Agers sacrificed middle-class standards of living to embark on their voyages of self-discovery does not change the fact that their preference for spiritual satisfaction over material satisfaction has very little appeal to those still denied the latter. There is all the difference in the world between the sectarian 'religions of the oppressed' that allow whole groups of people to make sense of their deprivations by turning them into marks of grace, and the occasionally ascetic spirituality of the comfortable who choose a little self-denial for their soul's sake. Hence we would expect—and observation bears this out—that New Agers will be middle class. We can be slightly more specific and expect that the spiritual dynamics of the New Age will have their greatest appeal, not uniformly to the middle class, but specifically to the university-educated middle classes working in the expressive professions: social workers, counsellors, actors, writers, and artists. We might guess that those drawn more to the new-science and new-ecology ends of the New Age will be people with an interest in science and science fiction. That certainly seems to be the case for UFO-ologists.

Though we can see how the promise of esoteric knowledge and power might appeal to the inadequate, it does not seem to be the case that the occult attracts people with major personality disorders. To see the attraction of the New Age as *compensation* for what is missing in someone's life is to overlook the point I made in the previous chapter about confidence. Revolutions are not normally led by the downtrodden when things are getting worse; they occur when real improvements produce rapidly rising expectations and they are led by people at the bottom layer of the privileged classes. You have to believe that something is absent from your life to be bothered to attend spiritual-growth courses, but equally well you have to have a degree of self-confidence to believe that such growth is possible.

There is a further connection which may not be as obvious. One subtle but pervasive feature of New Age thought which has been alluded to a number of times is its challenge to professional authority. In part, space has been created for the New Age by the gradually increasing and now apparently widespread suspicion of scientific and professional authority. Where sociologists of the 1950s actually defined professions in terms of a commitment to the social good rather than personal interest, we are much more likely to see professionals as being like other workers, as concerned for their own power and prestige as they are for such noble goals as the pursuit of knowledge, justice, and health. As scientists are more and more deployed on *both sides* of public arguments about the costs and benefits of new technologies, so they are seen to be fallible.[44]

Those people who offer alternative therapies and new science are, with varying degrees of self-awareness, claiming that they are as discerning as the members of professions whose narrow-mindedness they criticize. Such a claim is more likely to come from people educated to a similar degree, though not necessarily in the same disciplines, as those whose professional monopoly they repudiate.

What is clear from even a cursory acquaintance with the New Age is that it appeals more to women than to men.[45] This is not unprecedented or unexpected. While the official positions of the major Christian churches are monopolised or dominated by men, a majority of the congregations are women, and women have for centuries been the mainstay of the churches, even those such as the Catholic Church which are explicitly and ideologically patriarchal.

Women have long held founding and leading roles in deviant religious movements, especially those that stress charisma and spirit possession. One could mention the twelfth-century mystic Hildegard of Bingen or the fourteenth century Dame Julian of Norwich. From the nineteenth century one could note Madame Blavatsky and Annie Besant, two of the founders of Theosophy, Ellen White of the Seventh Day Adventists, Mary Baker-Eddy of

Christian Science, or Ann Lee, who founded the Shakers. The first seances of modern spiritualism were conducted by the Fox sisters.

It is a rough-and-ready picture, but, in terms of gender, the New Age divides. The parapsychology and esoteric knowledge side tends to be male. The healing, channelling, and spirituality side tends to be female. Eileen Caddy was one of the founders of the seminal Findhorn community. Jill Purce, Nicki Scully, Xandria Williams, and June Marsh Lazar are just some of the many women lecturers and trainers. Just as in the mainstream churches, women form the majority of the market for New Age products. My own rough count of some 500 people entering the hall for the Mind, Body, and Spirit convention in 1993 gave a female-to-male ratio of about 2 to 1.

Why women should be more interested in matters spiritual than men is an enormous subject and I can only sketch an answer by drawing attention to two general areas. First, there is the *focus* of religious activity. The churches have always been interested in the control of sexuality and in the instruction of the next generation, both matters which are concentrated on the domestic hearth and in which women have a major role to play. With secularization and the withdrawal of the churches from public and political life, religion becomes increasingly concentrated on the family, the home, and sexual and social reproduction—activities in which women are traditionally socialized to give a lead. To return to the simplified division of the social world to which I have referred a number of times in this book, the increasing divide between the private world and the public world, with religion relegated to the former, increases its relevance for women and diminishes it for men. One sees this very clearly in the way in which religious officials such as pastors deal far more with women than with men, so much so that clergymen (especially the celibate clergy of the Catholic Church) are often regarded as being a little effeminate themselves.

But as well as there being an obvious resonance between spirituality and the traditional roles of women, there is also a resonance with conceptions of femininity which even quite radical feminists endorse. Although there is a feminist position which argues that there are no significant differences between men and women which are not the product of gender socialization (and hence which cannot be changed), more common is the claim that women are essentially if not enormously different (and superior) to men in character because their child-bearing and rearing experiences make them less confrontational, less aggressive, less goal oriented, less domineering, more co-operative, and more caring.[46] Where men wish to achieve, women wish to feel. This would certainly fit with the expressive emphasis of the New Age as much as with more traditional religions.

There is also a crucial point about roles *per se*. As I have already described and illustrated, the New Age rests on the premiss that the self is basically good and that problems stem from its being confined by institutional roles. In that sense, the critique of gender roles that is at least implicit in New Age thought is even more far-reaching than that of much feminist literature. It is not only the present patriarchal roles which need to be challenged. Rather it is the whole practice of encouraging people to interact on the basis of roles which must be replaced by 'authenticity'. I have made the point a number of times that the actual consequences in the real world of much New Age reorientation may be very slight (in that the changes are changes in attitude to circumstances rather than changes in circumstances). A more refined version of that observation is that, in so far as there is reorientation, it is in the private world of personal relationships. Although there are 'new men' who are attracted to the idea of changing gender roles, it is obvious that any restructuring will have greater appeal to the group most likely to benefit from the change—that is, to women.

The observation about gender needs to be tied to that about class. There are as few working-class women in the New Age as there are working-class men. This can be put in the context of social change— why are New Age ideas more popular and respectable now than thirty years ago?—if we appreciate the role of the university-educated middle classes in promoting the individualistic ethos of consumerism. This is the grand irony of the New Age. Most New Agers (even those who offer human-resource training for capitalist corporations) see themselves as being in some major sense at odds with the culture of late capitalism; they like to think of themselves as 'alternative'. In small matters they might be. Even in some quite major life-style choices, they might be deviating. But there is one sense in which the New Age is a perfect product of its time: an exemplification of modernity rather than a rejection of it. It is the acme of consumerism. It is individualism raised to a new plane. The eclecticism of the New Age is not just a matter of being tolerant of behavioural differences or of supposing that we all have an equal right to act as we wish provided it is does not harm others. It is going further than that to suppose not only that we can all discern the truth, but that what we all variously discern is all true. The individual consumer is not only the final arbiter of what he or she wants to believe and practise but also the final arbiter of truth and falsity. It is individualism taken to the level of epistemology, so that in place of the sectarian arguments over which revelation best embodied the one truth, there is complete relativism. The name Solipsism was given to a school of philosophy that argued that one could have knowledge only of oneself. In the New Age that is turned inside out. If under its many surface differences all of matter is really one unified energy field, then each of us is also everything else, and we can suppose that, by knowing ourselves and introspecting, we can know everything. In pragmatic terms, because we can know what works for us, we can know what works.

## The Significance of the New Age

It is one thing to note the existence of a phenomenon; it is another to assess its significance. In modern egalitarian societies one obvious way of gauging the impact of any specific movement which embodies a cultural innovation is to count the numbers of people involved in it, but for client and for audience cults in a cultic milieu this is clearly impossible and we are forced to estimate. The counter-cultural end of the New Age is certainly very small. Though at its height Findhorn attracted hundreds of young people, most stayed for short periods. Even if the number who have stayed at Findhorn for any length of time reached ten thousand (and it might be some way short of that), this would be less than the membership of Ian Paisley's Free Presbyterian Church of Ulster and far less than the number of people lost to the Christian Churches in Scotland in a decade. The more mainstream spiritualized human potential organizations will have influenced more people. Heelas estimates that, in the final year of its operations (which ran from 1977 to 1984), Exegesis trained more than 6,000 people. Insight claims over 100,000 participants world-wide since 1978. Between 1977 and 1984 about 8,000 people in Britain took est training courses and the movement claims more than two million participants since 1971.

Even a cautious estimate indicates that at least three million in countries ranging from Canada to New Zealand have participated in these and other 'est-like' movements since the early 1970s. In Britain, the most conservative estimate is that 50,000 have been involved. Numbers swell considerably if other forms of self religiosity are included.[47]

On top of that we would expect a considerable multiplier. It is in the very nature of cultic involvement that people acquire expertise and then pass on what they have learnt (or a diluted or mixed version of what they have learnt) to their partners and friends.

Beyond the people who have become personally involved in the New Age, there may well have been important changes in the general cultural climate. It is certainly the case that a diluted form of the holism of new science has become well established. We now have 'Well Woman' clinics which pay at least lip service to the idea that a person's health should be looked at *in toto* and in its personal and social context and not be viewed as a set of unconnected problems to be managed separately. Our respect for the enormous accomplishments of modern science and medicine (a man on the moon and a five-organ transplant) is tempered by fears of that power to intervene (Chernobyl and the Thalidomide babies). The contrast between the natural and the technological is well established, with a strong preference for the former and with a quite implausible range of consumer products now being advertised as natural, traditional, and country style. Even quite esoteric therapies have been incorporated in the product ranges of conventional capitalist enterprises. The Body Shop, a soap and cosmetics company that has created a highly successful international corporation on the appeal of its politically correct 'natural' products and minimalist packaging, in 1992 adopted aromatherapy and marketed a range of essential oils with a handy leaflet which boasts:

### AROMATHERAPY THE BODY SHOP WAY

To clear away much of the mysticism and doubt that surrounds aromatherapy, we've put together our own range that anybody can enjoy, regardless of age, sex or way of life. We want to make it as easy as possible for people to find out just how good aromatherapy can make them feel.

There's nothing complicated about our range and you don't need any specialist knowledge to use it. Here's how easy it is—when you're soaking in a relaxing bath, why not treat your face to an aromatherapy mask? or skip a cup of coffee in the morning and try showering with our reviving shower oil instead. The uses of aromatherapy are endless. Build it into your daily routine and you'll soon reap the benefits.

224 RELIGION IN THE MODERN WORLD

A year later, Marks and Spencer PLC, the epitome of the solid respectable quality supermarket, followed suit with its range of aromatherapy bubble bath liquids.

Just as TM successfully took the Hinduism out of yoga, the Body Shop has taken the esoteric knowledge out of essential oils. Further to reduce the already minimal change in life-style demanded by these consumerist versions of the original practices, the Body Shop suggests meditating while wearing the aromatherapy mask, thus saving twenty minutes!

*Good Housekeeping*, the Marks and Spencer of women's magazines, has published a directory of 'Complimentary Health' which, with no critical or evaluative comment, happily lists, among others, 'Crystal Therapy' ('for example, amber is meant to help digestive problems and malachite to cure inflammation') and 'Polarity Therapy' ('based on the theory that your chakras, or central energy sources, are neutral and that all points beyond them are positive or negative. . . . Illness occurs when the flow of energy through the body is slowed down or blocked. When this happens practitioners will place their hands on the body . . . to correct the balance and flow of energy').[48] And it is the lack of judgement which is significant about the mainstreaming of the New Age. Where once such respectable and popular leaders of opinion and disseminators of information as major periodicals, the electronic media, and educational institutions would have felt a responsibility critically to evaluate cultural innovations, now they simply present a cafeteria counter and allow the consumers to make their own choices, not only about what is good or moral, but also about what cures ailments and explains the nature of the universe.

At the risk of making the same point too often, I return to my main concern. What matters for our understanding of the role of religion in society is not how many people consume a particular set of ideas or a particular therapy but what difference such consumption makes. Much of New Age thought and practice is of limited salience, even for the believers and practitioners. Most of the people interested in holistic alternative medical therapies regard them as additions, rather than as alternatives, to conventional medicine. Aromatherapy may be widely publicized in women's magazines (where interestingly it appears alongside cosmetic routines) and offered in an Aberdeen physiotherapy clinic, but it has not displaced conventional medicine, which still occupies an extremely powerful position and still continues to define and manage large areas of social life.

I have already made the point that, for the vast majority of those people who have undertaken est or similar training, whatever the extent of their inner transformation, there has been no corresponding external effect. Even when New Age thought does have a major impact on the lives of individuals, we can make the same point as was made by the new religious movements of the 1970s. There is little or no impact on the world at large. The state, civic society, the polity, and the economy remain unaffected. In so far as any New Age interests have achieved some impact, it has been because they have coincided with more powerful and mundane forces. In so far as Western European governments are now interested in ecology, it is because appeals have been successfully made to self-interest and not because we have come to believe that the world is really a super-organism called Gaia.

In summary, New Age religion cannot aspire to promote radical and specific change because it does not have the cohesion and discipline of the sect. The New Age will not have the impact that Methodism had. But, as has already happened with aspects of its environmentalism and its holistic approach to health, some of its ideas may find themselves stripped of their more esoteric parts and accepted into the cultural mainstream. More important than its immediate impact on the lives of individuals is the part that it plays as symptom and as cause in the erosion of faith in orthodoxies and the authority of professional knowledge. For all its talk of community, the New Age is the embodiment of individualism.

## Notes

1. William Bloom, *The New Age: An Anthology of Essential Writings* (London: Rider/Channel 4, 1991), p. xviii.
2. For a general introduction, see ibid. For an introduction to the academic literature, see Paul Heelas, 'The New Age in Cultural Context: The Pre-Modern, Modern and Post-Modern', *Religion*, 23 (1993), 103–16, and the other essays in that issue. See also the essays in *Religion Today*, 9/3 (Summer 1994).
3. On client and audience cults, see Rodney Stark and William S. Bainbridge, *The Future of Religion: Secularization, Revival and Cult Formation* (Berkeley and Los Angeles: University of California Press, 1985), 27–9.
4. *Fortean Times*, 67 (Feb.–Mar 1993).
5. Of course, some of this represents coalescence and shifting of what was already going on in other places and in more diffuse forms. None the less no commentator has suggested that there has been no real growth.

6. Peter Brierley, *The New Age is Coming* (Research Monograph 35; London: MARC Europe, 1991).
7. Element catalogue, July–December 1992.
8. *Bookseller*, 14 Jan. 1994.
9. Brierley, *The New Age*, summarizes the frequency tables from the project.
10. New Life Workshop, advertising leaflet (Spring 1993).
11. Inner Sound and Voice Workshops, advertising leaflet (1993).
12. Eileen Caddy and Liza Hollingshead, *Flight into Freedom: The Autobiography of the Co-Founder of the Findhorn Community* (Longmead, Dorset: Element, 1988), 87.
13. Jeremy Slocombe and Eve Ward, 'Willing to Change: An Interview with Eileen Caddy', *One Earth: The Findhorn Foundation and Community Magazine*, 12 (Winter 1993–94), 9.
14. J. Gordon Melton, Jerome Clark, and Aidan A. Kelly, *New Age Almanac* (New York: Visible Ink, 1991), 39.
15. Ibid. 40.
16. The Lazaris Material, advertising leaflet (1993) produced by the New Magick Company. Lazaris is channelled by Jack Pursel, a former insurance executive; see ibid. 66–7.
17. Bloom, *The New Age*, p. xvi.
18. For a wide-ranging introduction to the sociology of intentional communities, see Rosabeth Moss Kanter, *Commitment and Community: Communes and Utopias in Sociological Perspective* (Cambridge, Mass.: Harvard University Press, 1972). For a comprehensive discussion of the related concept of total institutions, see C. A. McEwen, 'Continuities in the Study of Total and Nontotal Institutions', *Annual Review of Sociology*, 6 (1980), 143–85.
19. Bloom, *The New Age*, p. xvii.
20. Ibid.
21. There are, of course, considerable arguments about what makes some knowledge 'scientific' and allows other ideas to be dismissed as 'pseudo-science'. Without wishing to enter a complex debate, I would note that, while we may have a strong sense that, for example, astronomy and astrology are two very different beasts, there is no ready check list of characteristics that we can use unambiguously to differentiate the two kinds of animal. Attempts by philosophers of science to delineate science's constitutive features have been inconclusive. Sociological studies of how science is actually done suggest that 'the erratic and messy course of scientific controversy only acquires the formally rational structure which accords with prevailing principles of validity through *hindsight*, and by glossing over the operation of numerous arbitrary factors which closer analysis shows to be implicated in the course of events' (Roy Wallis, 'Science and Pseudo-Science', *Social Science Information*, 24 (1985), 598). W. H. Newton-Smith (*The Rationality of Science* (London: Routledge & Kegan Paul, 1981)) suggests that, rather than look for one single demarcating criterion, we should recognize that the success of those ideas we regard as 'scientific' rests on them having some, but not necessarily all, of the following characteristics. First, the development of scientific knowledge is cumulative. A good scientific theory will either preserve and continue the observational successes of its predecessors or have dramatic observational successes in areas where existing theory is unsuccessful; that is, science grows by building on the

successes of good theories and filling in the gaps they leave. Secondly, there is 'fertility': does the theory offer scope for future development and ideas to guide future research? Thirdly, science is critically empirical. Any new theory should have a good track record of observational success (and preferably it should have this despite serious attempts to prove it wrong; there is no idea so preposterous that it cannot find enough supporting evidence to convince the uncritical). Also important is the extent to which the theory supports other theories by explaining their laws, or by compatibility with them; that is, science is theoretically cumulative. Then there is the issue of how a new theory deals with failure. Can it sensibly be adjusted and improved in the face of observational failure or, like Marxist havering on the failure of class struggle, do such adjustments look like excuses? Internal consistency is a further important consideration.

22. Melton, Clark, and Kelly, *New Age Almanac*, 96–7.
23. Ibid. 118–9.
24. Liz Hodgkinson, *Spiritual Healing: Everything You Want to Know* (London: Piatkus, 1990).
25. New Life Workshop, advertising leaflet (1993). There is an interesting relationship with tradition suggested by the copyrighting of the name.
26. Quoted in R. Laurence Moore, 'Spiritualism and Science: Reflections on the First Decade of the Spirit Rappings', *American Quarterly*, 24/4 (1972), 483.
27. In the 150 years since Franz Anton Mesmer's theory of animal magnetism was formulated, the therapeutic claims of magnetic waves have never been rigorously tested, though it would be relatively simple to do so. It is interesting to note that the makers of magnetic wave beds in Britain specifically avoid making any therapeutic claims for their product but self-employed magnotherapists do make such claims to clients (*You and Yours*, BBC Radio Four, 8 July 1994).
28. Bach was struck off the British Medical Register in 1936 on the technical ground that he had been using unqualified assistants. See Melton, Clark, and Kelly, *New Age Almanac*, 184–5. As an aside, it is worth noting that the scientific establishment has often laid itself open to the New Age critique of its blinkered nature by using such technicalities to supress rivals rather than confront their arguments.
29. Melton, Clark, and Kelly, *New Age Almanac*, 198–202.
30. Eileen Campbell and J. H. Brennan, *Dictionary of Mind, Body and Spirit* (London: Aquarian, 1994), 182–3.
31. E. E. Evans-Pritchard, *Witchcraft Oracles and Magic among the Azande* (Oxford: Oxford University Press, 1968), 69–70.
32. Ibid. 70.
33. Carol Riddell, *The Findhorn Community: Creating a Human Identity for the 21st Century* (Forres: Findhorn Press, 1990), 15.
34. James Lovelock 'A Quest for Gaia', *New Scientist*, 6 Feb. 1975, and *Gaia: A New Look at Life on Earth* (Oxford: Oxford University Press, 1979).
35. There is an interesting argument which bears on the major issue of the possibility of secularization. Stark and Bainbridge believe that the spiritualization of elements of the human-potential movement is evidence for their general claim about the unsatisfactory nature of naturaluistic beliefs. Wallis and Bruce see it rather as a consequence of success and the diffuseness of the beliefs which

228   RELIGION IN THE MODERN WORLD

informed human-potential movements. 'The very success of its methods gave
rise to new questions, awakened new interests, and thus provoked further
search . . . as followers and practitioners sought to find a general explanation
and plan behind the effects of diverse particular practices and remedies. . . . we
are suggesting that increasing the spiritual elements in the Human Potential
Movement offers viable solutions to problems caused, not by the failure of the
movement to produce the goods, but by the diffuseness of the movement's ideology' (Roy Wallis and Steve Bruce, 'The Stark–Bainbridge Theory of Religion:
A Critical Analysis and Counter Proposals', *Sociological Analysis*, 45 (1984), 23).
See also Roy Wallis, 'The Dynamics of Change in the Human Potential
Movement', in Rodney Stark (ed.), *Religious Movements: Genesis, Exodus and
Numbers* (New York: Paragon House, 1985), 129–56.

36. Karel Dobbelaere and Lilianne Voyé, 'From Pillar to Postmodernity: The
Changing Situation of Religion in Belgium', *Sociological Analysis*, 51 (1990),
S1–S13. One suspects that the figures included some respondents who were
thinking of a more traditionally Christian notion of life after death.

37. Robert Tisserand, *Aromatherapy for Everyone* (Harmondsworth, Middx.: Arcana,
1990), 3.

38. The beauty of homeopathy is that, just as no orthodox scientist can construct
an explanation of how a drug so diluted that no trace of it can be found by conventional chemical methods can have any beneficial effects, so it cannot be
accused of harmful effects. However, there is increasing concern that some
alternative and traditional remedies (the use of chromium orotate, ginseng,
and raspberry leafs as dietary supplements, for example) are poisonous; see Liz
Hunt, 'Calls for Better Control of "Natural Remedies" ', *Independent on Sunday*,
19 Sept. 1993. There are also the related ethical issues of selling desperately ill
people treatments that are useless and, worse, discouraging people from
undergoing useful conventional therapies. In 1991 two British doctors were
struck off the Medical Register for selling inefficacious 'Maharishi Ayur-Veda'
therapy to AIDS sufferers.

39. See Rosie Waterhouse and Phil Reeves, 'Author of Child Sex Abuse Book is
Sued', *Independent*, 15 May 1994; Rosie Waterhouse and Sarah Strickland,
'Abuses of Memory', *Independent on Sunday*, 1 May 1994; Simon Hoggart,
'Tricks of Memory', *Observer Magazine*, 27 Mar. 1994; and Christopher Reed,
' "Incest" Father Sues "Quack" Therapists', *Observer*, 17 Apr. 1994.

40. Cayce (1877–1945) was an American clairvoyant, influenced by Theosophy,
who offered 'distance' cures for ailments. Through his son's organizational
skills in publishing and distributing his works, Cayce became popular in the late
1970s.

41. Riddell, *The Findhorn Community*, 86–7.

42. Jeremy Slocombe, 'Last Thoughts', *One Earth: The Findhorn Foundation and
Community Magazine*, 14 (Summer 1994), 19.

43. Judith L. Boice, *At One with All Life: A Personal Journey in Gaian Communities*
(Findhorn: Findhorn Press, 1989).

44. This argument has been elegantly made by Steven Yearley, 'The Social
Authority of Science in a Post-Modern Age', (unpublished inaugural lecture,
University of Ulster, 1994).

45. See Riddell, *The Findhorn Community*, and Boice, *At One with All Life*.

46. For understanding women's attraction to the New Age, of course, it does not

THE NEW AGE 229

matter whether the generally agreed-upon differences in male and female character are a result of biological or social differences. It only matters that there be present such discernible differences.

47. Paul Heelas, 'The Sacralization of the Self and New Age Capitalism', in Nicholas Abercrombie and Alan Warde (eds.), *Social Change in Contemporary Britain* (London: Polity Press, 1992), 143–4.
48. *Good Housekeeping*, Oct. 1993.

# 9

# CONCLUSION

THE European Reformation in the sixteenth century marked a vital change: the world would never be the same again. With it we entered modernity. This does not mean that a religious revolution on its own caused the world to shift on its axis. In many respects the Reformation innovations in religious culture were a response to preceding social, economic, and political changes. None the less the rise of Protestantism was an important emblem of changes already underway, a decisive accelerator of those changes, and an original cause of further upheaval. The Reformation hastened the rise of individualism and of rationality, and both of these were fundamentally to change the nature of religion and its place in the world. Individualism threatened the communal basis of religious belief and behaviour, while rationality removed many of the purposes of religion and rendered many of its beliefs implausible. The term 'implausibility' has been used quite deliberately to shift our attention away from the lay concern with the truth or falsity of religion. Being right and being believed are not the same thing and the first does not always lead to the second. What is important for the career of any ideas or body of ideas is the environment of social circumstances and social relationships that makes them more or less likely to be believed.

The full impact of individualism took four centuries to be felt. Logically one would have expected it to have lead quickly to complete fragmentation. If fifty very different people read the Bible and attempted to discern God's will, one might expect to get fifty different answers. That did not happen; instead three or four different answers emerged, each corresponding to major social and regional cleavages. Instead of collapsing into thousands of small fragments, like a car-windscreen shattering, the religious culture cracked into a small number of large shards.

The cohesion of the religious culture of Western Europe in the early modern period can be explained as follows. First, the people of the seventeenth, eighteenth, and early nineteenth centuries differed from us in living fairly narrow lives. They were not yet sufficiently affluent nor was the division of labour so extensive that they would do very different kinds of jobs, live in very different kinds of circumstances, or see the world in very different ways. As a consequence, the fragmentation of culture and ideology occurred only slowly. When the Quakers and Baptists and Presbyterians and Anglicans were arguing with each other in the eighteenth century, they were earnestly contesting which of them had the divine truth. But they argued within a fairly narrow range of possibilities and, most importantly, they all accepted an important starting assumption: that truth was unitary and indivisible. The Protestants' rejection of the priesthood meant that every individual had to discern God's will and respond, but they were all Christians and there was only one Christ and one God. They each read the Bible, but there was only one Bible. They were each guided by the in-dwelling Holy Spirit, but there was only one Holy Spirit. So there could only be one correct interpretation. This was a pre-hermeneutic world. The notion that the perspective and interests of the reader so influence the interpretation of any text that it makes little sense to talk of a *correct* reading had not yet become widespread.

Furthermore, the sovereign individual, though promised by the Reformation, was slow to emerge from social and political domination. So long as many people lived in tied cottages on estate villages or their urban equivalent, independence of mind was a luxury to be entertained only by the small number of people with independent means.

Thirdly, there is an obvious but important point about the passage of time and the gradual increase in the range of beliefs which has become available in the culture. The leaders of the Reformation—Luther, Calvin, and Zwingli—had been raised in the medieval Christian Church. They shared many of the beliefs of the organization they sought to change. As each century has passed and we have moved further and further away from that time, so, like a funnel, the range of ideas that can be entertained has broadened but until the end of the last century people still spoke a fairly common ideological language, and so long as they did that there was no need to succumb to relativism.

We might think of the third period in my model—the late modern period—as ideological promiscuity. In the early modern period there was considerable individual shifting as people looked for the religion that they thought closest approximated to God's wishes, but most seekers were not eclectic. Every time Elizabeth Taylor gets married she promises herself and the world's media that this is the real one. All the previous marriages were mistakes but now she has found the right man and this one will last for eternity, until, two years later, it also fails. This is what Americans quaintly call *serial monogamy* and it is quite different from promiscuity, where one maintains at the same time a number of relationships and is not exclusively committed to any of them.

In the religious life of the Western world, the big change—from serial dogmatism to promiscuous liberalism—comes around the start of this century when the degree of social and cultural pluralism forces the denominational attitude to become common. Each major religious organization revised its self-perception from claiming an exclusive relationship with the divinity to supposing that it represented simply one of many roads to God.

This trajectory can be described in terms of the place of the individual in the dominant religious culture and in terms of the organizational types delineated in Chapter 4. With modernization, the focus of religious activity and the location of religious authority shift from professionals representing the people (the cathedral or 'church') to the sovereign consuming individual of late modernity (the 'cult'), with an intervening early modern stage in which individualism is restrained because life circumstances are sufficiently common for large numbers of people to be able 'voluntarily' to sink their own individuality into the 'sect' and the 'denomination'.

At the risk of stating the obvious, I should insert, as an aside, an important qualification. This account is in the first instance only relevant to those societies which evolved basically egalitarian cultures and democratic polities. Clearly the corrosive influence of cultural pluralism will have very different consequences in an authoritarian society where an élite insists on maintaining the superiority of its religion and is able to withstand challenge. As I have just noted, fragmentation can be retarded by the exercise of political power and, in the case of the English and Scottish reformations, it was. One also has the interesting inverse case of state-imposed secularity in those countries where Communist governments worked strenuously to eradicate religious belief and practice. However, in both examples the effect was a delay, not a fundamental change of direction.

Within this simple story line of change from church to sect to denomination to cult, there are many distinctive dramas. In a variety of ways introduced in Chapter 5, social circumstances can provide religion with roles other than bridging the natural and supernatural worlds. Ethnic conflicts, major cultural transitions, and class conflicts can sustain communities and, with them, communal religion or, as is happening with the spread of Pentecostalism in the Third World, give large numbers of people good reason to align themselves with sectarian religion. Where, as in the United States, the social structure is open enough for sectarians to create their own sub-societies and subcultures, sectarians can recreate and sustain the 'church' form of religion. But, for those people whose circumstances do not give religion the opportunity to perform such social functions, churches and sects evolve into denominations and denominations decline. The diminishing number of people who continue to do religion do it in an increasingly individualistic and idiosyncratic manner.

The best image I can find for this is the 'pick-and-mix' sweet counter. Sweets used to be stored in their separate jars and sold in weights, with different prices for different sorts of sweets. In about 1966 Woolworth's had the brilliant idea of responding to the enormous variety of sweets then available by having a large counter with buckets of different sorts of sweets, a set of scales, bags, and a little shovel. Instead of being served, the customer served himself by taking a bag and putting into it a few of this sort and few of that sort and then having it weighed and paying. Customers could now construct precisely their own desired mix of sweets. This eclecticism is the characteristic form of religion in the late modern period. It may not yet be the most common, but it represents in religious culture the dominant ethos of late capitalism: the world of options, lifestyles, and preferences.

The great nineteenth-century denominations will endure. They may be nearly devoid of function and barely demarcated from the surrounding culture, but inertia will preserve them for some time to come. Sects will continue where the society allows them the social space. The decline of the dominant religious traditions will allow the flowering of alternative ideas and therapies, and the failure of rationality to meet the expectations it has aroused will mean an enduring demand for such products. However, the relativism at the heart of the cultic milieu will prevent any of these innovations acquiring the social power or influence of previous religious innovations.

Little originality is claimed for the main argument of this book. Though the precise assembly may be novel, the key components are sociological orthodoxy and the main illustrations are the common currency of modern historians. In part I have been motivated by a desire to reassert the value of the work of Max Weber, Ernst Troeltsch, Bryan Wilson, David Martin, and Peter Berger. Too often the secularization account of religious change is presented in pastiche and caricature. My explanation of the decline of the popularity and importance of religion in the modern world does not suppose that patently false superstitions will be replaced by patently obvious truth as people become better educated or that modern people will become self-consciously committed to an atheistic and materialistic view of themselves and the universe. We have not all become committed rationalists; rather, in the phrase popularized by Weber, most of us have become religiously 'unmusical'. Like the truly tone-deaf, we know about music, we know that many people feel strongly about it, we might even be persuaded that, in some social sense, it is a good thing, but still it means nothing to us.

Belief in the supernatural has not disappeared. Rather the forms in which it is expressed have become so idiosyncratic and so diffuse that there are few specific social consequences. Instead of religiosity expressing itself in new sects with enthusiastic believers, it is expressed through piecemeal and consumerist involvement in elements of a cultic world. To pursue Weber's music metaphor, the orchestras and mass bands with their thunderous symphonies have gone. Handfuls of us will be enthusiastic music-makers but, because we no longer follow one score, we cannot produce the melodies to rouse the masses.

# Bibliography

BAILEY, EDWARD, 'The Implicit Religion of Contemporary Society: An Orientation and a Plea for its Study', *Religion*, 13 (1983), 69–83.

BAINBRIDGE, WILLIAM S., and STARK, RODNEY, 'Formal Explanation of Religion: A Progress Report', *Sociological Analysis*, 45 (1984), 145–58.

BALLARD, R., and BALLARD, C., 'The Sikhs: The Development of Southern Asian Settlements in Britain', in J. L. Watson (ed.), *Between Two Cultures* (Oxford: Blackwell).

BARCLAY, HUBERT F., and FOX, A. W., *A History of the Barclay Family with Pedigrees from 1067 to 1933* (London: St Catherines Press, 1934).

BARKER, DAVID, HALMAN, LOEK, and VLOET, ASTRID, *The European Values Study 1981–1990 Summary Report* (London: European Values Study Group/Cook Foundation, 1992).

BEASLEY-MURRAY, P., and WILKINSON, A., *Turning the Tide: An Assessment of Baptist Church Growth in England* (London: Bible Society, 1981).

BECKER, GARY, 'The Economic Approach to Human Behavior', in Jon Elster (ed.), *Rational Choice* (Oxford: Blackwell, 1986), 108–22.

BECKFORD, JAMES A., 'New Wine in New Bottles: A Departure from Church–Sect Conceptual Tradition', *Social Compass*, 234 (1976), 71–85.

BECKWITH, IAN, 'Religion in a Working Men's Parish', *Lincolnshire History and Archaeology*, 4 (1969), 29–38.

BENNETT, WILL, 'Cult Denies Child Sex Abuse', *Independent*, 2 July 1993.

BEN-TAL, DANNY, 'Welcome to Club Meditation', *Independent Weekend*, 28 Aug. 1993.

BERGER, PETER L., *The Sacred Canopy: Elements of a Sociological Theory of Religion* (New York: Doubleday, 1967).

—— 'Substantive Definitions of Religion', *Journal for the Scientific Study of Religion*, 13 (1974), 125–33.

—— *Facing up to Modernity: Excursions in Society, Politics and Religion* (Harmondsworth, Middx.: Penguin, 1979).

—— *The Heretical Imperative: Contemporary Possibilities of Religions Affirmation* (London: Collins, 1980).

—— BERGER, BRIGITTE, and KELLNER, HANSFRIED, *The Homeless Mind* (Harmondsworth, Middx.: Penguin, 1974).

—— and LUCKMANN, THOMAS, *The Social Construction of Reality* (Harmondsworth, Middx.: Penguin, 1973).

BETTEY, J. H., *Church and Community: The Parish Church in English Life* (Bradford-on-Avon, Moonraker Press, 1979).

BEZILLA, ROBERT (ed.), *Religion in America 1992–93* (Princeton: Princeton Religion Research Centre, 1993).

BIBBY, REGINALD, 'The State of Collective Religioisity in Canada: An Empirical Analysis', *Canadian Review of Sociology and Anthropology*, 16 (1979), 105–16.

—— 'Searching for Invisible Thread: Meaning Systems in Contemporary Canada', *Journal for the Scientific Study of Religion*, 22 (1983), 101–19.

—— 'Religious Encasement in Canada', *Social Compass*, 32 (1985), 287–303.

—— and BRINKERHOFF, MARTIN, 'The Circulation of the Saints: A Study of People who Join Conservative Churches', *Journal for the Scientific Study of Religion*, 112 (1973), 273–85.

—— —— 'When Proselytizing Fails: An Organizational Analysis', *Sociological Analysis*, 35 (1974), 189–200.

—— —— 'Circulation of the Saints Revisited: A Longitudinal Look at Conservative Church Growth', *Journal for the Scientific Study of Religion*, 22 (1983), 253–62.

—— and WEAVER, HAROLD R., 'Cult Consumption in Canada: A Further Critique of Stark and Bainbridge', *Sociological Analysis*, 46 (1985), 445–60.

BISSET, P., 'Size and Growth', in Peter Brierley and Fergus Macdonald (eds.), *Prospects for Scotland: From a Census of the Churches in 1984* (London: MARC Europe, 1985), 17–25.

BLOOM, WILLIAM, *The New Age: An Anthology of Essential Writings* (London: Rider/Channel 4, 1991).

BOICE, JUDITH L., *At One with All Life: A Personal Journey in Gaian Communities* (Findhorn: Findhorn Press, 1989).

BOUMA, GARY D., 'The Real Reason One Conservative Church Grew', *Review of Religious Research*, 20 (1979), 127–37.

—— 'Australian Religiosity: Some Trends since 1966', in Alan W. Black and Peter E. Glasner (eds.), *Practice and Belief: Studies in the Sociology of Australian Religion* (Sydney: Allen & Unwin, 1983), 15–24.

—— and DIXON, BEVERLY R., *The Religious Factor in Australian Life* (Melbourne: MARC Australia, 1991).

BREAULT, KEVIN D., 'New Evidence on Religious Pluralism, Urbanism and Religious Particiaption', *American Sociological Review*, 54 (1989), 1048–53.

BRIERLEY, PETER, *A Century of British Christianity: Historical Statistics 1900–1985 with Projections to 2000* (Research Monograph 14; London: MARC Europe, 1989).

—— *The New Age is Coming* (Research Monograph 35; London: MARC Europe, 1991).

—— *'Christian' England: What the English Church Census Reveals* (London: MARC Europe, 1991).

—— *Reaching and Keeping Teenagers* (London: Christian Research Association, 1993).

—— and HISCOCK, VAL, *UK Christian Handbook 1994/95 Edition* (London: Christian Research Association, 1993).

—— and MACDONALD, FERGUS, *Prospects for Scotland: From a Census of the Churches in 1984* (London: MARC Europe, 1985).

BRIGGS, JOHN, 'Report of the Denominational Enquiry Group to the Baptist Union Council' (unpublished paper, 1979).

British Parliamentary Papers, *1851 Census, Great Britain, Report and Tables on Religious Worship, England and Wales, 1852–53* (Cork: Irish University Press reprint, 1970).

BROWN, ANDREW, 'Birth Celebration without Religion Offered', *Independent*, 23 July 1994.

BROWN, CALLUM, *The Social History of Religion in Scotland since 1730* (London: Methuen, 1987).

—— 'Did Urbanization Secularize Britain?', *Urban History Yearbook* (1988), 1–14.

—— 'A Revisionist Approach to Religious Change', in Steve Bruce (ed.), *Religion and Modernization: Sociologists and Historians Debate the Secularization Thesis* (Oxford: Oxford University Press, 1992), 31–58.

—— *The People in the Pews: Religion and Society in Scotland since 1780* (Glasgow: Economic and Social History Society of Scotland, 1993).

BROWN, FORD K., *Fathers of the Victorians: The Age of Wilberforce* (London: Cambridge University Press, 1961).

BRUCE, STEVE, 'The Student Christian Movement: A Nineteenth Century New Religious Movement and its Vicissitudes', *International Journal of Sociology and Social Policy*, 2 (1982), 67–82.

—— 'Authority and Fission: The Protestants' Divisions', *British Journal of Sociology*, 36 (1985), 592–603.

—— *No Pope of Rome: Militant Protestantism in Modern Scotland* (Edinburgh: Mainstream, 1985).

—— *God Save Ulster! The Religion and Politics of Paisleyism* (Oxford: Oxford University Press, 1986).

—— 'Protestantism and Politics in Scotland and Ulster', in J. K. Hadden and A. D. Shupe (eds.), *Prophetic Religions and Politics* (New York: Paragon House, 1986), 410–29.

—— *The Rise and Fall of the New Christian Right: Conservative Protestant Politics in America 1978–1988* (Oxford: Oxford University Press, 1988).

—— 'Modernity and Fundamentalism: The New Christian Right in America', *British Journal of Sociology*, 41 (1990), 477–96.

—— *A House Divided: Protestantism, Schism and Secularization* (London: Routledge, 1990).

—— *Pray TV: Televangelism in America* (London: Routledge, 1990).

—— 'Pluralism and Religious Vitality', in Steve Bruce (ed.), *Religion and Modernization: Sociologists and Historians Debate the Secularization Thesis* (Oxford: Oxford University Press, 1992), 170–94.

BRUCE, STEVE, 'Funding the Lord's Work: A Typology of Religious Resourcing', *Social Compass*, 39 (1992), 93–101.

—— 'Religion and Rational Choice', *Sociology of Religion*, 54 (1993), 193–205.

—— KIVISTO, PETER, and SWATOS, WILLIAM H. (eds.), *The Rapture of Politics: The Christian Right as the United States Approaches the Year 2000* (New Brunswick, NJ: Transaction, 1994).

—— and WRIGHT, C., 'Law, Religious Toleration and Social Change', *Journal of Church and State*, 37 (1995), 103–20.

BUDD, SUSAN, *Varieties of Unbelief: Atheists and Agnostics in English Society 1850–1960* (London: Heinemann, 1977).

BUGLIOSI, VINCENT (with GENTRY, CURT), *Helter Skelter: The Manson Murders* (Harmondsworth, Middx.: Penguin, 1977).

BULL, MALCOLM, and LOCKHART, KEITH, *Seeking a Sanctuary: Seventh-Day Adventism and the American Dream* (New York: Harper & Row, 1989).

BURLEIGH, J.H., *A Church History of Scotland* (Oxford: Oxford University Press, 1973).

CADDY, EILEEN, and HOLLINGSHEAD, LIZA, *Flight into Freedom: The Autobiography of the Co-Founder of the Findhorn Community* (Longmead, Dorset: Element, 1988).

CAIRNS, DAVID S., *The Army and Religion: An Enquiry and its Bearing upon the Religious Life of the Nation* (London: Macmillan, 1919).

CAMPBELL, COLIN, 'The Cult, the Cultic Milieu and Secularization', in Michael Hill (ed.), *A Sociological Yearbook of Religion in Britain—5* (London: SCM Press, 1972), 119–36.

—— 'The Secret Religion of the Educated Classes', *Sociological Analysis*, 39 (1978), 146–56.

CAMPBELL, EILEEN, and BRENNAN, J. H., *Dictionary of Mind, Body and Spirit* (London: Aquarian, 1994).

CAPLOW, THEODORE, 'Contrasting Trends in European and American Religion', *Sociological Analysis*, 46 (1985), 101–8.

—— BAHR, HOWARD M., and CHADWICK, B. A., *All Faithful People: Change and Continuity in Middletown's Religion* (Minneapolis: University of Minnesota Press, 1983).

CARROLL, JACKSON W., and LONG MARLER, PENNY, 'Culture Wars? Insights from Ethnographies of Two Protestant Seminaries', *Sociology of Religion*, 56 (1995), 1–20.

CARTER, LEWIS F., 'The "New Renunciates" of the Bhagwan Shree Rajneesh: Observations and Identification of Problems of Interpreting New Religious Movements', *Journal of the Scientific Study of Religion*, 26 (1987), 148–72.

—— *Charisma and Control in Rajneeshpuram: The Role of Shared Values in the Creation of a Community* (Cambridge: Cambridge University Press, 1990).

CAYLEY, C., *The Leeds Guide: Giving a Concise History of that Rich and Populous Town* (Leeds, 1808).

COLEMAN, JOHN A., 'Church–Sect Typology and Organizational Precariousness', *Sociological Analysis*, 29 (1968), 550–66.

COLLINSON, PATRICK, *The Religion of Protestants: The Church in English Society 1559–1625* (Oxford: Oxford University Press, 1982).

—— *Godly People: Essays on English Protestantism and Puritanism* (London: Hambledon Press, 1983).

CONDRAN, JOHN G., and TAMNEY, JOSEPH B., 'Religious "Nones", 1957 to 1982', *Sociological Analysis*, 46 (1982), 415–23.

COX, JEFFREY, *The English Churches in a Secular Society: Lambeth, 1870–1930* (New York: Oxford University Press, 1982).

CRESSY, DAVID, 'Purification, Thanksgiving and the Churching of Women in Post-Reformation England', *Past and Present*, 141 (Nov. 1993), 106–46.

CROMARTIE, MICHAEL (ed.), *No Longer Exiles: The Religious New Right in American Politics* (Washington: Ethics and Public Policy Centre, 1993).

CROSS, CLARE, *Church and People 1450–1660* (London: Fontana, 1970).

CURRIE, ROBERT, *Methodism Divided* (London: Faber & Faber, 1968).

—— GILBERT, ALAN D., and HORSLEY, LEE, *Churches and Churchgoers: Patterns of Church Growth in the British Isles since 1700* (Oxford: Oxford University Press, 1977).

DAVIS, DEBORAH, with DAVIS, BILL, *The Children of God: The Inside Story by the Daughter of the Founder Moses David Berg* (Grand Rapids, Mich.: Zondervan, 1984).

DEMPSEY, KEN, 'Is Religion Still Relevant in the Private Sphere? The State of Organized Religion in an Australian Rural Community', *Sociological Analysis*, 50 (1989), 247–63.

DE KLERK, WILLIAM W., *The Puritans in Africa: A Story of Afrikanerdom* (Harmondsworth, Middx.: Penguin, 1974).

DICKENS, A.G., *The English Reformation* (London: Fontana, 1967).

DOBBELAERE, KAREL, and VOYÉ, LILIANNE, 'From Pillar to Postmodernity: The Changing Situation of Religion in Belgium', *Sociological Analysis*, 51 (1990), S1–S13.

DRUMMOND, ANDREW L., and BULLOCH, JAMES, *The Scottish Church 1688–1843* (Edinburgh: St Andrew Press, 1973).

—— —— *The Church in Victorian Scotland 1843–1874* (Edinburgh: St Andrew Press, 1975).

—— —— *The Church in Late Victorian Scotland 1874–1900* (Edinburgh: St Andrew Press, 1978).

DURKHEIM, EMILE, *Suicide* (London: Routledge Kegan Paul, 1970).

—— *The Elementary Forms of the Religious Life* (London: George Allen & Unwin, 1971).

EDWARDS, CHRISTOPHER, *Crazy for God: The Nightmare of Cult Life* (Englewood Cliffs, NJ: Prentice-Hall, 1979).

EVANS-PRITCHARD, E.E., *Witchcraft Oracles and Magic among the Azande* (Oxford: Oxford University Press, 1968).

FERN, DEANE W., *Third World Liberation Theologies* (Maryknoll, NY: Orbis, 1986).

—— *Profiles in Liberation: 36 Portraits of Third World Theologians* (Mystic, Conn.: Twenty-Third Publications, 1988).

FINKE, ROGER, 'Religious Deregulation: Origins and Consequences', *Journal of Church and State*, 32 (1990), 609–26.

—— 'An Unsecular America', in Steve Bruce (ed.) *Religion and Modernization: Sociologists and Historians Debate the Secularization Thesis* (Oxford: Oxford University Press, 1992), 145–69.

—— and IANNACCONE, LAURENCE R., 'Supply-Side Explanations for Religious Change', *Annals of the American Academy of Political and Social Science*, 527 (1993), 27–39.

—— and STARK, RODNEY, 'Religious Economies and Sacred Canopies: Religious Mobilization in American Cities, 1906', *American Sociological Review*, 53 (1988), 41–9.

—— —— *The Churching of America 1576–1990: Winners and Losers in our Religious Economy* (New Brunswick, NJ: Rutgers University Press, 1992).

FITZGERALD, FRANCES, 'A Reporter at Large: Rajneeshpuram', *New Yorker*, pt. I (11 Sept. 1986), 46–96, and pt. II (29 Sept. 1986), 83–125.

FLETCHER, RONALD, *The Making of Sociology*, i. *Beginnings and Foundation* (London: Nelson, 1971).

FREUD, SIGMUND, 'The Future of an Illusion', in *Civilization, Society and Religion etc.* (Pelican Freud Library, 12; Harmondsworth, Middx.: Penguin, 1986).

FULTON, JOHN, *The Tragedy of Belief: Division, Politics and Religion in Ireland* (Oxford: Oxford University Press, 1991).

GARDINER, W. H. T., *'Edinburgh 1910': An Account and Interpretation of the World Missionary Conference* (Edinburgh: Oliphant, Anderson & Ferrier, 1910).

GALLUP, GEORGE, H., Jr., *The Gallup International Public Opinion Polls: Great Britain 1937–1975* (New York: Random House, 1976).

—— and JONES, SARAH, *100 Questions and Answers: Religion in America* (Princeton: Princeton Religion Research Centre, 1989).

GARVEY, JOHN H., 'Fundamentalism and American Law', in Martin Marty and R. Scott Appleby (eds.), *Fundamentalisms and the State: Remaking Politics, Economics and Militance* (Chicago: University of Chicago Press, 1993), 28–49.

GAUSTAD, EDWIN S., *Historical Atlas of Religion in America* (New York: Harper & Row, 1962).

GELLNER, ERNEST, *Nations and Nationalism* (Oxford: Blackwell, 1983).

—— *Plough, Sword and Book: The Structure of Human History* (London: Paladin, 1991).

GERARD, DAVID, 'Religious Attitudes and Values', in Mark Abrams, David

Gerard, and Noel Timms (eds.) *Values and Social Change in Britain* (London: Macmillan, 1985), 50–92.

GERTH, HANS H., and WRIGHT MILLS, C., *From Max Weber: Essays in Sociology* (London: Routledge, 1970).

GEORGE, CAROL V. R., *God's Salesman: Norman Vincent Peale and the Power of Positive Thinking* (New York: Oxford University Press, 1994).

GIDDENS, ANTHONY, (ed.), *Human Societies: A Reader* (Cambridge: Polity Press, 1992).

GILBERT, ALAN D., *Religion and Society in Industrial Society: Church and Chapel and Social Change 1740–1914* (London: Longmans, 1976).

GILKEY, LANGDON, *Creationism on Trial: Evolution and God at Little Rock* (Minneapolis: Winston Press, 1985).

GILLIOMEE, HERMANN, 'The Growth of Afrikaner Identity', in Heribert Adam and Hermann Gilliomee (eds.), *Ethnic Power Mobilised: Can South Africa Change?* (New Haven: Yale University Press, 1979), 83–125.

GIORGI, LIANA, 'Religious Involvement in a Secularized Society: An Empirical Confirmation of Martin's General Theory of Secularisation', *British Journal of Sociology*, 43 (1992), 639–56.

GILL, ROBIN, 'Secularization and Census Data', in Steve Bruce (ed.), *Religion and Modernization: Sociologists and Historians Debate the Secularization Thesis* (Oxford: Oxford University Press, 1992), 90–117.

—— *The Myth of the Empty Church* (London: SPCK, 1993).

GLENNY, MISHA, *The Rebirth of History* (Harmondsworth, Middx.: Penguin, 1990).

GOODRIDGE, R. MARTIN, 'The Ages of Faith: Romance or Reality', *Sociological Review*, 23 (1975), 381–96.

GRAHAM, H. G., *The Social Life of Scotland in the Eighteenth Century* (London: A. & C. Black, 1937).

GRAY, ROBERT Q., *The Labour Aristocracy in Victorian Edinburgh* (Oxford: Oxford University Press, 1976).

GREELEY, ANDREW M., *Religious Change in America* (Cambridge, Mass.: Harvard University Press, 1989).

GULA, JOZEF, 'Catholic Poles in the USSR during the Second World War', *Religion, State and Society*, 22 (1994), 9–35.

GUNTER, BARRIE, and VINEY, RACHEL, *Seeing is Believing: Religion and Television in the 1990s* (London: John Libbey/Independent Television Commission, 1994).

HADAWAY, C. KIRK, MARLER, PENNY L., and CHAVES, M., 'What the Polls Don't Show: A Closer Look at US Church Attendance', *American Sociological Review*, 58 (1993), 741–52.

HADDEN, JEFFREY K., 'Toward Desacralizing Secularization Theory', *Social Forces*, 65 (1987), 587–611; repr. in slightly abridged form as Reading 48 in Anthony Giddens (ed.), *Human Societies: A Reader* (Cambridge: Polity Press, 1992), 230–7.

HADDEN, JEFFREY K., and SHUPE, ANSON D., 'Introduction', in Hadden and Shupe (eds.), *Prophetic Religions and Politics: Religion and the Political Order* (New York: Paragon House, 1986).

—— —— *Televangelism: Power and Politics on God's Frontier* (New York: Henry Holt, 1988).

HALÉVY, LIE, *A History of the English People in 1815* (London: Penguin, 1937).

HALL, JOHN H., *Gone from the Promised Land: Jonestown in American Cultural History* (New Brunswick, NJ: Transaction, 1987).

HAMILTON, BERNARD, *Religion in the Medieval West* (London: Edward Arnold, 1986).

HAMMOND, PHILLIP E., and WARNER, KEE, 'Religion and Ethnicity in Late-Twentieth-Century America', *Annals of the American Academy of Political and Social Science*, 527 (May 1993), 55–66.

HARE, AUGUSTUS J. C., *The Gurneys of Earlham* (London: George Allen, 1897).

HARRELL, DAVID E., *All Things Are Possible: The Healing and Charismatic Revivals in Modern America* (Bloomington, Ind.: Indiana University Press, 1975).

—— *Oral Roberts: An American Life* (Bloomington, Ind.: Indiana University Press, 1985).

HAY, DAVID, and MORISY, ANN, 'Reports of Ecstatic, Paranormal or Religious Experience in Great Britain and the United States: A Comparison of Trends', *Journal for the Scientific Study of Religion*, 17 (1978), 255–68.

—— —— 'Secular Society/Religious Meaning: A Contemporary Paradox', unpublished paper, 1981.

HEELAS, PAUL, 'Western Europe: Self-Religions', in Stewart Sutherland and Peter Clarke (eds.), *The World's Religions* (London: Routledge, 1988), 925–31.

—— 'Exegesis: Methods and Aims', in Peter Clarke (ed.), *The New Evangelists: Recruitment, Methods and Aims of New Religious Movements* (London: Ethnographica, 1988), 17–41.

—— 'Western Europe: Self-Religions', in Stewart Sutherland and Peter Clarke (eds.), *The Study of Religion: Traditional and New Religion* (London: Routledge, 1991), 167–73.

—— 'The Sacralization of the Self and New Age Capitalism', in Nicholas Abercrombie and Alan Warde (eds.), *Social Change in Contemporary Britain* (Cambridge: Polity Press, 1992), 139–66.

—— 'Cults for Capitalism? Self-Religions, Magic and the Empowerment of Business', in John Fulton and Peter Gee (eds.), *Religion and Power, Decline and Growth: Sociological Analyses of Religion in Britain, Poland and the Americas* (London: British Sociological Association Sociology of Religion Study Group, 1991), 27–41.

—— 'The New Age in Cultural Context: The Pre-Modern, Modern and Post-Modern', *Religion*, 23 (1993), 103–16.

HELLER, ZOE, 'The Mall of God', *Independent on Sunday Review*, 2 June 1991, pp. 2–7.

HELWEG, ARTHUR W., *Sikhs in England* (Delhi: Oxford University Press, 1986).

HEMPTON, DAVID, *Methodism and Politics in British Society, 1750–1850* (London: Hutchinson, 1987).

—— 'Popular Religion and Irreligion in Victorian Fiction', *Historical Studies*, 16 (1987), 185–6.

HERBERG, WILL, *Protestant–Catholic–Jew: An Essay in American Religious Sociology* (Chicago: University of Chicago Press, 1983).

HERVIEU-LÉGER, DANIÈLE, *Vers un nouveau christianisme: Introduction à la sociologie du christianisme* (Paris: Cerf, 1986).

—— 'Religion and Modernity in the French Context: For a New Approach to Secularization', *Sociological Analysis*, 51 (1990), S15–25.

HILL, MICHAEL, and BOWMAN, RICHARD, 'Religious Adherence and Religious Practice in Contemporary New Zealand: Census and Survey Evidence', *Archives de sciences sociales des religions*, 59 (1985), 91–112.

HILL, ROSALIND, 'From the Conquest to the Black Death', in Sheridan Gilley and W. J. Sheils (eds.), *A History of Religion in Britain: Practice and Belief from Pre-Roman Times to the Present* (Oxford: Blackwell, 1994), 45–60.

HODGKINSON, LIZ, *Spiritual Healing: Everything You Want to Know* (London: Piatkus, 1990).

HOGGART, RICHARD, *The Uses of Literarcy* (Harmondsworth, Middx.: Penguin, 1962).

HOGGART, SIMON, 'Tricks of Memory', *Observer Magazine*, 27 Mar. 1994.

HOLLINGER, DENNIS, 'Enjoying God Forever: An Historical/Sociological Profile of the Health and Wealth Gospel in the USA', in John Fulton and Peter Gee (eds.), *Religion and Power: Decline and Growth* (London: British Sociological Association Study Group of Religion, 1991), 53–66.

HORNSBY-SMITH, MICHAEL P., *The Changing Parish: A Study of Parishes, Priests and Parishioners after Vatican II* (London: Routledge, 1989).

—— *Roman Catholics in England* (Cambridge: Cambridge University Press, 1987).

HUGHES, PHILLIP J., 'Types of Faith and the Decline of Mainline Churches', in Alan W. Black (ed.), *Religion in Australia: Sociological Perspectives* (Sydney: Allen & Unwin, 1991), 92–105.

—— *Religion: A View from the Australian Census* (Sydney: Christian Research Association, 1993).

HUNT, LIZ, 'Calls for Better Control of "Natural Remedies" ', *Independent on Sunday*, 19 Sept. 1993.

HUNTER, JAMES DAVIDSON, *Evangelicalism: The Coming Generation* (Chicago: University of Chicago, 1987).

IANNACCONE, LAURENCE R., 'The Consequences of Religious Market Strucutre', *Rationality and Society*, 3 (1991), 156–77.

INGLIS, KEITH, S., 'Patterns of Religious Worship in 1851', *Journal of Ecclesiastical History*, 11 (1960), 74–87.

IRWIN, G. A., and VAN HOLESTEYN, J. J. M., 'Decline of the Structured Model of Electoral Competition', *Western European Politics*, 12 (1989), 21–41.

ISICHEI, ELIZABETH, *Victorian Quakers* (Oxford: Oxford University Press, 1970).

JANOVITZ, MORRIS, *The Last Half-Century: Societal Change and Politics in America* (Chicago: University of Chicago Press, 1978).

JELEN, TED G., 'The Effects of Religious Separatism on White Protestants in the 1984 Presidential Election', *Sociological Analysis*, 48 (1987), 30–45.

—— *The Political Mobilization of Religious Beliefs* (New York: Praeger, 1991).

JOHNSON, BENTON, 'A Critical Appraisal of the Church–Sect Typology', *American Sociological Review*, 22 (1957), 88–92.

—— 'On Church and Sect', *American Sociological Review*, 28 (1963), 539–59.

—— 'Church and Sect Revisited', *Journal for the Scientific Study of Religion*, 10 (1971), 124–37.

JOHNSTON, H., 'The Marketed Social Movement: A Case Study of the Rapid Growth of TM', *Pacific Sociological Review*, 23 (1980), 333–54.

JOHNSON, PHILLIP E., *The Shopkeepers' Millennium: Society and Revival in Rochester, New York, 1815–37* (New York: Hill & Wang, 1978).

JOHNSON, STEPHEN D., TAMNEY, JOSEPH B., and BURTON, R., 'Factors Influencing Vote for a Christian Right Candidate', *Review of Religious Research*, 31 (1990), 291–304.

JUDAH, J. STILLSON, *The History and Philosophy of the Metaphysical Movements in America* (Philadelphia; Westminster Press, 1968).

—— *Hare Krishna and the Counter Culture* (New York: Wiley, 1974).

KALDOR, PETER, *Who Goes Where? Who Doesn't Care* (Homebush, NSW: Lancer, 1987).

KALSI, SEWA SINGH, *The Evolution of a Sikh Community in Britain* (Leeds; University of Leeds Department of Theology and Religious Studies, 1992).

KANTER, ROSABETH MOSS, *Commitment and Community: Communes and Utopias in Sociological Perspective* (Cambridge, Mass.: Harvard University Press, 1972).

KELLEY, DEAN, *Why the Conservative Churches are Growing* (New York: Harper & Row, 1972).

KERNS, PHIL (with WEED), *People's Temple, People's Tomb* (Plainfield, NJ: Logos International, 1979).

KNOTT, KIM, 'Other Major Religions', in T. Thomas (ed.), *The British: Their Religious Beliefs and Practices 1800–1986* (London: Routledge, 1986), 133–57.

LACQUER, T. W., *Religion and Respectability: Sunday Schools and Working Class Culture 1780–1850* (New Haven: Yale University Press, 1976).

LANTERNARI, VITTORIO, *The Religions of the Oppressed: A Study of Modern Messianic Cults* (New York: Alfred A. Knopf, 1963).

LASLETT, PETER, *The World We have Lost* (London: Methuen, 1983).

LENSKI, GERHARD, *The Religious Factor* (New York: Doubleday, 1963).

LERNOUX, PENNY, *Cry of the People* (Harmondsworth, Middx.: Penguin, 1980).

LESSNOFF, MICHAEL, 'Protestant Ethic and Profit Motive in the Weber Thesis', *International Journal of Sociology and Social Policy*, 1 (1981), 1–30.

—— *The Spirit of Capitalism and the Protestant Ethic: An Enquiry into the Weber Thesis* (Cheltenham: Edward Elgar, 1994).

LIEBMAN, CHARLES, S., 'Extremism as a Religious Norm', *Journal for the Scientific Study of Religion*, 22 (1983), 75–86.

LOFLAND, JOHN, *Doomsday Cult: A Study of Conversion, Proselytization and Maintenance of Faith* (Englewood Cliffs, NJ: Prentice-Hall, 1966).

LOVELOCK, JAMES, 'A Quest for Gaia', *New Scientist*, 6 Feb. 1975.

—— *Gaia: A New Look at Life on Earth* (Oxford: Oxford University Press, 1979).

LYND, ROBERT S., and LYND, HELEN J., *Middletown: A Study in Contemporary American Culture* (New York: Harcourt, Brace & Co., 1929).

McCONELL, D. L., *A Different Gospel: A Historical and Biblical Analysis of the Modern Faith Movement* (Peabody, Mass.: Hendrickson, 1988).

McEWEN, C. A., 'Continuities in the Study of Total and Nontotal Institutions', *Annual Review of Sociology*, 6 (1980), 143–85.

McLEOD, HUGH, 'White Collar Values and the Role of Religion', in Geoffrey Crossick (ed.), *The Lower Middle Class in Britain 1870–1914* (London: Croom Helm, 1977).

McMULLIN, ERNAN, 'Science and the Catholic Tradition', in Ian G. Barbour (ed.), *Science and Religion* (London: SCM Press, 1968), 30–42.

MANNHEIM, KARL, *Essays on the Sociology of Knowledge* (London: Routledge & Kegan Paul, 1952).

MARSHALL, GORDON, *Presbyteries and Profits: Calvinism and the Development of Capitalism in Scotland 1560–1707* (Oxford: Oxford University Press, 1980).

—— *In Search of the Spirit of Capitalism: An Essay on Max Weber's Protestant Ethic Thesis* (London: Hutchinson, 1982).

MARTIN, DAVID, 'Sect, Order and Cult', in Martin, *Pacifism* (London: Routledge & Kegan Paul, 1965).

—— *The Dilemmas of Contemporary Religion* (Oxford: Blackwell, 1978).

—— *A General Theory of Secularization* (Oxford: Blackwell, 1978).

—— *Tongues of Fire: The Explosion of Protestantism in Latin America* (Oxford: Basil Blackwell, 1990).

MARTIN, HUGH, and PAYNE, E. A., *A Christian Yearbook* (London: SCM Press, 1943).

MARTIN, JAMES M., *Actualizations: Beyond est* (San Francisco: San Francisco Book Co., 1977).

MARTIN, SEAMUS, 'Latin Hymns Echo of Old Era', *Herald*, 6 Sept. 1993.

MARTY, MARTIN, and APPLEBY, R. SCOTT (eds.), *Fundamentalisms Observed* (Chicago: University of Chicago Press, 1987).

—— —— (eds.), *Fundamentalisms and the State: Remaking Polities, Economies and Militance* (Chicago: University of Chicago Press, 1993).

MELTON, J. GORDON, *Encyclopedic Handbook of Cults in America* (New York: Garland, 1986).

—— *The Encyclopedia of American Religions* (Detroit: Gale, 1989).

—— CLARK, JEROME, and KELLY, AIDAN, A., *New Age Almanac* (New York: Visible Ink, 1991).

MERTON, ROBERT K., *Science, Technology and Society in the 17th Century* (New York: Fertig, 1970).

MICHELS, ROBERT, *Political Parties: A Sociological Study of the Oligarchic Tendencies of Modern Democracy* (New York: Free Press, 1962).

MOEN, MATTHEW C., *The Transformation of the Christian Right* (Tuscaloosa, Ala.: University of Albama Press, 1992).

MOL, HANS (ed.), *Western Religion: A Country by Country Sociological Inquiry* (The Hague: Mouton, 1972).

MOODIE, T. D., *The Rise of Afrikanerdom* (Berkeley and Los Angeles: University of California Press, 1975).

MOORE, R. LAURENCE, 'Spiritualism and Science: Reflections on the First Decade of the Spirit Rappings', *American Quarterly*, 24/4 (1972), 474–500.

NEUHAUS, RICHARD, *The Naked Public Square: Religion and Democracy in America* (Grand Rapids, Mich.: Eerdmans, 1984).

NELSON, GEOFFREY K., 'The Concept of Cult', *Sociological Review*, 16 (1968), 351–62.

NEWTON, SMITH, W. H., *The Rationality of Science* (London: Routledge & Kegan Paul, 1981).

NEILL, STEPHEN, *A History of Christian Missions* (Harmondsworth, Middx.: Penguin, 1975).

NIEBUHR, H. RICHARD, *The Social Sources of Denominationalism* (New York: Meridian, 1962).

NIELSEN, JORGEN, *Muslims in Western Europe* (Edinburgh: Edinburgh University Press, 1992).

NIELSEN, NIELS, *Revolutions in Eastern Europe: The Religious Roots* (Maryknoll, NY: Orbis, 1991).

NORMAN, EDWARD, *Christianity in the Southern Hemisphere* (Oxford: Oxford University Press, 1981).

OBELKEVITCH, JAMES, *Religion and Rural Society: South Lindsay 1825–1875* (Oxford: Oxford University Press, 1976).

—— 'Religion', in F. M. L. Thompson (ed.), *The Cambridge Social History of Britain 1750–1950*, iii. *Social Agencies and Institutions* (Cambridge; Cambridge University Press, 1990), 311–56.

OZMENT, STEVEN, *Protestants: The Birth of a Revolution* (London: Fontana, 1993).

PARKER, D., and PARKER, H., *The Secret Sect* (Pendle Hill, NSW: The Parkers, 1982).

PATTERSON, G., 'The Religious Census: A Test of its Accuracy in South Shields', *Durham County Local History Society Bulletin* (Apr. 1978), 14–17.

PRYCE, KEN, *Endless Pressure: A Study of West Indian Life-Styles in Bristol* (Harmondsworth, Middx.: Penguin, 1979).

RAISTRICK, ARTHUR, *Quakers in Science and Industry* (London: David & Charles, 1968).

REED, CHRISTOPHER, ' "Incest" Father Sues "Quack" Therapists', *Observer*, 17 Apr. 1994.

RIDDELL, CAROL, *The Findhorn Community: Creating a Human Identity for the 21st Century* (Forres: Findhorn Press, 1990).

RIESBRODT, MARTIN, *Pious Passions: The Emergence of Modern Fundamentalism in the United States and Iran* (Berkeley and Los Angeles: University of California Press, 1993).

RIEFF, PHILIP, *The Triumph of the Therapeutic* (Harmondsworth, Middx.: Penguin, 1973).

ROBBINS, THOMAS, *Cults, Converts and Charisma: The Sociology of New Religious Movements*, special issue of *Current Sociology*, 36 (1988).

ROCHFORD, E. BURKE, *Hare Krishna in America* (New Brunswick, NJ: Rutgers University Press, 1985).

ROOF, WADE CLARK, and MCKINNEY, WILLIAM, *American Mainline Religion: Its Changing Shape and Future* (New Brunswick, NJ: Rutgers University Press, 1987).

ROOKSBY, DONALD A., *The Quakers in North-West England*, i. *The Man in Leather Breeches* (Colwyn Bay, Clwyd: The Author, 1994).

ROOZEN, DAVID A., and CARROLL, JACKSON, W., 'Recent Trends in Church Membership and Participation: An Introduction', in Dan R. Hoge and David A. Roozen (eds.), *Understanding Church Growth and Decline, 1950–1978* (New York: The Pilgrim Press, 1979).

ROSE, PHILLIP, *Social Trends 23* (London: Her Majesty's Stationery Office, 1993).

SAHLINS, MARSHALL, *Stone Age Economics* (Chicago: Aldine, 1972).

SCHNEIDER, LOUIS, and DORNBUSCH, SANFORD M., 'Inspirational Religious Literature: From Latent to Manifest Functions of Religion', *American Journal of Sociology*, 62 (1957), 476–81.

SEMMEL, BERNARD, *The Methodist Revolution* (London: Heinemann, 1974).

SHINER, LARRY, 'The Concept of Secularization in Empirical Research', *Journal for the Scientific Study of Religion*, 6 (1967), 207–20.

SHINN, LARRY D., 'Conflicting Networks: Guru and Friend in ISKCON', in Rodney Stark (ed.), *Religious Movements: Genesis, Exodus and Numbers* (New York: Paragon House, 1985), 95–114.

SIGELMANN, L., and PRESSER, S., 'Measuring Public Support for the New Christian Right: The Perils of Point Estimation', *Public Opinion Quarterly*, 52 (1988), 325–37.

SILVA, JOSÉ, and MIELE, PHILLIP, *The Silva Mind Control Method* (New York: Pocket Books, 1977).

SIMPSON, GRANT, 'The Declaration of Arbroath Revitalised', *Scottish Historical Review*, 56 (1977), 11–34.

SIMPSON, JOHN H., 'Moral Issues and Status Politics', in Robert C. Liebman and Robert Wuthnow (eds.), *The New Christian Right: Mobilization and Legitimation* (New York: Aldine, 1983), 188–207.

SLOCOMBE, JEREMY, 'Last Thoughts', *One Earth: The Findhorn Foundation and Community Magazine*, 14 (Summer 1994), 19.

—— and WARD, EVE, 'Willing to Change: An Interview with Eileen Caddy', *One Earth: The Findhorn Foundation and Community Magazine*, 12 (Winter 1993/4), 9.

SOUTHER, R. W., *Western Society and the Church in the Middle Ages* (Harmondsworth, Middx.: Penguin, 1970).

SPUFFORD, MARGARET, *Small Books and Pleasant Histories* (London: Methuen, 1981).

—— 'Can We Count the "Godly" and the "Conformable" in the Seventeenth Century?', *Journal of Ecclesiastical history*, 36 (1985), 428–38.

STARK, RODNEY, 'Modernization, Secularization and Mormon Success', in Thomas Robbins and Dick Anthony (eds.), *In Gods We Trust: New Patterns of Religious Pluralism in America* (2nd edn.; New Brunswick, NJ: Transaction, 1991), 201–18.

—— 'Europe's Receptivity to New Religious Movements', *Journal for the Scientific Study of Religion*, 32 (1993), 389–97.

—— and BAINBRIDGE, WILLIAM S., 'Of Churches, Sects and Cults', in Stark and Bainbridge, *The Future of Religion: Secularization, Revival and Cult Formation* (Berkeley and Los Angeles: University of California Press, 1985), 19–37.

—— —— *The Future of Religion: Secularization, Revival and Cult Formation* (Berkeley and Los Angeles: University of California Press, 1985).

—— —— *A Theory of Religion* (New York: Peter Lang, 1987).

—— and IANNACCONE, LAURENCE R., 'A Supply-Side Reinterpretation of the "Secularization" of Europe', *Journal for the Scientific Study of Religion*, 33 (1994), 230–52.

STONE, E. L. G., 'The Appeal to History in Anglo-Scottish Relations between 1291 and 1401: Part 1', *Archives*, 9 (1969–70), 11–21.

SVENNEVIG, MICHAEL, HALDANE, IAN, SPEIRS, SHARON, and GUNTER, BARRIE, *Godwatching: Viewers, Religion and Television* (London: John Libbey/Independent Broadcasting Authority, 1989).

SYMONDSON, A., *The Victorian Crisis of Faith* (London: SPCK, 1970).

TAMBIAH, S. J., 'The Ideology of Merit and the Social Correlates of Buddhism in a Thai Village', in Edmund R. Leach (ed.), *Dialectics in Popular Religion* (Cambridge: Cambridge University Press, 1968), 41–121.

TANNER, MARCUS, 'Serbia Tries to Rid Itself of a Turbulent Priest', *Independent on Sunday*, 7 Nov. 1993.
—— 'God Invoked by Rivals in Montenegro', *Independent*, 1 Nov. 1993.
THOMAS, KEITH, *Religion and the Decline of Magic* (Harmondsworth, Middx.: Penguin, 1973).
THOMPSON, KENNETH, *Emile Durkheim* (London: Tavistock, 1982).
TILL, BARRY, *The Churches Search for Unity* (Harmondsworth, Middx.: Penguin, 1972).
TIPTON, STEVEN M., *Getting Saved from the Sixties: Moral Meaning in Conversion and Cultural Change* (Berkeley and Los Angeles: University of California Press, 1982).
TISSERAND, ROBERT, *Aromatherapy for Everyone* (Harmondsworth, Middx.: Arcana, 1990).
TOMKA, MIKLÓS, 'The Changing Social Role of Religion in Eastern and Central Europe: Religion's Revival and its Contradictions', *Social Compass*, 42 (1995), 17–26.
TROELTSCH, ERNST, *The Social Teaching of the Christian Churches* (Chicago: University of Chicago Press/Midway repritns, 1976).
VAN MEERBACK, ANNE, 'The Importance of a Religious Service at Birth: The Persistent Demand for Baptism in Flanders', *Social Compass*, 42 (1995), 47–58.
VAN ZANDT, DAVID E., *Living in the Children of God* (Princeton: Princeton University Press, 1991).
VINCENT, THOMAS, *The Shorter Catechism Explained from Scripture* (1674; Edinburgh: Banner of Truth Trust, 1980).
WALLIS, ROY (ed.), *Sectarianism: Analyses of Religious and Non-Religious Sects* (London: Peter Owen, 1975).
—— *The Road to Total Freedom: A Sociological Analysis of Scientology* (London: Heinemann, 1976).
—— *The Rebirth of the Gods?* (Belfast: Queen's University, 1978).
—— *Salvation and Protest: Studies of Social and Religious Movements* (London: Frances Pinter, 1979).
—— 'Inside Insight', *New Humanist*, 95 (Autumn 1979), 94.
—— 'Sociological Reflections on the Demise of the Irish Humanist Association', *Scottish Journal of Sociology*, 4 (1980), 125–39.
—— 'Being with Werner', *New Humanist*, 96 (Spring 1981), 23.
—— 'Charisma, Commitment and Control in a New Religious Movement', in Roy Wallis (ed.), *Millennialism and Charisma* (Belfast: Queen's University, 1982), 73–140.
—— *The Elementary Forms of the New Religious Life* (London: Routledge, 1984).
—— 'Science and Psuedo-Science', *Social Science Information*, 24 (1985), 585–601.
—— 'The Dynamics of Change in the Human Potential Movement', in

Rodney Stark (ed.), *Religious Movements: Genesis, Exodus and Numbers* (New York: Paragon House, 1985), 129–56.

WALLIS, ROY (ed.), 'Figuring Out Cult Receptivity', *Journal for the Scientific Study of Religion*, 25 (1986), 494–503.

—— 'Hostages to Fortune: Thoughts on the Future of Scientology and the Children of God', in David G. Bromley and Phillip E. Hammond (eds.), *The Future of New Religious Movements* (Macon, Ga.: Mercier University Press, 1987), 80–90.

—— and BRUCE, STEVE, 'The Stark–Bainbridge Theory of Religion: A Critical Analysis and Counter-Proposals', *Sociological Analysis*, 45 (1984), 11–27.

—— —— 'Homage to Ozymandias: Reply to Bainbridge and Stark', *Sociological Analysis*, 46 (1985), 73–6.

—— —— 'The Threatened Elect: Presbyterians in Ulster and South Africa', in Wallis and Bruce, *Sociological Theory, Religion and Collective Action* (Belfast: Queen's University, 1986), 261–91.

—— —— 'Secularization: Trends, Data and Theory', *Research in the Social Scientific Study of Religion*, 3 (1991), 1–31.

WARNER, R. STEPHEN, 'Work in Progress towards a New Paradigm for the Sociological Study of Religion in the United States', *American Journal of Sociology*, 98 (1993), 1044–93.

WASHINGTON, PETER, *Madame Blavatsky's Baboon: Theosophy and the Emergence of the Western Guru* (London: Secker, 1993).

WATERHOUSE, ROSIE, and REEVES, PHIL, 'Author of Child Sex Abuse Book is Sued', *Independent*, 15 May 1994.

—— and STRICKLAND, SARAH, 'Abuses of Memory', *Independent on Sunday*, 1 May 1994.

WEBER, MAX, *Economy and Society* (Berkeley and Los Angeles: University of California Press, 1978).

—— *The Protestant Ethic and the Spirit of Capitalism* (London: George Allen & Unwin, 1976).

WHITING, ROBERT, *The Blind Devotion of the People: Popular Religion in the English Reformation* (Cambridge: Cambridge University Press, 1989).

WHITNEY, JANET, *Elizabeth Fry: Quaker Heroine* (London: Harrap, 1951).

WHYTE, JOHN H., *Church and State in Modern Ireland, 1923–1970* (Dublin: Gill & Macmillan, 1970).

WILCOX, CLYDE, *God's Warriors: The Christian Right in Twentieth Century America* (Baltimore: Johns Hopkins University Press, 1992).

WILSON, BRYAN R., 'An Analysis of Sect Development', *American Sociological Review*, 24 (1959), 3–15.

—— *Religion in Secular Society* (London: C. A. Watts, 1966).

—— 'Religion and the Churches in America', in William G. McLoughlin and Robert N. Bellah (eds.), *Religion in America* (Boston: Houghton Mifflin, 1968), 73–110.

—— *Contemporary Transformations of Religion* (Oxford: Oxford University Press, 1976).

—— *Religion in Sociological Perspective* (Oxford: Oxford University Press, 1982).

—— 'Morality in the Evolution of the Modern Social System', *British Journal of Sociology*, 36 (1985), 315–32.

—— 'The Functions of Religion: A Reappraisal', *Religion*, 18 (1988), 199–216.

—— 'How Sects Evolve: Issues and Inferences', in Wilson, *The Social Dimensions of Sectarianism: Sects and New Religious Movements in Contemporary Society* (Oxford: Oxford University Press, 1990).

—— 'The Persistence of Sects', *Diskus*, 1 (1993), 1–12.

—— and DOBBELAERE, KAREL, *A Time to Chant: The Soka Gakkai Buddhists in Britain* (Oxford: Clarendon Press, 1994).

WITHRINGTON, DONALD J., 'The 1851 Census of Religious Worship and Education: With a Note on Church Accommodation in Mid-19th Century Scotland', *Records of the Scottish Church History Society*, 18 (1974), 133–48.

WOLFE, JOHN N., and PICKFORD, M., *The Church of Scotland: An Economic Survey* (London: Geoffrey Chapman, 1980).

WOLFE, KENNETH, *The Churches and the British Broadcasting Corporation 1922–1956* (London: SCM Press, 1984).

WUTHNOW, ROBERT, 'Recent Patterns of Secularization: A Problem of Generations', *American Sociological Review*, 41 (1976), 856–67.

—— *The Restructuring of American Religion* (Princeton: Princeton University Press, 1988).

YEARLEY, STEVEN, 'The Social Authority of Science in a Post-Modern Age' (unpublished inaugural lecture, University of Ulster, 1994).

YEO, STEPHEN, *Religion and Voluntary Organizations in Crisis* (London: Croom Helm, 1976).

# INDEX